CONCISE DICTIONARY OF CHRISTIAN ETHICS
Edited by Bernhard Stoeckle

Concise Dictionary of Christian Ethics

Edited by Bernhard Stoeckle
with contributions by
J. Dominian, Anton Vögtle, Laurence Bright, O.P.,
and others

A Crossroad Book
THE SEABURY PRESS . NEW YORK

The Seabury Press
815 Second Avenue
New York, N.Y. 10017

© 1979 Search Press London
Printed in Great Britain

Library of Congress Cataloging in Publication number: 79-50666

ISBN 0-8164-0357-0

Contents

Main articles

vi

Prefatory Note

This volume is intended specifically as a dictionary and not as a handbook or manual (with all the systematic divisions and categories that that implies). It is not offered as an exhaustive guide to moral doctrine. At present it is impossible to set out an authoritative theological ethics in anything like a handy one-volume format, if indeed it is possible to put forward anything at all in the old confident style.

The use of the word 'Christian' in the title does not mean that we claim that Christians have an essentially distinct morality: one different, that is, from the morality proper to non-Christians, and excluding all communication with other human ethical systems, ideas and research. The word 'Christian' has a twofold reference here: to the conviction that humanity cannot be realized and fulfilled without reference to an absolute guarantee which precedes all human legitimation: without reference, in other words, to transcendence or religiousness. This awareness prevents moral endeavours from becoming aims in themselves and anything like the dictatorship of a total autonomy of worldly reality, or a divinization of human morality. It also calls on that unconditional sense of responsibility that should inhere in any properly conceived study of ethics, and reminds us of the centrality of an ethics of belief, of faith.

The transcendence to which the Christian must always refer is of course biblical revelation. That means, however, that the transcendence which is believed and which empowers and enlivens the moral striving of Christians is none other than the radical human love of God made 'flesh' in Jesus Christ. This action which made God man's neighbour demands that all Christians should open themselves to any facts, discoveries, theories, research and so on that are humanly significant; it also demands that Christians should take absolutely seriously the unconditional worth and dignity which revelation grants to every human personality, and to all individual responsibility. Theological ethics has to engage in an intensive and broad-based confrontation with human problems, and that requires critical study and knowledge of the human sciences. Hence this book is, we hope, consistently open to the suggestions of the sciences, while it shuns the dictatorship of any party-line, ecclesiastical or other, and offers basic guidelines for all interested Christians who wish to consider or reconsider the fundamentals of ethics at the present time. If it affords an initial attitude to and understanding of the problems involved and the immense amount still to be discovered about human nature, and leads readers to a more profound investigation of the complexities, it will have done its work.

THE EDITORS

Articles originally in German were translated into English and shorter, unsigned definitions were supplied by Rosaleen Ockenden, David Smith, Francis McDonagh, John Griffiths, Edward Quinn, Colin Carr, W.H. O'Hara, M. Chaytor and Michael Callaghan.

A

Abortion. See *Birth control*.

ABSTINENCE

1. General. Abstinence or renunciation has to do with refusal, keeping at a distance, withdrawing claims; in other words with courses of action which are by their nature concerned with stopping by free choice, either temporarily or permanently, fulfilment or enrichment, mainly of instinctual demands. Until recently the influence of emancipatory ideologies and anti-repressive education made abstinence an object of suspicion, and 'immediate satisfaction' of all desires as they arise (see *Time*) is still a popular precept. Now, however, it is beginning to be realized that the humanization of man and the world requires considerable readiness for frustration and self-imposed rejection of one's own desires, and of stimuli, offers, and possibilities of consumption. In particular, concern to preserve a livable future highlights the urgency of abstinence (see *Environment*). Nevertheless, if abstinence is to be convincingly presented as an inescapable demand of human existence it must be related to securely based scientific knowledge.

2. The psychological aspect. Psychoanalytical studies have shown one way of distinguishing abstinence from other forms of behaviour, notably repression and suppression. Repression means a process or mechanism which operates for the most part unconsciously, both as regards the repressed material and as regards the activities of the personality which carry out the repression. By means of these activities unwanted id-impulses or their derivatives

1

(memories, fantasies, emotions) are denied access to consciousness. However, the act of repression creates a permanent or at least long-lasting opposition between the ego and the id of the psyche at the point of repression. The main cause of this is the continued transfer of instinctual energy to the repressed material which under unfavourable conditions may develop into a subsidiary mental centre and provoke conflicts (counter-cathexis). Suppression, unlike repression, is said to be a conscious activity, a decision to forget something and not to think about it any more (*ignorantia affectata; indifference*, q.v.), though it is impossible to draw a clear line between the two.

3. *The basic structure of abstinence*. Every instance of abstinence is part of an independent and responsible process of decision taking place in a situation of conflict or choice. The main influence in the process is the realization that the only way to secure some urgently desired object or to attain some urgently sought end is to abandon the pursuit of other aims which one regards in themselves as important (here the act of suppression may well prove very useful). If abstinence is to succeed in this context it requires an adequate sense of external reality, a solid basis of ego-strength (ego-weakness makes a person incapable of acts of abstinence), a personal model of meaning, and an ability to try out courses of action and calculate possible consequences. Specifically, abstinence as a free, personal decision is always subject to two sets of pressures: subjective, from one's personal aims, and those of the intersubjective relations I and you and I and community. Hence abstinence never occurs for its own sake.

4. *Theological significance*. A Christian cannot allow himself any illusions about the status of abstinence as an integral part of the life of faith. The believer sees abstinence in terms of his re-enactment of God's radical love for man as exemplified once and for all in Jesus's self-abasement and sacrifice even in death on the Cross. Only in the light of this love is the full extent of human nature's involvement with 'sarx' revealed (see *Body*), and the believer therefore regards abstinence not as alienating repression and an obstacle to his search for identity (*q.v.*), but a genuine

healing force in human nature and an instrument for bringing him more swiftly to his goal (1 Cor 9.25; 2 Tim 2.4).

In terms of its objects, the New Testament message regards it as most urgent to abstain from wealth, insistence on getting one's due (see the Sermon on the Mount), irreconcilability, revenge and enmity. The most important thing, however, is that every act of abstinence should be recognizable as an act done out of love. If this connexion is missing, even the highest acts of abstinence are worthless (1 Cor 13.3). All forms of abstinence inspired by condemnation of God's good creation are also to be rejected (1 Tim 4.1-4) (*World, q.v.*). *See Asceticism.*

Bibliography: A Blueprint for Survival. London, 1972. **Forrester, J.**: World Dynamics. Cambridge, Mass., 1970. **Hengel, M.**: Property and Riches in the Early Church. London & Philadelphia, 1975. **Roszak, T.**: The Making of a Counter Culture. New York & London, 1972. **Schnackenburg, R.**: The Moral Teaching of the New Testament. London, 1965. **Schumacher, E.F.**: Small is Beautiful. London & New York, 1970. **Ward, B. & Dubos, R.**: Only One Earth. London, 1974.

B. Stoeckle

ACHIEVEMENT

The successful completion of a human act, especially one showing resolve. The full subjective ordination of a human act to its proper, therefore moral and ultimate end.

Bibliography: Atkinson, J.W. (Ed.): Motives in Fantasy, Action, and Society. Princeton, N.J., 1958. **Cardenal, E.**: Love. London, 1974. **Horkheimer, M. & Adorno, T.**: The Dialectic of Enlightenment. London & New York, 1974. **McClelland, D.C.**: The Achieving Society. Princeton, N.J., 1961.

ACTION

Action or 'activity' is a general term for human behaviour as distinct from the behaviour of animals in the sense of the

3

reflective, intentional and goal-directed aspects of the human. Action which is human includes a causally 'responsible' conditioning of effects which the actor directs towards intended goals or aims by the choice of certain means conditioned by inner and outer circumstances and conditions (motives, needs, social norms and rôles). See *Norm*.

H. Oberhem

Activity. See *Action*; *Behaviourism*.

ADDICTION

The victim of addiction is ill or potentially ill. He desires pleasure or substitute satisfaction by the inappropriate because excessive consumption of one or more drugs ranging from opiates, barbiturates, hypnotics through alcohol, cannabis, hallucinogens, to stimulants and of course nicotine. Addiction features a psychological and often also a physical dependence on the drug, and therefore an overwhelming desire or compulsion to take it continually, often whatever the circumstances. Various psychological and physical injuries can result for addicts of various types. Ethics allows the use of such substances by a medical practitioner and use by individuals for improvement of health, the attainment of a certain degree of euphoria, the increase of companionability and the suppression of pain and mourning, but not when damage to health or the possibility of ill-effects exceeds the known or reasonably expected benefits. The cure or treatment of the various states of addiction depends on various psychological and physical findings and remedies, but also on the ability of the individual to win self-respect and knowledge, which requires sympathy, understanding and help in his condition from family, friends, and all those round him.

Bibliography: Bean, P.: The Social Control of Drugs. London, 1974. **Blum, E.M. & Blum, R.H.**: Alcoholism: Modern Psychological Approaches to Treatment. San Francisco, 1967. **Chein, I., Gerard, D.L., Lee, R.S. & Rosenfeld, E.**: Narcotics, Delinquency and Social Policy: The Road to H. London, 1964. **Franks, C.M.**: 1970 Alcoholism. In: **Costello, C.G. (Ed)**.: Symptoms of Psychopathology: A Handbook. New York, 1970. **Judson, H.**: Heroin Addiction in Britain. New York, 1974. **Rosenthal, M.S.**: The Phoenix House Therapeutic Community: An Overview. In: **Steinberg, H. (Ed.)**: Scientific Basis of Drug Dependence. London, 1969. **Teasdale, J.D.**: Drug Dependence. in: **Eysenck, H.J. (Ed.)**: Handbook of Abnormal Psychology. London, 2 1971. **Trouton, D. & Eysenck, K.J. (Eds.)**: The Effects of Drugs on Behaviour. In: **Eysenck, H.J. (Ed.)**: Handbook of Abnormal Psychology. London, 1960. **Vaillant, G.E.**: The Natural History of Urban Drug Addiction – Some Determinants. In: **Steinberg, J. (Ed)**: Scientific Basis of Drug Dependence. London, 1969, **Wilner, D.M. & Kassebaum, G.G. (Eds)**: Narcotics. New York, 1965. **World Health Organisation Expert Committee on Drug Dependence**: Sixteenth Report. WHO Technical Report Series, No. 407, 1969. Twentieth Report, 1974. **Zwerling, I & Rosenbaum, M.**: Alcohol Addiction and Personality (Non-psychotic Conditions). In: **Arietti, S. (Ed.)**: American Handbook of Psychiatry, Vol. 1, New York, 1959, 623-44.

R. Völkl

AGGRESSION

Unprovoked offensive action or attack by an individual or individuals on an other or others. Theories of the causation of aggression may be divided into two groups: those which see it as the result of pent-up or frustrated drives or inward psychic energy, and those which see it as engendered mainly or wholly by external stimuli or learning: these are theories of *endogenous* versus *exogenous* causation. Treatment recommended by the two schools differs accordingly, the endogenists advising the 'release' of aggression in mildly aggressive or non-aggressive action, the exogenists advising the avoidance of aggressive stimuli and experience, and the inculcation of appropriate social behaviour. The view taken in moral theology must depend on the notion of person and freedom, and appropriate observation of behaviour.

Bibliography: Berkowitz, L. : Aggression: A Social Psychological Analysis. New York, 1962. Dollard, J., Doob, L., Miller, N., Mowrer, O & Sears, R.: Frustration and Aggression. New Haven, 1939. Freud, S.: Beyond the Pleasure Principle. London, 1948. Lorenz, K.: On Aggression. New York & London, 1966. Montagu, M.F.A. (Ed.): Man and Aggression. New York, 1968. Storr, A.: Human Aggression. New York, 1968.

AGING

1. Fundamental aspects. Aging is a basic phenomenon of life. Its biological, psychological, social and sociological aspects are the concerns of the various branches of gerontology (the scientific and especially medical study of the aging process, old age, and the problems met with by old people). It is important to recognize that aging is neither a disease nor a misfortune but a qualitative transformation and a quite normal process. The aging process is part of the life process and comprises a progressive diminution of the possible and the indeterminate and a continuous acquisiton of the realized and confirmed; it includes, therefore, the positve aspect of increased emphasis and the negative aspect of a certain degree of impoverishment. It is essential to understand and to accept this as a normal event if one is to treat one's own aging appropriately or, as the case may be, behave correctly towards the aged.

Nevertheless, people experience the problems of aging as those of an irreversible process of change (biomorphosis) of the organism and its functions, a reduction of stimulus perception and therefore slower responses, a diminution of adjustability and adaptability, inadequate performance from the sense organs, and sickness and suffering in forms largely unexperienced in the course of life up to now. For the aging person all these experiences stress the inevitable finiteness of human existence. Theologically speaking, they show him that wearing down is part of the condition of a created being. In our present-day society, affected as it is by the youth cult, and by the ethics of achievement and consumption, the experience of aging is qualified by typical reactions to it and devaluation of it.

The loss of one's job or professional rôle and therefore to a considerable degree of social function is tantamount to a kind of 'social death' which can also seriously transform and disturb family life and often lead to loneliness for the aging man or woman. Such factors can help to induce moral inadequacies, such as self-righteousness, and obstinate, dogmatic and cantankerous behaviour (cf Eph 6.4); meanness, silliness (e.g., juvenilism); and various forms of what might be called senile egotism, can appear or gain intensity.

On the other hand, notable positive aspects of a 'happy old age' are a changed and to some extent more profound level of achievement through increased professional experience, better judgment, greater reliability and stability, maturity and independence, inward enrichment, and the greater freedom which can also result from solitude (a not wholly negative state)—a truly dignified composure in regard to the things and values of this world. This can (all the more since aging is often accompanied by increased religious receptivity) gain in theological depth in the knowledge that not aging as such but 'being in Christ' (cf Gal 3. 28) and appropriate moral behaviour are decisive (cf Wis 4. 8f, 16). Moral behaviour includes here good neighbourliness and mediation of knowledge, experience and wisdom through word and example marked by kindness and patience (cf 1 Tim 5. 9f; Tit 2. 2-4).

2. *Moral application*. Learning how to age is not only possible but the task of one's whole life (to be prepared for by physical and mental as well as spiritual training). It is necessary always (and nowadays especially in jobs and professions) to be prepared to change and relearn. Such readiness can be assisted by critical evaluation of each phase of the life-cycle and activity, and by preparation for a well-occupied old age, for instance by engaging in independent out-of-work or 'leisure-time' pursuits which will fill and compensate the even greater leisure and solitude to come. Aging has to be learned in accordance with religious and moral attitudes and since an egotist can never age in a full sense, the best preparation for aging is instruction in

correct behaviour towards others, and not least religious mastery of guilt (*q.v.*) and suffering, and courageous acceptance of the transience and pilgrim nature of human existence (cf Hebr 13. 14).

Since there have never been so many people around as there are today, and the numbers will grow; since in fact society is 'growing older', it has to learn how to accept the 'fourth generation' and no longer to treat them as a marginal group but (especially since there have never been so many 'young', active old people) to take note of their importance (for instance, for consumption) and their 'power' (as voters, for example). Society must no longer treat the aged as a 'social burden'. In view of the rapid process of change, they deserve respect even as bearers of tradition and inertia; the forgotten fourth commandment deserves rediscovery in the Church too (see *Memory*), and the self-awareness and self-respect of older people ought to be strengthened. All this is essential 'gerontology' and a form of help for the aged which is very much needed at present, even in the family circle where a kind of distant intimacy is too often practised. Just caring for the old in the conventional material sense is not enough, even though such a social service is important for solitary individuals; it is just as important, for instance in the parish, to enlist the aged in the service of others (in, say, honorary posts where their expertise can be put to good use). In addition, opportunities to meet others (in clubs and societies for older people, for example), cultural pursuits and entertainment are necessary to counteract the isolation even of those living in homes for the aged. Obviously the Church's work for the aged includes a preparation for a 'good' death, but in contrast to the one-sided stress on that common in the past, the emphasis in church action for the aged is on helping them to lead a more fulfilled life in their 'third age'.

Bibliography: Birren, J.E.: The Psychology of Aging. Englewood Cliffs, New Jersey, 1964. **Boros, L.:** The Moment of Truth. London & New York, 1965. **Choron, J.:** Death and Western Thought. New York, 1963. **Hinton, J.:** Dying. Harmondsworth, 1967. **Rahner, K.:** On the Theology of Death. London & New York, 1965. **Welford, A.T.:** Ageing and Human Skill. London, 1958. *R. Völkl*

Alcoholism. See *Addiction.*

ALIENATION

Estrangement of the individual from self, an other, others, society or God. The non-realization or inadequate realization of one's true self or ultimate end. The feeling of pointlessness or inappropriateness induced by a society whose dominant goals negate those desired by the individual.

Bibliography: **Marcuse, H.**: Eros and Civilization. Boston, 1955. **Id.**: One-dimensional Man. Boston, 1964. **Marx. K.**: The Economic and Philosophic Manuscripts of 1844. New York, 1964. **Schacht, R.**: Alienation. New York & London, 1971.

ALMS

In any society in which there are obvious extremes of wealth, the giving of alms is highly regarded. This was true of the Israel that produced the Old Testament, where justice and righteousness were equated with the giving of alms to the poor and needy of the land. Almsgiving characteristically receives a theological reason; in Deuteronomy, for instance, generosity to the poor is linked with God's generosity to the nation when he redeemed them from Egyptian bondage.

The obligation of almsgiving is still central to the New Testament, though we are apt to overlook the strong theologies behind it, and assume that it is merely a matter of practical charity. Two chapters of 2 Corinthians (8 and 9) are taken up with the collection being instituted for the poverty-stricken Jerusalem church. For Paul it is the visual form of his theology of the church as Christ's risen body. The giving church is identified with the one who 'though he was rich, yet for your sake he became poor, so that by his poverty you might become rich' (2 Cor 8.10). In Matthew's theology it is the recipient who is identified with Jesus: 'as you did it to one of the least of these my brethren

9

you did it to me' (Mt 25.40).

There is, of course, no simple way to apply these requirements to the totally different form of a modern western society. In a capitalist context the giving of aid to developing countries, for instance, both allows them to consume more of the goods that have to be produced if capitalism is to continue, and masks the fact of their exploitation through the West's control of prices paid for raw materials. Aid has been shown to be an excellent investment. No doubt the biblical requirement to give alms can be translated into something along the lines of a requirement to bring about a planned society in which each receives according to their need, but little seems to have been done by the official churches to express this point of view to their members.

L. Bright

ALTRUISM

Non-egostistical interest in and concern for the happiness and ultimate salvation of others.

ANTHROPOLOGY

The theory or doctrine of man concerned with scientific and systematic research into his nature, his development and his behaviour. Christian ethics is currently interested in all anthropological research since ethics is concerned with the nature of man in the world. In order to decide what man should do, science and philosophy must be constantly consulted to discover what man is. The basic moral question is 'What should we do' (before God and according to Christ)? It is of course sometimes difficult to decide to what extent we should listen to the statements of the sciences in determining that question's answer. It would be justifiable to ignore a philosophical approach which saw man as totally negative in himself in the face of God—a position which dialectical theology is often not far from adopting. It would be false too to see the biblical message and revelation only as existential clarifications of the situation and goals of men in the world. Excessive anthropocentrism is dangerous, as is a magical understanding of God operating in so to speak competition with the laws of nature—like some arbitrary jack-in-the-box somewhere inside it all.

A legitimate Christian ethics consults all the sciences from comparative psychology (which discovers more about human nature from the comparative study of animals and human beings) to genetics (and the study of inherited characteristics). A legitimate Christian ethics would reject a restriction of its knowledge to revelation because that would in fact contradict revelation, which shows man at the centre of the world.

Bibliography: Benedict, R.: Patterns of Culture. Boston, 1934. **Browning, D.:** Act and Agent: An Essay in Philosophical Anthropology. London, 1964. **Buber, M.:** Knowledge of Man, ed. by M. Friedmann. London, 1966. **Bultmann, R.:** Theology of the New Testament, 2 vols. London. 1952-55. **Cairns, D.:** The Image of God in Man. London, 1953. **Heidegger, M.:** Being and Time. London, 1962. **Kroeber, A.L.:** Anthropology Today. New York, 1965. **Leach, E.R.:** Rethinking Anthropology. London, 1961. **Levi-Strauss, C.:** Structural Anthropology. New York, 1963. **Lindzey, G.,** (Ed.): Handbook of Social Psychology. Cambridge, Mass., 1954. **Platt, J.:** New Views on the Nature of Man. London, 1965. **Robinson, H.W.:** The Christian Doctrine of Man, London, 1911. **Stacey, W.D.:** The Pauline View of Man. London, 1956.

H. Kramer

Apathy. See *Indifference*.

Armaments. See *Capitalism; Conflict*.

Ascesis. See *Asceticism*.

11

ASCETICISM

The Greek word *askesis* has the sense of 'training', 'taking exercise'. Clearly any serious approach to life, whether religious or secular, calls for some self-discipline. The problem is to determine how much is desirable; it has been answered quite differently by, say, Confucianism in China and certain types of Hinduism in India. Christians throughout history have veered uneasily between these two extremes.

Two factors lying behind this alternation deserve special mention. The relative importance of the material world, and the human body in particular, over against soul or spirit, has been understood very differently through Christian history, to which the formative first century that saw the production of the New Testament is no exception. Certainly Christianity inherited from Judaism a very firm view of the value of the material. The world, God's creation, is said to be thoroughly good by all the Old Testament authors. So is the human body; Israel saw no need to distinguish it sharply from a separate spiritual part. Consequently asceticism had no place, except for certain ritual purposes; the Greek tendency to denigrate the body, seen at its extreme in a Diogenes, was totally alien to Israel.

No doubt the Greek-Hebrew antithesis can be exaggerated, and there is no linear progression of Greek infiltration from the earliest to the latest New Testament writings; yet there is certainly a contrast between, say, Paul and John. Paul is true to the Old Testament tradition in never rejecting the world and its values, though these have to be radically transformed in Christ. But John, for whom the church was predominantly gentile, saw 'the world' as essentially evil, 'the lust of the flesh and the lust of the eyes and the pride of life'. Over against this stands the church, seen as so changed in Christ that it lives by a sole commandment, love of one's (Christian) brother. John undoubtedly opposed the growing popularity of gnosticism in the late first-century world (salvation comes through knowledge granted to an esoteric group) yet equally surely it left its mark on his thought.

The second factor determining Christian attitudes to asceticism was eschatology. In the earliest period there was a strong sense that the end of all things was near at hand, so that many things had to be rejected even though there would have been nothing to object to in less crisis-ridden times. Paul is inconsistent here. For instance in 1 Cor 6 he judges sexual morality through relationship with the body of Christ; in 1 Cor 7 he gives the imminent end as a reason for preferring celibacy to marriage.

With the passage of time this factor became less important, and the church accepted that it had to guide its members through normal life in the world. This is reflected in the quite different emphases the gospel writers give to their central character. Mark, for whom the time is still short, presents Jesus as a mysterious doer of great deeds; Matthew, perhaps twenty years later, sees the need for a giver of new laws to regulate the church's life, and a little later still Jesus becomes in Luke the humane and gracious figure at the centre of world-history. Consequently emphasis on ascetic rejection of the world's values is almost non-existent in Luke.

In John, however, the failure of the end to come had a nearly opposite effect. The end-time does not come because it already has come, though not for the whole world, only for the church. John's church, living by love alone, already living out the future, is in stark contrast with the world. For it, then, the asceticism of living unspotted by the world is a necessity.

The point of this brief exegesis is to show that no unique Christian teaching on asceticism is revealed in the New Testament. At certain periods of history, such as the 'flight to the desert' in the third century and after, or with the Jansenist tendencies in the Counter-Reformation church, asceticism has been highly regarded. At other times it has been played down, as in the relaxed atmosphere of the high Middle Ages or in the strongly secularized church of post-Vatican II. Both positions can claim New Testament authority, leaving us happily free to choose.

L. Bright

AUTHORITY

The decisive educational influence of one person on

another in terms of knowledge, decision and action for a short or long period, can be of great help to a person's self-determination. Various cultural factors affect authority relationships, above all simplicity and complexity, personal closeness and distance, stability and change. In institutional authority relations there is the danger of alienation (*q.v.*) resulting from the absolutization of formal functions through the increase of elements of domination and power. Anti-authoritarian and even anarchist movements and impulses are the results of abuses of authority in institutions. Authority properly exercised must rely on mutual respect, commonly recognized values and goals, and a sense of service. Obedience is an open reception of the demands and possibilities of the personal or communal fulfilment of existence. It requires criticial ability and distance as well as co-operation on the part of those in a relationship of authority and obedience. In religion, divine authority of course exceeds all human conceptions of it, but is shown in revelation as always entering into dialogue. Authority in the Church is either the mediation of divine authority for the obedience of faith or, as leadership within the community, a form of human authority whose competence and legitimation are primarily determined by the commonly experienced presence of Christ, his spirit and his power in the faith of the Church. It is a hierarchy of functions in which witness and service are pre-eminent. The maturity which ecclesiastical obedience demands consists in living out one's belief as fully as possible *in the community*.

Bibliography: Adorno, T.W., Frenkel-Brunswik, E., Levinson, D.J. & Sanford, R.N.: The Authoritarian Personality. New York, 1950. Dominian, J.: Authority.London, 1976. Lash, N.: Authority. London, 1976. Rahner, K.: Meditations on Freedom and the Spirit. London & New York, 1976. Id.: Beliefs, Attitudes and Values. San Francisco, 1968. Russell, B.: Authority and the Individual. London, 1949.

R. Hofmann

B

Behaviour. See *Action; Behaviourism*.

BEHAVIOURISM

The stimulus-and-response scheme of human action (*q.v.*) which rejects or plays down introspective, 'mental' aspects of behaviour. The study of various notions of human behaviour put forward by leading behaviourists, and by other psychologists who lay more stress on post-Freudian notions of impulse or drive, can help anyone making a Christian ethical judgment of a situation to assess the difficulties or unexpected side-effects which arise when a specific individual tries to keep to specific (ecclesiastical) norms. Understanding of the operation of learning in human psychology and of the possible nature and effects of human biology will correct easy reference to nature and physiology, so often met with in ethical argumentation.

Bibliography: **Bandura, A.**: Principles of Behaviour Modification. New York, 1969. **Broadbent, D.E.**: Behaviour. London, 1961. **Hull, C.L.**: Principles of Behaviour. New York, 1943. **Miller, G.A., Galanter, E. & Pribram, K.H.**: Plans and the Structure of Behaviour. New York, 1960. **Pavlov, I.P.**: Conditioned Reflexes. London, 1927. **Rahner, K.**: Theological Investigations, Vol. 1, London, 1961; Vol 2. London, 1963. **Skinner, B.F.**: The Behaviour of Organisisms. New York, 1938. **Id.**: Science and Human Behaviour. New York, 1953.

BEHAVIOURISM

Behavioural Research. See *Behaviourism*.

Belief. see *Faith*.

BIBLICAL ETHICS

I. OLD TESTAMENT ETHICS

1. Foundation: From the standpoint of comparative religion 'Israel's existence before Yahweh' is correctly described as 'ethical religion'. Even for the priestly office 'ethics has priority over ritual' (Hempel). The source and ground of Old Testament ethics is the Yahweh revelation. The latter consists in the self-presentation of the one God as 'Yahweh': that is, as the God who turns personally and decisively to the world and man, directing them in creation and history to an absolute future, summed up by Paul in the expression: 'God everything to every one' (1 Cor 15.28).

Man ('as partner of God') is expected to respond to God's turning to him with the free offer of a covenant partnership by realizing himself in an active 'Yes' to Yahweh and thus 'in, through and with Yahweh' to turn to the world and the human community in thought, word and deed. Thus 'service to the world' and 'service to man' are raised in the Old Testament to the level of 'service to Yahweh.'

2. The decalogue: The most compact expression of Old Testament ethics is the decalogue. In Exodus 20.1-17 it is the centrepiece of the present Sinai-pericope (19-24); in Deuteronomy (5.6-21), as a direct utterance of God, it forms the basis of Moses' sermon on the law. Its proclamation is centred mainly in the official Yahweh cult. In the light of this the 'ten words' have been described as 'apodictic Yahweh-law'. But the form of direct precept and prohibition, which is characteristic of the decalogue, has its origin in the directives for living laid down by the clan and the teachers of wisdom, family and school. Thus the 'ten words' are as much a part of *ethics (q.v.)* as of law.

As a comparison of the two versions makes clear, the decalogue has a history of growth. Nevertheless, Israel's

16

belief that it was composed by Moses is correct in the sense that, with the Yahweh-proclamation, the 'Yes' to Yahweh had to embrace also the 'Yes' to Yahweh's human community (see above, 'Foundation'). In fact, only two hundred years after Moses, the officially appointed court-prophet, Nathan, reminded David that his adultery with Bathsheba and the murder of her husband were contrary to the will of Yahweh as revealed in tradition (cf. 2 Sam 12). Consequently the revelatory character of the decalogue must be maintained in principle, even though it appears in its present detailed form to be a growth structure (of revelation!).

The basic structure of the decalogue as a 'Torah'—that is, a guide and consequently an initiation of the people of God into its future, which lies in Yahweh himself—takes the form of a fillet cross: a 'vertical' contains duties to God; but it carries also a 'horizontal' on which appear duties to the human community. Both dimensions of human self-realization 'before Yahweh' are indissolubly tied to one another. Any merely 'cultic practice' is consequently excluded from the outset.

Does the decalogue however not consist too much in prohibitions and too little in positive directives? Apart from the fact that in Hebrew the linguistic form 'you shall not' (in the sense that 'otherwise you are not the people of Yahweh') is chosen, the ten commandments are meant simply to mark out the sphere of salvation within which the people of God has to go on its ways in order to remain in possession of salvation (in anticipation of the end-time). But at the same time these demarcation points provide an invitation to fill in the sphere thus marked out with positive action.

The ethic of human fellowship is an essential characteristic of the 'ethical decalogue'. Its Deuteronomic version works this out already in the Sabbath precept, which is justified 'socially' (Deut 5.14). The sixth and eighth commandments also (in the Lutheran and the Catholic enumerations) are formulated against the background of human fellowship (and not of an abstract 'scale of values'). It is a question here of concrete goods of life: parents, love, marriage, freedom and possessions ('stealing' includes deprivation of freedom— theft [q.v.]), honour. Through its *indispensable inter-personal dimension the decalogue places the human ethic in the centre of the biblical religion and thus secures it against any hazards.*

3. *The ethics of the prophets*: The Yahwistic basic directives, which found their definitive expression in the existing decalogue, served the prophets as a standard for their indictments and directives. Amos, the first of the 'writing prophets' (about 760 B.C.) made *mispat*— that is, social justice—the main theme of his preaching (5.24). He had to deliver Yahweh's sentence of death to Israel, since men were degraded among Yahweh's people by their more highly placed 'fellow men' to become mere objects of the drive for possessions, power and pleasure (2.6-8, etc.). According to Hosea (about 745 B.C.), Yahweh's instruction to Jacob already ran: 'Hold fast to love (= *hesed* = attachment) and justice, and wait continually for your God' (Hos 12.6). The most significant ethical saying which Hosea attributes to God runs: 'I desire steadfast love (*hesed*) and not sacrifice, the knowledge of God, rather than burnt offerings' (6.6 = Mt 9.13; 12.7). To know God or Yahweh, for Hosea, is to know his will and to live by it according to the decalogue (4.1f). For Isaiah (from 740 B.C.) the basic attitude towards Yahweh is one of humble faith (7.9), but its fruits must be 'justice and righteousness' (1.21; 5.7). The 'good', without which Jerusalem is like Sodom and Gomorrha (1.9), according to Isaiah, means: 'Seek justice, correct oppression; defend the fatherless, plea for the widow' (1.17). About 700 B.C. Micah sums up revealed ethics in the lapidary dictum: 'He has showed you, O man, what is good; and what does the Lord require of you but to do justice, and to love kindness, and to walk humbly before your God?' (6.8). In order to demonstrate the equal importance of the relationship with God and the relationship with our fellow-men (cf. Mt 22.39), Micah even mentions the 'horizontal' in the first place. Both Zephaniah (from 630) and Jeremiah (from 625) likewise stand for the ethic of human fellowship (cf. Zeph 1.8f; 2.3; 3.3f; Jer 5.1ff; 7.21ff). It is the same with Ezekiel during the Exile (18.6ff; 22.6ff) and Zechariah after the Exile (7.8ff), and again with Trito-Isaiah (58.1ff: fasting means doing the works of justice and love) and Malachi (3.5).

To sum up: The prophets as 'heralds of God's will by vocation' are in principle already the advocates of what we call human rights. But behind what they understand as 'human' is Yahweh with all the weight of his divinity.

4. *The ethics of the wisdom teaching*: The early tribal wisdom in Israel certainly helped to prepare and to sustain the ethics of the decalogue and the prophets. In court wisdom the basic question, 'How successful is my life before men and before God?', is more clearly set against the background of interpersonal achievement; but at the same time God's presence (cf. Prov 15.3; 22.12) is not simply forgotten. The post-exilic wisdom teaching on the other hand (beginning with Prov 1-9) drew its directives again more from the tradition of revelation as recorded in Scripture than from reflection on the experience of life. At the same time the ethics of the decalogue and the prophets was given new expression in concrete rules of life.

A. Deissler

II. NEW TESTAMENT ETHICS

1. *Jesus' moral directives*: Jesus did not teach any ethics. Nevertheless it is sufficiently clear from our sources that his proclamation of God and of the reign of God already dawning in his work is aimed at transforming human behaviour and consequently also existing conditions. At the same time Jesus' agreement with the Old Testament Jewish tradition of faith appears to have an unmistakable character of its own. John the Baptist still concentrates on the threat of Yahweh's avenging judgment in order to justify his call to repent, to seize on the final offer of salvation. Jesus on the other hand stresses mainly the other belief firmly rooted in Israel's tradition: Yahweh as the absolutely holy and the one who demands holiness is also the one whose love, transcending all human standards (cf.Mt 20.1-15), will not let him be diverted from his salvific intentions. Hence the calls to salvation ('beatitudes'), hence — for instance — Jesus' characteristic way of addressing God as 'loving Father'. This certainty of the God approaching to save his sons and daughters is the sustaining ground and driving force of a new life, outlined by Jesus in word and

deed as obligatory but not determined in its details by casuistry.

Confronted by the God who bestows salvation we can only take up the receptive attitude of a child (Mk 10.15), only surrender ourselves to him trustfully (for God cares for us: cf. Mt 6.25f, 28-30; 10.29,31 and par.) and entirely (God or money: Mt 6.24 par.). Everything—and this means first of all his becoming Lord—is to be expected and sought from him (Our Father) before whom even the authority of the state is restricted in its scope (as in the question of the imperial tax: Mk 12.17).

The norm of the devotion required—which is certainly not to be understood as merely passive—is in the first place God's revealed will. Jesus sets this before his hearers in its absolutely essential requirements (cf. the unification of love of God and love of neighbour in Mark 12.28-34) and in its pristine clarity (for example, in the rejection of divorce) in the form of examples: in regard to relations with our fellow men (Mt 5.21-22a), *marriage* (*q.v.*) (5.27f) and *truth* (*q.v.*) (5.33f). In any case it is man's inward disposition which is required and this no 'law' can reach. Here each man is aware of his *guilt* (*q.v.*). Jesus says nothing about original sin or the struggle between flesh and spirit, but clearly states that evil springs from man's heart (Mk 7.15) (*world* [*q.v.*]); in the parables too he refers to this situation of guilt (the demands he makes however imply personal responsibility and also the possibility of fulfilment).

In the Our Father, besides seeking forgiveness for sins already committed, we ask also to be preserved from fresh sins. This can come about in fact in virtue of faith in God's salvific will which is effective even now. The love of God experienced in this way reaches its goal only in the 'response' of forgiveness by man to man (the behaviour of the first servant in Matthew 18.23ff is 'impossible'; cf. the supplementary clause in the petition for forgiveness in the Our Father).

The ultimate consequence of living in the light of God's salvific will is love of enemies. The scandal, obvious to everyone, of God the Creator bestowing his love on all, both good and bad, is to be the model of the behaviour required in realizing God's sonship (Mt 5.44f): here God in his goodness, bestowing his love also on his 'enemies', on sinners, is himself the 'norm' (Lk 6.36). According to this example, loving enemies does not mean meekly putting up with evil but mastering it by love. Only in this way is it possible to break out of the vicious circle of hatred in all dimensions of existence. In this connexion the paradoxical examples of 'repayment' which are chosen only clarify the degree of love required, even though there are circumstances which permit nothing more than the endurance of evil or a prayer for the persecutors. Even here, however, Jesus did not restrain initiative but called for it. He himself gave an example: in his openness towards people regarded as separated from God, in order to bring them back to him. He demanded this openness from his disciples, trying to convince them of the law of the love of God, who wants nothing for himself but life for the sinner, while the latter has only to accept the reconciliation he is offered (Lk 15.11-32). It is the anticipation, the most certain pre-supposition and the goal of the life which is laid open in turning to the God of love—that is, in conversion—to the advent of the reign of this God.

P. Fiedler

2. Ethics of the New Testament community

The development towards a 'Christian' ethics, which began after Easter, can scarcely be summed up in a brief formula. Here it must also be remembered that the witnesses heard in the New Testament, representing about three generations, write mainly with a pastoral concern and in each case bring diverse interests and varying degrees of reflection to bear on the concrete and constantly changing situations and queries of the people whom they are addressing.

Jesus' demand for whole-hearted commitment to the will of God who gives salvation remains the basic norm of behaviour. That is why—as the Synoptic gospels in particular testify—the essential contents of Jesus' proclamation of God and God's kingdom survive in the primitive community and in the communities outside Palestine. Jesus' requirement of love represents a positive radicalizing of the moral precepts of the decalogue and is understood as the embodiment of all commandments, as 'the fulfilling of the law' (Rom 13.8-10; Gal 5.14); it was regarded as the

21

supreme norm throughout the whole time up to James, John and 1 John, although it naturally found different concrete expressions with reference to particular situations—for example, as 'love for the brethren'. And in particular Jesus' message of the primacy of God's anticipatory salvific action is fully maintained: according to this, faith in the crucified and risen Messiah, Jesus, permitted the theo-logical substantiation of ethics to be extended by an expressly Christo-logical substantiation.

Paul can understand Jesus' atoning death (1 Cor 15.3b) in the last resort only as the insurpassable manifestation of God's redeeming love and Jesus Christ's loving devotion (Rom 5.6-8; Gal 2.20). In virtue of the self-communication of God's 'righteousness' received in faith, through which the baptized person has become 'a new creation' (2 Cor 5.17), the indicative of the salvation-event—appropriated in baptism—and the imperative of existential realization as description of the Christian's historical being are necessarily objectively connected (Rom 6.1ff; 8.1ff). The Pneuma and the freedom bestowed by him have to be proved in renunciation of sin, of the 'works of the flesh', and in 'the fruit of the Spirit', which includes 'joy' and 'peace' as well as moral behaviour (Gal 5.13ff); and the latter is inconceivable (1 Cor 8.10,13) without active love, 'the law of Christ' (Gal 6.2). But the reverse side of this eschatological existence of the believer is the dialectical 'as though not' of 1 Corinthians 7.29-31, which however must be distinguished from the Gnostic-dualist contempt for the *world* (*q.v.*); this is shown, among other things, by Paul's remarks on *marriage (q.v.)* and celibacy (1 Cor 7) and especially in his insistence that all spheres of human life provide scope for serving God in the midst of the ordinary routine of the world (Rom 12.1f).

Although Paul can cite numerous other motives for his exhortations (for example, the will of God, the honour of God, the example of Jesus and of the apostles, the public reputation of the community, and especially reward or punishment at the judgment, and the brevity of the time that remains), the decisive norm and motivation of his ethical instruction remains the new creation achieved in Christ and the membership of the 'body of Christ' involved in this. In this sense his ethic is a purely 'Christian' ethic, a 'community-ethic', which sees individuals as members of the body of Christ who are expected in virtue of the 'charism' bestowed on them to make their contribution to the 'edification'—the building up—of the community. Since what are known as 'virtues' are ultimately effects of the Pneuma it is not by chance that the term *arete* or *virtue* (*q.v.*) in the sense of personal achievement is used only sporadically. Nevertheless, Paul—who adopts also the hellenistic term *'conscience'* (*q.v.*) for the Christian's duty of moral decision—can very well encourage a Gentile Christian community not to be behind their neighbours in doing whatever Hellenism conventionally regards as good and laudable (phil 4.8). In the same sense he demands obedience to the existing authorities in the pagan state (Rom 13.1-7). In view of the hope of an imminent parousia he could not be expected to go beyond the traditional elements of instruction (as known already in the Synagogue) or to reflect—for instance—on the possible perversion of political power (cf. Revelation), still less to provide a stimulus for actively changing political and social conditions (for example, the question of slavery: 1 Cor 7.17ff; Phm). It must however be recognized that his theology contains permanently relevant basic statements on ethical behaviour in the world and that the requirement of *'agape'*, understood radically, involves a 'revolutionary' trend which breaks through and surpasses the contemporary material-ethical judgments.

The Christological-pneumatological substantiation of moral behaviour is also largely maintained in post-apostolic times (Col; Eph; 1 Pet; Jn; 1 Jn). After that, negative phenomena of ordinary life increasingly come to the fore and have to be mastered: the threat to orthodoxy from seductive false doctrines mainly Gnostic in character (esp. Jude; 2 Pet; Past); fatigue and sluggishness (Heb 12; Rev 2-3 and *passim*) with a corresponding emphasis on the necessity of 'good works' (Jas; Rev; Past) and a list of minimal moral requirements for Church ministries (Past; esp. 1 Tim 3.1ff); the distress caused by the sins of Christians—extending even to apostasy—and the problem of dealing with sinners (1 Jn; Jn 20.22f; Mt 18.15ff); also unwillingness to follow Christ in bearing undeserved disgrace and suffering (Mk 8.34 par; Heb 12.13; Jas 5.11; 1 Pet 2 and *passim*) and to

23

accept martyrdom at a time of great persecution (Rev). As time stretched out it became increasingly necessary to formulate practical rules for organizing the life of the individual and the community. Consequently recourse was had to a greater extent than formerly to the rich parenesis of Jewish Old Testament tradition and widespread traditions of popular philosophy. Thus what were known as 'household codes' were taken over and given a Christian emphasis (Col 3f; Eph 5; 1 Pet 2f; 1 Tim 2; Tit 2) as the 'simplest attempts at a morality of social duties' (Schelkle). Typical also is the increasing acceptance of basic ideas of hellenistic morality and religiosity (Tit 2.12 and *passim*). The sense of the special character of Christian ethics however was never lost. This is shown for example, in the fact that even in largely hellenized lists of virtues 'faith' and 'love' are stressed on each occasion by being placed at the beginning or end of the enumeration (Col 3.14; Past; 2 Pet 1.5-7). What the New Testament books of the post-apostolic age expressly underline is the Pauline maxim of an active faith (Gal 5.6) and the permanent requirement of living a Christian life oriented to the concrete world, to a world changing then as it is changing now.

Bibliography: OT: Dakin, D.M.: Peace and Brotherhood in the Old Testament. London, 1956. **Gelin, A. & Descamps, A.**: Sin in the Bible. London, 1967. **Jones, O.R.**: The Concept of Holiness. London, 1962. **Kimpel, B.**: Moral Principles in the Bible. London, 1956.

Bibliography: NT: Alexander, A.: The ethics of St Paul. London, 1920. **Andrews, M.E.**: The Ethical Teaching of Paul. London, 1934. **Baker, E.**: The Neglected Factor – The Ethical Element in the Gospel. London, 1963. **Davies, W.D.**: The Setting of the Sermon on the Mount. London, 1964. **Dewar, L.**: An Outline of New Testament Ethics. London, 1949. **Enslin, M.A.**: The Ethics of Paul. London, 1930. **Furnish, V.P.**: Theology and Ethics in Paul. Nashville & New York, 1968. **Id.**: The Love Command in the New Testament. Nashville & New York, 1968. **Henry, C.**: Christian Personal Ethics. London, 1957. **Lillie, W.**: Studies in New Testament Ethics. London, 1963. **Manson, T.W.**:

Ethics and the Gospel. London & New York, 1960.
Marshall, L.H.: The challenge of New Testament Ethics.
London, 1950. **Murray, J.**: Principles of Conduct. London,
1964. **Sanders, J.T.**: Ethics in the New Testament. Philadel-
phia, 1975. **Schnackenburg, R.**: The Moral Teaching of the
New Testament. London & New York, 1965. **Scott, C.A.**:
New Testament Ethics. London, 1936² **Scott, E.**: The Ethical
Teaching of Jesus. London, 1924. **Wilder, A.N.**: Eschatol-
ogy and Ethics in the Teaching of Jesus. London & New
York, 1950².

A. Vögtle

Biology. See *Behaviourism*.

BIRTH CONTROL. I

The task of regulating births is one that confronts every
married couple today. Knowing that they should give a
personal form to their marriage and that they are able to
prevent conception, they are faced with the need for
responsible parenthood. For the sake of their marriage and
the education of their children, they will not simply leave
the creation of new life to chance. On the contrary, they
will give careful thought to the timing and circumstances of
each birth. They will be guided by their consciences in their
duty to plan their family and, if necessary, to prevent
conception.

In many parts of the modern world, a population
explosion has taken place, whereas there is a marked
decline in the birth-rate in the highly industrialized countries. Because of this, there is a great need for the whole
problem of birth control to be studied sociologically and
scientifically and to be widely discussed at all levels. State
intervention in the prevention of births, however, should at
the most play only a subordinate part. It is the task of each
married couple to make decisions in this sphere. Nonetheless, there is a need for information about the implications
and methods of birth control and the prevention of
conception. The procreation of new life, for example,
outside marriage, without regard to the necessary con-

ditions for any suitable education of the child, is ultimately an act of irresponsibility. The person who has an intimate sexual relationship before or outside marriage, resulting in the procreation of new life, is bound to accept responsibilty for this act, together with the other parent, but may not be able to decide about the child's future existence. In addition to this irresponsible procreation of new life, however, there is also another—negative and materialistic—attitude that is common among married couples (and landlords) today with regard to children and especially families with many children. This attitude has to be regarded as basically immoral.

2. Unacceptable methods of birth control. Killing or aborting the foetus or child have to be rejected as negative methods of birth regulation. There are also serious moral objections to the practice of preventing the fertilized ovum from embedding in the uterus after the male and female cells have merged together to form a zygote, thus marking the biological commencement of new human life (the 'coil'). A positive method of birth control such as artificial insemination in the case of infertility on the part of the husband has also been seen as unacceptable.

3. Methods of regulating conception. The moral dimension of the choice of the method used in preventing conception is not primarily dependent on the purely biological or physiological aspect of the sexual act. It is determined far more by the significance of the whole encounter between the two partners.This encounter is, after all, in its intention, a physical expression of the love of the two partners for each other and their readiness to hand on life. The traditional teaching of the Church, proposed as official (magisterial) teaching, but not defined as infallible in the encyclical *Humanae Vitae*, describes the prevention of conception by artificial means as morally evil in itself. According to *Humanae Vitae*, then, the only permissible methods are either complete continence or observation of so-called 'safe' periods (the rhythm or temperature method). Many moral theologians have, however, argued that there are sound objective reasons for choosing other methods. The German bishops have, for example, declared that married couples

26

can, under certain conditions, act according to their consciences and make a responsible personal decision regarding the choice of method. On the other hand, however, this choice cannot be left entirely to the married couple. There is, for instance, a great difference between preventing conception temporarily by following an artificial or other method and preventing it permanently by means of an irreversible operation (sterilization). The latter can only be seriously considered as an ultimate possibility where there is an absolute contra-indication with regard to new life and where one or both partners have shown intolerance towards other methods of preventing conception. Complete continence can be too heavy a burden for the couple to bear and the rhythm method often proves unreliable or psychologically unacceptable because the marriage cannot be conducted according to the calendar. Such artificial devices as the condom and the pessary may be disturbing to the personal act of self-giving in physical love and they are often as unsafe as withdrawal (*coitus interruptus*), which can place such a strain on the man that the result is unsatisfactory and damaging to the harmony of the marriage relationship. The hormonal method of preventing ovulation (the pill) has proved to be the least detrimental of all to the personal expression of sexual love and it may well be the safest. It should, however, only be employed subject to medical discretion, since it is clearly a radical intervention in the hormone balance of the woman's body. Any moral evaluation of the various methods of preventing conception is ultimately a question of the personal maturity and responsible attitude of the partners themselves.

Bibliography: **Dominian, J.**: Proposals for a New Sexual Ethic. London, 1977. **Egner, G.**: Birth Regulation and Catholic Belief. London, 1967. **Kosnik, et al.** : Human Sexuality: New Directions in (American) Catholic Thought. London & New York, 1977. **Pyle, L.**: The Pill. London, 1967. **Roberts, T.D. et al.**: Contraception and Holiness. New York, 1964; London 1965.   *J. Gründel*

BIRTH CONTROL. II

Birth control is any means used by either sex to prevent

conception. Methods have varied over the ages but from the nineteenth century onwards techniques have become increasingly refined, so that today natural, mechanical and hormonal methods are used individually or in combination to give a very high degree of conception avoidance.

Birth regulation—that is, the responsibility of married couples to decide the timing, spacing and size of their family, and to act accordingly—has now been accepted by Christianity as an essential part of married life. There are still differences of opinion regarding the means used for birth regulation. The Catholic Church adheres officially to the view that all forms of artificial birth control are immoral and that only the natural periods of fertility and infertility in the woman's cycle should be used. The papal encyclical *Humanae Vitae* (1968) reiterated the view that any use whatever of marriage must retain its natural potential to procreate human life. This teaching remains the formal position of the Catholic Church, even though the teaching remains controversial among Catholics themselves.

The important point, however, is that whatever means of birth regulation are used, the result is an ever-increasing control by the married of the moment of fertilization. This means that the overwhelming majority of sexual acts within marriage will not be connected with procreation. The twentieth century is witnessing the end of an era when sexual intercourse was intimately related to procreation. A new meaning for human sexuality is now emerging.

This meaning might be expressed as sex as a precious gift of God. Sex is a bodily language which conveys love by affirming and confirming the life of the couple. Every sexual act has the potential of expressing thanksgiving and gratitude for the past, mobilizing hope for the future and reconciliation in the presence of conflict, and confirming the couple's sexual identity. Coitus is able to facilitate the life of the couple, and through them the life of the children who will emerge as the new meaning of human sexuality.

Bibliography: Abbott, W. & Gallagher, J.: The Documents of Vatican II. New York, 1966. **Billings, J.**: Natural Family Planning: The Ovulation Method. Collegeville, 1972. **Curran, C.**: Contemporary Problems in Moral Theology. Notre Dame, 1970. **Dedek, J.**: Contemporary Medical Ethics. New

York, 1975. **Dominian, J.**: Authority. London, 1976; 'Birth Control and Married Love' in *The Month*, London, March 1973. The Church and the Sexual Revolution. London, 1971. Proposals for a New Sexual Ethic. London, 1977. **Egner, G.**: Birth Regulation and Catholic Belief. London, 1971. Ethical and Religious Directives for Catholic Health Facilities. Washington, 1971. **Häring, B.**: Medical Ethics, Notre Dame, 1972. **C.E. Curran,** Ed: Contraception: Authority and Dissent. New York, 1969. What does Christ Want. South Bend, 1968; **Hoyt, R, Ed.**: The Birth Control Debate. Kansas City, 1968. **Kosnik, A., et al**: Human Sexuality. New York, 1977. **Noonan, J.**: Contraception. Cambridge, 1965. **Pope Paul VI**: Humanae Vitae. Rome, 1968. **Pope Pius XI**: Casti Connubii. Rome, 1930. **Pyle, L.**: The Pill. London, 1967. **Schillebeeckx, E.**: Marriage. London, 1976. Marriage: Human Reality and Saving Mystery. New York, 1965. **Uricchio, W., Ed.**: Proceedings of a Research Conference on Natural Family Planning. Washington, 1973. **Vorgrimler, H., Ed.**: Commentary on the Documents of Vatican II, vol. 5. London & New York, 1969. **Wassmer, T.**: Christian Ethics for Today. Milwaukee, 1969.

J. Dominian

Birth Prevention. See *Birth control*.

BODY

Christianity has been accused of hostility towards the body and of regarding it as totally opposed to the soul. This criticism is not without foundation.

A hostile attitude towards sexuality has characterized Christianity throughout history. Platonic and Gnostic ideas were accepted at a very early stage by the Church, leading to an identification of concupiscence (which was regarded as the result of original sin) with the natural and spontaneous reactions of human impulses (especially sexual urges). In their moral teaching about man, Christian theologians consequently contrasted matter and spirit, body and soul and sensuality and reason, always devaluing the first of each of these contrasting pairs. Because of this

29

dualism, the body and its structure of sexual and other impulses (see *Sex*) came to be seen as a force that threatened man's spiritual quest for perfection and had to be tamed and as far as possible restricted in its demands. The negative results of the application of this teaching were discernible in the emergence of an aggressive policy of dark and ominous pronouncements in the sphere of faith.

At the same time, however, it is not difficult to detect nowadays a new hostility towards the body that has almost exclusively profane origins. It has been brought about by the great influence exerted by industrial technology with its effect of reducing man to an object, and by the current ideological emphasis on activity, by the schizoid fanaticism of contemporary intellectual endeavour and by the absolute value given to the search for pleasure (*q.v.*) and the narcissistic worship of the body.

1. *Anthropological understanding*. Our present understanding of man and his behaviour does not allow us to say that he is simply a biological or physiological organism or a mere body or corporeality. To say this would give rise to the misunderstanding that man 'has' his body as something additional which is related only externally to this essential, personal being and without which he is still able to assert himself. Although the distinction between *res extensa* and *res cogitans* was clearly formulated by Descartes, the dualistic divsion of man into 'body' and 'soul' that became so firmly rooted in Western thought cannot be attributed exclusively to Cartesian influence. On the other hand, it is clear that man is not purely body and that he does not simply 'have' his body, but 'is' really body (in the same sense as he 'is' also 'soul'). It is also apparent to us today that the human body is not a mere container that is filled by the soul yet cannot really provide a proper home for it.

Many anthropologists believe that body and soul are two different aspects of a single human reality and that, according to this whole view of man, the human body does not simply end at man's finger tips, in other words, it does not incorporate within itself only what is contained by the epidermis. These anthropologists claim, then, that the wider, extended bodily environment of man also belongs to his body (secondary or extended corporeality). It ought not

to be difficult for Christian theologians to accept such a
holistic view of man, since the entire biblical teaching
testifies to the fact that man is both body and soul and any
division or opposition between body and soul is alien to
Scripture. 'Body' in the New Testament means man as a
whole and as a person in the concrete (see Rom 6. 12; 12.
1). Human life was conceivable to the biblical authors only as
corporeal (see 2 Cor 5. 1-10). When there is any question, in
the writings of Paul, for example, of a conflict between
'flesh' and 'spirit', this does not mean that the author
believed that there was a natural state of hostility existing
between the natural body and the natural spirit (or soul). It
points rather to his conviction that man, who is caught up
in sin and selfishness, is always resisting God's will.

Despite the fact that man is body, he is, unlike an
animal, able to enter into a relationship with his body and
regard it in a hostile, reserved, critical or loving way, care
for it or neglect it. In this, his relationship is not with
something else, but with himself, with the result that it
basically orientated towards an ideal self-understanding
and absence of problems (Wyss). Disturbances such as
pain, illness and certain critical phases (puberty, for
example) and the need to manipulate the body can reduce
the body to the level of an object and, under certain
circumstances, may even alienate it and place it over and
against man. In this way, man's original unity with his
body can be temporarily or even permanently changed.
What is perhaps most important in this context is that
man's identity with his body, in the sense of a close and
effective association with it, enables man to trust himself
and others, opens the way to social communication (q.v.)
and harnesses his impulses, desires, will and thinking so
that he really enters into a living relationship with the
world and his being in the world is thus fully realized.

In the light of our present understanding of this relationship as a state of being together in complete identity,
two ways of associating with the body strike us as clearly
wrong—on the one hand, an excessive preoccupation with
the body (resulting, for example, in narcissism or
hypochondria) and, on the other, treating the body as an
enemy or as an object of revulsion (Sartre). The consequences of the second attitude can, in extreme cases, be

31

that the whole shape of the body becomes neglected, dirty and unrecognizable. This hostility towards the body also occurs when it is exploited or violated or when excessive demands are made on it or it is used as an instrument to achieve certain ends. Whatever form hostility towards the body may take, it always results in a loss of living and fluent communication with the world, a destruction of true spontaneity and a narrowing and hardening of man's whole sphere of interest and concern. In addition, there is always a danger that man's relationship with his fellow men will become one of manipulation.

2. Theological interpretation. We do not yet know enough about the urgent anthropological demands made in the light of the structure and behaviour of the human body to be able to produce a really effective theology or ethical study of the body. All that we possess at present are indications of what is right and what is wrong in individual cases. It is therefore necessary to apply our existing anthropological assumptions to values that are rooted in a transempirical and valid image of man (see *Freedom*). It is possible for this need to be in accordance with Christian teaching in a very special way. In the first place, this is because the image of man that is presented to the Christian believer shows that the human body is the result of God's good act of creation, raised, in the form of the incarnate Word, to a level of exceptional honour and distinction. In the second place, it is also because man's body has been given an assured future by the fact of the Lord's resurrection (see *Hope*). The Christian understanding of and attitude towards the body is therefore bound to be decisively fashioned by this scriptural teaching about the future of man and his body. The present situation of lowliness and corruption in which the body is placed (see Phil 3. 21; 2 Cor 4. 7) has to be seen in the eschatological perspective of power and glory (see 1 Cor 15. 43; Col 3. 4; Phil 3. 20). The present darkness that covers man's corporeality is enlightened by the promise of future salvation (*q.v.*), so that 'we groan and long to put on our heavenly dwelling' (2 Cor 5. 1) and yearn for the redemption of the body (see Rom 8). What is more, our anticipation of God's future defines our moral responsibility with regard to our corporeality here and now quite clearly. According to Paul, 'the body is not meant for immorality, but for the Lord' (1 Cor 6. 13). The conclusion that the Christian must draw from this teaching is that he should not treat his body as though it were without significance with regard to salvation. He is therefore morally obliged not to use it or let it be used as an object that is different from the rest of his humanity or as a commodity that can be situated in a zone beyond all good and evil. The body, then, has a just claim to be treated with respect and modesty (see *Chastity*). Whenever the body is not treated as intimately affected by God's promise, then our attitude towards it is likely to be exposed to no less uncertainty. We shall, in other words, be without the liberating certainty of what will happen to the body.

3. *The moral task*. Since, as Karl Rahner has said, the true end of man, who will never be an angel, is the 'personalization of the material', a process which will be completed 'in the resurrection of the flesh', the Christian's response to this promise must be that he is ready to accept his body without reserve and will then do everything possible to ensure that his corporeal life will not be repressed or denied, but will be fully integrated into his whole personal being. This means above all that he will be free, unrestrained and entirely without resentment in his attitude towards the natural values of the body (see for example, *Sex*), open to beauty, strength and physical prowess, happy if the body is enriched in any way and ready to promote anything that will receive the natural values of the body and help them to be expressed. Because of this, the Christian will be resolutely opposed to the present fashionable neglect of the body that is based on a nihilistic philosophy or resignation. In the perspective of God's ultimate salvation, it is right to care for one's own body, since this expression of the Christian's full consent to the future gives a temporary foresight here and now into what transfigured man will be. Such a full acceptance of the reality of the body, however, also requires an equally full acceptance of the fact that our present corporeal state is limited by suffering and death. This means that the Christian will reject any unreal optimism that claims that

BODY

it is possible to achieve here and now a utopian state of corporeality which is untouched by suffering, death and decay. Finally, our consent to the body in our present situation of human brokenness and imperfection can also be given while we at the same time renounce the possibility of fulfilment here and now. This is all the more important when we recognize how seriously our natural corporeal values are threatened by exploitation, such as exhibitionism and greedy consumer needs. It is an important service to creation to keep one's distance from this type of exploitation and thus to ensure that the values of the body are not levelled down, prostituted or made into objects. Man's consciousness of himself, which is so necessary for his sense of personal identity, is also brought about in the same way, but it is worth noting that the object that is freely renounced (see *Abstinence*) can still be perceived in its claim to value. This is especially so if it is renounced for a long time or permanently. It would be fundamentally wrong to try to make such a renunciation subjectively easier by devaluing the object, subjecting it to defamation or simply calling it evil.

Bibliography: Fisher, S. & Cleveland, S.E.: Body Image and Personality. New York & London, 1958. **Kosnik, A., et al.**: Human Sexuality: New Directions in (American) Catholic Thought. New York & London, 1977. **Schilder, P.**: The Image and Appearance of the Human Body. London, 1935. **Thielicke, H.**: Ethics of Sex. London, 1975.

B. Stoeckle

C

Calumny. See *Honour*.

Capital. See *Capitalism; Freedom; Justice; Marxism; Theft*.

CAPITALISM

1. The term 'capitalism' refers to the conditions of life in a society in which the different social levels, the authority and the influences exerted on and by men are determined above all by the economy and in particular by the regulation of the means of production and the relationships of ownership and property. There is, in the special procedures and levels of interest that characterize a capitalist society, a certain commercial orientation which can be described as the group attitude of entrepreneurship (Weber). This is closely linked in capitalism with the view that has prevailed since the seventeenth and eighteenth centuries, namely that 'luxury helps to strengthen those economic structures that were already beginning to emerge previously, that is, the capitalist structures. All those who welcome economic progress are therefore bound to favour the growth of luxury' (W. Sombart). As Voltaire so wittily and yet mysteriously expressed it, 'Abundance is an extremely necessary thing'.

A certain unease is often felt in this context and the biblical curses pronounced over the rich and condemnations of wastefulness and living at the expense of others come readily to mind. This feeling is often increased by the suspicion that the capitalist 'system' is to blame when the surplus saved by certain economic units ('satellites') is disappropriated and monopolized by other units that are economically and politically more powerful ('monopolies') (R. Olmedo). Such criticisms are common in the current atmosphere of hostility to capitalism, a climate in which it is difficult to form a balanced judgment of its positive achievements. Any view that is not actively critical of capitalism is indeed regarded by many people today as anti-social. This, of course, points directly back to the origin of the concept 'capitalism', when it was used as a polemical term or counter-concept in the struggle in which socialists, drawing their inspiration from Marx's teaching and seeing themselves as the indirect heirs of capitalism, tried to strike a blow at that economic system and mentality which was hostile rather than simply alien to socialism.

2. *Structures and problems.* Capitalism in contemporary society can hardly be regarded as an orderly and unified whole. The word 'system' is really out of place here. There is a great deal to be said in favour of the argument that capitalism has never existed in the sense of an 'all-embracing unification of the social and economic structure'. Capitalism has been characterized as a 'primacy of economic and rational calculation', which is open to so many different possible political and social forms that any reference to the profit-making interest of the armaments industry in capitalism can, for example, be qualified by the comment that members of a 'pure' capitalist society ought to be 'essentially unwarlike in their attitude' (Behrendt) because of the fundamental need to reject all state intervention and all conflict conditioned by the state. It is therefore not simply by chance that the defenders of capitalism have identified the time of what Otto Spengler called 'unlikely peace', that is, between 1871 and 1914, with the period of 'high capitalism'. According to Marxist-Leninist critics of capitalism, however, this 'high' period was the one during which the state ruthlessly carried out a policy of violence in order to make its rich members richer, in other words, the period of imperialistic capitalism. Such inner contradictions in the attempt to define capitalism can,

however, be understood if they are seen as mutually complementary statements. After all, the unprejudiced observer knows that he must be on his guard against making overall judgments and seeking all-embracing models. Instead of trying to make a global survey of the capitalist system and its consequences, then, it is perhaps better to say that both agrarian-feudal forms of society and also (and especially) the economic processes in industrialized societies have elements of capitalism and these can be regarded by capitalism in a technological and a sociological sense.

Capitalism made human labour available in a new way, engaging on a very large scale in hitherto unknown means of production (or 'capital'). This process was in no way simply accepted—it was socially desired because of its economic utility. It also brought in its wake a very rapid development in technology. At the same time, it placed many workers in the position of being objects with regard to the means of production that had to be used. Many critics of society have defined this situation (not very convincingly) as an arbitrary exploitation of the structures, resulting in human labour becoming devoid of meaning ('alienation').

From the political point of view, a more successful form of criticism of capitalism can be summarized in the following way. The worker is reduced to the level of an object in the capitalist economy because his position as a wage-earning labourer is separated from the means of production, which cannot be appropriated by him and is therefore alien. In this process of separation, the labour ('goods') that can be purchased by the capitalist (entrepreneur) on the labour market must be bought at a price that will make the engagement of that labour profitable (see *Humanity*). This results in a numerical minority controlling all the power that can be put to economic use in an acquisitive society (capital) and arranging the economic processes (although not exclusively) to suit its own purposes.

Capitalism, then, can be regarded, with certain gradations of emphasis, as the market economy of bourgeois society. On the one hand, this has an effect on social relationships, in which the unequal and one-sided distribution of the means of acquisition (capital) is not diminished or cancelled out. In addition, this inequality, which is an essential part of the 'rules of the game', also serves to justify the inner contraditions that are present in the essentially class structure of modern society, which is based on the possession or non-possession of capital. On the other hand, however, capitalism also gives an increasingly 'bourgeois' colouring to the whole way of life of the wage-earning workers in any dynamic society. This is even the case when the economic processes have been firmly based on the principle of common ownership of the means of production in a centralized and bureaucratic organization (state capitalism). The movement that can often be observed in certain spheres in a social market economy towards a form of capitalism that is socially moderated by the setting up of such goals as codetermination (*q.v.*) in management, social partnership and power-sharing by employees cannot simply be applied on a world-wide scale. We are not yet even in a position to glimpse the 'beginning of a situation in which the at present still problematical solidarity of the proletariat may develop into a solidarity of the whole of mankind' (Horkheimer)

3. *The Church's criticism of capitalism*. Paul VI has throughout his pontificate expressed quite pronounced criticism of capitalism (for the first time in his address on 8 June 1964). Apart from making certain concrete demands (such as calling for real checks on enterprises controlling the international markets), this criticism is concerned with the need to discover the causes underlying the 'imperialism of international capital', a task initiated by Pius XI in his encyclical *Quadragesimo anno*, 109. Paul VI has rejected an unrestrained liberal (Manchester) form of capitalism and has condemned such deficiencies in economic spirit and methods as unbridled competitiveness, an insatiable desire for profit and the habit of giving an absolute value to private ownership (*Populorum progressio*, 26).

Pius XI suggested that the capitalist economy as such was ambivalent or indifferent (*Quadragesimo anno*, 101) and this can be linked to the conviction that a rationally based interest in the profitability of the economy can best be guaranteed by free private initiative. At the same time, society has to be warned of the 'spirit' and programme of a form of capitalism which calls for an unreserved incorporation into what Behrendt has called a 'coherent structure of rationality, objectivity and calculation' so that the means of production may be rationally exploited. The question of justice in economic life and of an orientation in that life towards the common good should, moreover, not be confused with the problem of just behaviour in the economic market. A series of short articles on the part played by 'remunerative businesses' with such titles as 'Abortion' or 'The Conflict in Cyprus' could justly be brought together under the common heading of 'Inhumanity'. Von Nell-Breuning called the capitalist economy a 'temptation' and declared that 'man can expose himself to that temptation only for important reasons and if the necessary safeguards are provided'. There are abundant reasons, but insufficient safeguards. See *Marxism*.

Bibliography: **Blum, F.H.**: Ethics of Industrial Man. London, 1970. **Camara, H.**: Race Against Time. London, 1971. **Gollwitzer, H.**: The Rich Christians and Poor Lazarus. Edinburgh, 1971. **Macintyre, A.**: Marxism and Christianity. London, 1969. **Nunby, D. (Ed)**: Economic Growth in World Perspective. London, 1966. **Preston, R.H. (Ed)**: Technology and Social Justice. London, 1971. **Tawney, R.**: Religion and the Rise of Capitalism. London, 1926. **Whitely, D.E.H. (Ed)**: Sociology, Theology and Conflict. Oxford, 1969.

R. Henning

CELIBACY

A celibate (the word comes from Latin) is someone required or resolved not to marry; usually through a vow implying continence. Celibacy of course implies chastity, the virtue that regulates sexual behaviour within or outside marriage, but raises much wider problems in that it is a rejection of sexual behaviour altogether: a celibate is far more than a bachelor or a spinster. While celibacy as part of a chosen way of life, stemming from the so-called 'vow of chastity' made by members of religious orders and others, has not of recent years been a matter of much controversy within the Catholic Church, the celibacy required by the Western Church as a condition of ordination to the priesthood has.

There is no point in examining the biblical evidence in detail, since it has little bearing on the matter. Advice to avoid marriage is more common in the New Testament than the Old, where it is almost unheard of, but is fully accounted for by expectation of the end of the world. In any case such advice is offered to the Christian group as a whole, not to one part of it. When we meet with the first traces of an ordained hierarchy, in the Pastoral Epistles written at the end of the first century, bishops are merely told to be 'husbands of one wife' and not to marry again after bereavement.

Growing suspicion of the body and its sexuality, perhaps the result of Gnostic or Manichaean influence, led to the growing popularity of celibate life in the desert, lived by monks and other ascetics, and with it the first attempts to impose the discipline on priests as such, starting with Nicea. These were always resisted, especially in outposts of empire; as late as the twelfth century St Aelred came from a line of hereditary priests at Hexham. At length however legislation began to bite, and by the Reformation a theoretically celibate clergy was taken for granted in the West. This was reaffirmed at Trent, and again in the Decree on Priestly Formation of Vatican II. A flurry of encyclicals in the same sense, before and since, is perhaps the clearest indication that change will eventually come about.

The reason for this is that theological ideas about sexuality and about priesthood are themselves in flux. Since Freud it has become impossible to think of people as asexual; more positively, their sexuality is known to be an aid to their maturing growth. Again, the notion that a family would hinder devotion to God, or at least the parish, is hard to sustain now that there is no necessity for sexual activity to produce one. This is not an argument against freely chosen celibacy in the religious state, but it tells against required celibacy for the secular priest. He too is no longer set apart, in a quasi-magical way, from the community he serves; is he to be denied the help of a stable sexual relationship should he so wish?

Since so momentous a change in many centuries of tradition is unlikely to take place overnight, various half-way positions have been suggested. Donald Goergen has thought, for instance, that the exercise of a priest's sexuality short of the 'fully genital' would not violate the spirit of his requirement to be celibate. Since human beings are sexual through and through, however much they may have suppressed it, it is difficult to find a very profound difference between genital and non-genital activity. Here, as usual, alleviating reform is the enemy of necessary change.

Bibliography: Bailey, D.S.: The Man-Woman Relation in Christian Thought. London, 1959. Bassett, W., & Huizing, P., Eds.: Celibacy in the Church. New York, 1972. Blenkinsopp, J.: Celibacy, Ministry, Church. New York, 1968. Dominian, J.: Proposals for a New Sexual Ethic. London, 1977. Erikson, E.H.: Identity. London, 1968. Francoeur, R.: Eve's Spare Rib. New York, 1972. Frazier, C.A.: 'Origins of Clerical Celibacy in the Western Church' in Church History 41. London, 1972. Goergen, D.: The Sexual Celibate. New York, 1975. London, 1976 (cf bibliography). Kosnik, A., et al: Human Sexuality. London & New York, 1977. Lea, H.C.: History of Sacerdotal Celibacy in the Christian Church. New York, 1966. Winnicott, D.W.: The Maturational Processes and the Facilitating Environment. London, 1965.   L. Bright

CHASTITY

The inner readiness of a person fully to accept his sexuality, to acknowledge the sexual drives in their total personal and social context and to integrate them fully into the totality of human life. See *Marriage; Sex; Masturbation; Birth control; Body; Celibacy*.

CODETERMINATION

A condition of self-determination. It is a principle of social

41

anthropology that man finds himself only through social participation. Vatican II asserted not only that capital and labour are of equal title but that labour must have the priority. Unfortunately the participation of the individual in the control process of democratic society is far too distant, in fact anonymous. Systems of worker participation and management must ensure that the personal dignity of the individual at work and in work is respected and that such schemes are not merely designed to promote functionality and productivity—in other words, the system. The human goal is the appropriate participation of all in the areas of responsibility that concern them.

D. Mieth

Colonialism. See *Capitalism; Development aid; Freedom; Marxism; Socialism; Virtue.*

Commandments. See *Biblical ethics*.

COMMANDMENTS OF THE CHURCH

The five commandments traditionally binding the baptized from their seventh year: to keep holy Sunday and Holy Days; to hear mass on Sundays and Holy Days; to abstain and fast as required by the Church; to go to confession at least once a year, if in a state of mortal sin; to receive communion at Easter or thereabouts. Also those laws of the Church governing marriage, education and so on, which are introduced and modified from time to time in accordance with the constitution of the Church.

COMMUNICATION

1. The term 'communication' is used in the general sense of coming into a relationship with another person or with others or of being in that relationship, in which the persons involved either intentionally or unintentionally share themselves or something outside themselves with each other. Man's

existence is fundamentally one of dialogue and the individual can only really come to himself in being with others. For this reason, communication is an essential prerequisite for human life and social order. All human behaviour in any situation where man is together with his fellow men, either actively or passively, speaking or in silence and using language or purely physical means of expression, has this aspect of communication. In other words, whenever one person's action evokes reaction on the part of another, it is impossible for men not to communicate. The individual person learns the rules from the first moments of his existence, without even being conscious of them.

2. *Communication as a process and a phenomenon*. As the laws, structures, functions and effects of the human phenomenon of communication have become better known and their importance has been increasingly recognized over the past forty or so years, a science of communication has developed. In this science, an equal emphasis has been placed on theoretical study and practice. The exponents of this science have made it their aim to find out how men can communicate better with each other and how to understand each other and live in peace with each other with the help of better communication.

The process of communication has been shown to be very complex. Quite apart from whether this communication takes place between individuals (interpersonal communication), groups (group communication) or large numbers of people (mass communication), the phenomenon itself goes back to the same simple basic structure: a communicator (or source of information) conveys news (information) to a recipient. The essential feature of this conveying process is that it is reciprocal. The information produces in the recipient a reaction (of consent, rejection, contradiction, etc.), which in its turn, as 'feedback', informs the communicator about the effect produced by his information. This feedback influences his behaviour. Communication, then, never operates as a oneway process. It is always a cruciform process and is always accompanied by an exchange of rôles. All information, moreover, always contains, over and above the pure data (the factual content of the information or 'content aspect') that it incorporates, a reference to the way in which the communicator would like his information to be interpreted by the recipient. This indication of the communicator's own personal attitude contained within the information is known as the 'referential aspect'. Because of this, the communication process creates a network of relationships (communication system), the complexity of which is in accordance with the number of people involved, since the behaviour of each individual is determined by the behaviour of all the other individuals and also determines their behaviour.

For this and other reasons, communication is both necessary and, if it functions well, most suitable for all forms of interpersonal relationship. It can take the form of a dialogue (and overcome isolation or eliminate or at least to a great extent limit tensions). It also has an orientating function (imparting knowledge and bringing about changes, for example). Finally, communication is also socializing in its effects (creating community or increasing understanding) or, of course, precisely the opposite. Everyone is responsible for this.

Communication, as a means of conveying information, is also essentially an interchange of signs. At a certain point, the communication itself takes over from those participating in it and becomes objectivized in a sign. This sign does not, however, only or in precisely regulated combinations with other signs (the so-called syntactic aspect) represent what is meant (the sigmatic aspect). It also has of itself a definite meaning (the semantic aspect) and brings about in the recipient an intended attitude (the pragmatic aspect). Anyone who aims to communicate something to someone else has therefore to encode or encipher his information in such a way that the recipient is able to decode or decipher it. The sign chosen must therefore have a content of meaning that is understandable. The precondition for this intelligibility is, however, a semantic agreement or correspondence between the communicator and the recipient. In individual communication, this can certainly be created in each case in such a way that each sign is combined with each meaning. In the case of a really living and above all effective flow of communication, however, a carefully structured supply of signs and rules (in other words, a code) is indispensable.

3. *The significance of language.* Undoubtedly language is the most characteristic and effective of man's system of signs. With the help of language, he is able to transmit information of two kinds—notative information (that is, purely objective or lexical) and connotative (that is, concerned with emotion, judgment or values). This information can be about all kinds of matters (object-language) or even about language itself (meta-language). It can be in a scientific or theoretical form (artificial functional language) or in everyday or colloquial language. It is clear from the modern science of language (linguistics) that what we have here is a phenomenon existing at very many different levels with a variety of problems that can only be elucidated if a great number of individual disciplines are taken into consideration.

In this attempt to clarify the problems of communication, it is not simply a question of linguistic analysis, of language as a sign-system (semiotics) or of the interrelationship between the linguistic signs themselves (syntactics) or of their meanings (semantics). It is also not only a question of the origin of those linguistic signs or of their uses and effects (pragmatics). These questions are important, but we are above all concerned with the relationship between language and the speaker's understanding of the world and of himself (hermeneutics), the culture of every linguistic community (the study of the content of language) and the social context of those communities (socio-linguistics).

Language is much more than an abstract sign-system. It is in a close and living relationship with human life in all its dimensions and, as spoken language (speech, language game), it is part of a definite form of life. To understand language, then, it is simply not enough to know the traditional code. It is rather necessary to be familiar with the whole socio-cultural and social environment in which the language is used, because this is reflected and expressed in the language and helps to give it its essential form. Spoken communication is then only possible insofar as the communicator succeeds in overcoming regional, national, cultural and social linguistic barriers, in other words, in translating his communications into the context of living and understanding that belongs to the recipient.

Perhaps the greatest obstacle to communication is the

manipulation (*q.v.*) of language for the purpose of furthering or defending positions of power. True communication is also blocked whenever the informative element is subjected to the suggestive or when the aim of convincing the recipient is replaced by that of persuasion or indoctrination. This takes place in propaganda, in demagogic, ideological or polemical language and in cases of aggression, fantasy or oppression,. In all these instances, language is distorted into the very opposite of communication. Barriers are erected instead of bridges and polarities instead of communities.

As an interchange of signs, communication always has to be transmitted through signals. These may be optical (gestures, images, writing), acoustic (sounds or words) or audio-visual (a combination of sound and image). The typical difference between the two main forms of communication, interpersonal and mass communication, is, however, to be found at another level. The first takes place without any mediation, in direct face to face contact and in constant interaction between relatively few partners. The second, however, is mediated, that is, it takes place through a technical channel of contact (press, radio or television usually), with the result that time and place are to a great extent overcome and the information reaches a potentially unlimited number of recipients.

4. *The effect of communication.* This depends on the value and reliability of the information and the communicator's skill in imparting it (the order in which he presents positive and negative arguments, his use of emotional influences and so on), the accessibility, usefulness and redundance of the information (which is redundant in the technical sense here if it can still be understood, but is not too compressed, abstract or unusual) and finally the recipient's personality. (this includes his powers of receptivity or resistance, as determined by his intelligence and formation and by ethical and national factors, to rational or emotional influences.)

Even more decisive for the acceptance or rejection of information and therefore for its effect are the interests of the recipient and his group (family, church, social stratum). What is of importance, then, is the extent to which this information is able to fit into the recipient's system of values, beliefs and convictions (and those of his group) and the degree to which it can be effective in that system. The already existing attitudes of the recipient and his group are generally so prevalent, however, that he almost always selects, on the basis of his pre-understanding and even his prejudices (*q.v.*) the information that confirms and reinforces his view or the view held by his own group from the full range of information provided by the informants. At the same time as selecting, he also rejects, changes or even falsifies the information which does not confirm and reinforce his own attitude. It has been clearly demonstrated by those specializing in the science of communication that an authentic change of attitude can only be achieved in virgin territory or in a transformed climate of opinion (where, for example, there is dissatisfaction with the past and a search for new attitudes). Any really abrupt and radical change of attitude is most unlikely in a strongly defended traditional sphere.

These laws also apply to the effect of mass communication. The fact that this process takes place at the same time does not mean that it is at once accepted and that the information is assimilated in the same way by all the recipients. On the contrary, each individual member of the mass public always reacts according to the prevalent attitude of his intimate group. The consequence of this is to bring into operation the selective and interpretative mechanisms of the group. Communication is only effective if there is intense interaction between communicator and recipient. On the other hand, the feedback in mass communication is very weak because of the relatively rigid distribution of rôles between an interested 'communicator group' with a strong orientation towards the task of communication and an unlimited number of anonymous recipients. For this reason, mass communication has less power to convince those who receive it than interpersonal communication. Even when it succeeds in bringing about a genuine change of opinion under the conditions outlined above, then, it can only do this through a communication flow at two or more levels, in other words, step by step and in connexion with interpersonal relationships (formal and informal opinion forming).

These facts have to be taken into account by those

responsible for mass education, which should not, for example, aim at audio-visual domination or at appeals to the critical understanding of consumers. A far more acceptable aim is to develop authentic values among the members of intimate groups, who are ultimately responsible for the selection and assimilation of the information provided by the means of mass communication.

5. *Power and Communication*. Communication is inseparably linked with power. The man who makes decisions about codes, sign-systems and channels of contact has power. So does the man who functions as the second link in the chain of social communication and passes the information on either completely or in a distorted form. Even the man who either accepts or rejects information is exercising power, by his affirmation, devaluation or rejection of the other's world of meaning. The important question, then, is not whether power is present in the process of communication, but rather how it is exercised—is it, in other words, used in an authoritarian way, is it used to manipulate or is it used responsibly for the good of the whole? In a free democratic society, it is the task of those concerned with the political implications of communication to create suitable structures and at the same time to maintain a competitive offer and, by doing this, to fashion the process and organization of communication in such a way that the basic rights of the individual to freedom of opinion and information are preserved. The individual in turn has the task not only of observing these rights himself, but also of granting others full freedom to observe them as well.

Bibliography: Broadbent, D.E.: Perception and Communication. London, 1958. **Cherry, E.C.**: On Human Communication. Cambridge, Mass. & London, 1957 (2nd ed. 1966). **Mead, G.H.**: Mind, Self and Society. Chicago, 1934. **Morris, C.**: Signs, Language and Behaviour. New York, 1946. **Packard, V.**: The Hidden Persuaders. New York, 1957. **Smith, A.G. (Ed.)**: Communication and Culture. New York, 1966. **Wiener, N.**: Cybernetics. New York, 1961.

A. Elsässer

COMMUNISM

A social system in which goods are owned and available in common. The state in which all modes of social repression are superfluous, and in which antagonisms and aggression have disappeared, for all things are ordered automatically according to the principle 'from each according to his ability, to each according to his need' (Marx). See *Marxism*.

Community. See *Biblical ethics; Moral education; Family; Freedom; Marriage; Value.*

Compassion. See *Forgiveness; Mercy.*

Conduct. See *Action; Behaviourism; Ethics; Ethos.*

CONFLICT

1. Basic concept and distinctions to be drawn. A conflict is a relation of opposition between two or more acting units, when at least one of them is trying to prevail over the other. Conflict is not to be equated with tension; consequently it is only in an analogous sense that we can speak of the generation conflict and the like. Similarly, oppositions or rivalries cannot be called conflicts as long as they do not occupy the same field of action but produce a balance or are integrated. A distinction is drawn between conflicts between individuals, which are chiefly the concern of psychology, and social conflict, which is a subject of sociological inquiry. The dividing lines are, of course, fluctuating, because of their mutual conditioning. Psychologically, conflict is defined as 'a type of stimulus affecting the organism which sets up two or more incompatible responses of functionally equal strength' (B.A.Maher). Behaviourist research has investigated these stimulus-response patterns. Conflict within the individual has ethical significance as a conflict of conscience which, however, is not caused mechanically, but by the previous good decision. Social conflict may be divided into inter-social and intra-social conflicts. Inter-social conflict is a conflict between persons or groups who in their particularly intense interests (power, economic, emancipation) clash in regard to the same thing (field of conflict). Intrasocial conflict, on the other hand, is a contradiction inherent in one and the same social system which has erupted (class conflict, racial conflict). Research into conflict is of considerable interest for the social and political sciences. Schemes for the solution of conflicts are, however, dependent on value assumptions. For example, it is very important for the solution of conflicts whether the determining value is taken to be social integration or social innovation. If with the consensus theory society is regarded as a system of institutions and rôles relating to a regulated whole, then integration is the recurrent system-preserving theme. Conflicts are mishaps of the system. Within a theory of a system as open to correction, however, conflicts appear rather as learning processes in the system. Since K. Lewin, conflict research distinguishes three basic types of conflict: approach-approach conflict with equal attraction between different things or equal desire on the part of different agents; approach-avoidance conflict when the desire is coupled with resistance; avoidance-avoidance conflict when what is unwanted has to be reached because of compulsion. These basic models can be further elaborated and modified.

2. Moral relevance. Ethical importance attaches in particular to the investigation of group conflicts and analysis of conflicts between systems and within them, which is important for research into peace. In the genesis and and resolution of conflicts, power relationships play a big part; they must therefore not be overlooked in the analysis. It is clear that conflict study can provide ethics with important factual information, above all in the domain of social ethics (q.v.). Ethics, however, has also to scrutinize the ideas of value involved in models representing the origin and solution of conflicts. From the ethical point of view, conflict is fundamentally ambivalent; it is therefore neither bad in itself (harmonious thinking) or the good 'father of all things' (dialectic of history). Its destructive and constructive potentialities depend largely on what judgment is passed on circumstances, means and ends. Knowledge of how to regulate conflicts plays a rôle in problems of decision,

problems of integration (system-endangering conflicts) and problems of progress (innovating conflicts). The pugnacious element in man's individual and social self-realization is at all events not bad in itself, but takes its value or worthlessness from the relation in which it stands. The idea of a harmony without tension or of a basically passive attitude, is foreign to the Christian ethos (cf. for instance Mt 10.34; 11.12; Lk 13.22; 1 Cor 9.24 ff). The Christian ethical model for the solution of conflicts is consequently not that of harmony but of reconciliation (see *Love*), in which differences are not levelled out, but the elements of tension unfold their mutual fruitfulness.

Bibliography: **Epstein, S.**: The Measurement of Drive and Conflict in Humans: Theory and Experiment. In: **Jones, M.R. (Ed.)**: Nebraska Symposium on Motivation. Lincoln, 1962, 27-206. **Hull, C.L.**: A Behaviour System. New Haven, 1952. **Lewin, K**: A Dynamic Theory of Personality. New York, 1935. **Luria, A.R.**: The Nature of Human Conflicts. New York, 1932. **Yates, A.J.**: Frustration and Conflict. New York, 1962.

D. Mieth

CONSCIENCE

1. Place and value accorded to conscience in contemporary society. The fact that special importance is recognized as attaching to this subject, is significantly connected with modern endeavours to achieve *autonomy* in all domains of life. Even in dealing with morally important concerns modern man claims the right to self-determination. This means that in a previously unparalleled way he is thrown back on himself as soon as he is called upon to make a moral decision. It is true that the conditions of the contemporary world are not of a kind readily to satisfy the claim to moral autonomy and the implied wish for a personal life determined solely by one's own conscience. We must recall first of all the phenomenon of direction from outside ('other-directed man': Riesman) which compels people to conformist behaviour and thus considerably lessens their freedom of decision and conscience. There is also the fact that the technocratic structure of society to some extent promotes blurring of personal responsibility, for in this

51

system every one can shuffle off his responsibility onto others, which of course results in one individual finding himself shouldering a burden of responsibility which he is no longer able to bear. All this explains two things. The first is that conscience is assuming new forms. For example, it is increasingly assuming a private character as the individual's last chance of self-defence against the overwhelming weight of external compulsions. This also, of course, is a sign of the attempt to evade onerous obligations as far as possible. Then there is the functionalization of conscience, where conscience is no longer appealed to primarily for the sake of moral value-judgment, but rather in order to camouflage interests and justify needs. Secondly there is the phenomenon which must quite simply be called a 'revolt of conscience' (cf. for instance Camus, Gandhi, Solzhenitsyn, Horkheimer, Camara and also the protest movements among the younger generation).

2. *Meaning of the word.* As the prefix 'con-' indicates, 'con-science' points to a special kind of knowledge ('-science'). The older English word for it was 'inwit'. Conscience is from the Latin, where the word bore two meanings, self-awareness (*sui conscientia*), consciousness, memory, and conscience in the ethical sense. The literal sense, 'knowledge with another' (cf. Aquinas, S. Th. ka q 79 a13: *conscientia dicitur cum alio scientia*) defines conscience as an intersubjective phenomenon, as joint knowledge, co-knowledge, and this was understood as man's co-knowledge with God or God's joint knowledge with man.

3. *Biblical data.* The Old Testament has no special term for the reality signified by 'conscience' (An exception to this is Wis 17.11, derived from Hellenic modes of thought). It can nevertheless speak metaphorically on occasion of conscience as the voice of the divine judge (Gen 3.7-11; 4.10-12). In this connexion the terms 'heart' and 'kidneys' assume special importance. Since, generally speaking, the problem of man's relation to himself is less prominent in the Old Testament than his relation to God, conscience does not appear as a direct object of reflection. In the New Testament the word conscience (*syneidesis*) is not found in the gospels. On the other hand reference is constantly

made in Jesus' words to the heart of man; this is what represents the inner intention, conviction and attitude, and determines the moral value or worthlessness of an action. The position is different in the apostolic writings. The term conscience (*syneidesis*) is in current use with Paul. It serves him, as for instance in Romans 2.15, to denote that inward critical organ which makes it possible even for the heathen to live a life corresponding to that of a Jew according to the Law. The apostle leaves us in no doubt about the eminent rank of action in accordance with the judgment of conscience. It is true that 'whatever does not proceed from conviction (RSV: faith) is sin' (Rom 14.23), but the social responsibility incumbent on conscience is made equally clear. As can be seen from 1 Corinthians 8.7 ff, the Christian's *freedom* (*q.v.*) for tutelage of another's conscience is proclaimed. That is why regard must be had for the conscience of the weak. This can entail an obligation for the 'strong' to omit some action which can be done with a good conscience (eating of meats offered to idols) for the sake of a (still) wavering neighbour (see *Toleration*). The guideline of conscientious action is, therefore, love. The pastoral epistles insistently appeal to the believers' good conscience (Tit 1.15; 1 Tim 1.19; 4.2; 2 Tim 1.3). The Christological emphasis apparent in this, indicates that conscience in the Christian view is forward-looking and bound by Christ's law of love.

4. *Systematic analysis.* Any theological endeavour to elucidate the reality denoted by conscience, will have to face the question whether conscience is solely the product of immanent historical evolution or whether it also exhibits elements and structures which justify recognition of a meta-empirical transcendent root. An objective answer to this question will resist the temptation to operate with deductive arguments. It will have to proceed inductively, first (*a*) determining the anthropological position of conscience and then (*b*) by way of empirical pyschological clarifications.

(*a*) Human action and behaviour in general comprise the operation of three components. First there are the needs and drives, which indicate what the human being wants. Then there is the encounter with obligation, which notifies

53

the norm regulating vital activities and is called 'conscience'. Finally there is the act of will pronounced by the ego as judge. The relations between these three factors of desire, obligation and will, fall into extremely varied patterns. Nevertheless the human being knows that he ought not to do just anything that in itself he would like to, that sometimes he ought to do something which he does not like at all, and that his will in various ways does not correspond to what he ought to do, but only takes account of what he desires.

(b) In the early childhood stage itself, frequent identity of desire, obligation and will can be observed. The development of the small child, however, brings a distinct awareness of obligation and consciousness of the ego as source of decision becomes more explicit. In the psychoanalytic terminology of S. Freud, these three factors are termed id, superego and ego. The superego plays a decisive rôle in the emergence of conscience because, after the resolution of the Oedipus complex, it is in it that the introjected paternal authority is manifested. The stronger the Oedipus complex, the stronger the development of the superego. A strong superego affects the ego proportionally more, and produces anxiety, which appears to the ego as a troubled conscience (see Conflict).

A critical evaluation of this theory of conscience will certainly have to take into account its valuable features. For instance, it is correct to bring out the importance of the primary reference group (parents) for the formation of conscience. Conscience takes shape from others and through others; it is dependent on the human environment and the structures of authority that characterize it. Nevertheless, the conscience as 'judge and accuser', as manifested in the superego, is probably—at least in normal cases—a transitional stage in development towards a mature and adult conscience, though it must be admitted that many people never get beyond this genetically early stage. In most cases when people appeal to what they call their clear conscience but really mean simply what conforms to the generally prevailing morality or immorality, it is a matter not of the expression of a mature conscience, but of a hardened superego structure. Contemporary psychology has ceased to equate the origin of conscience with the formation of the superego, and tries to find bases for the formation of conscience in the development of narcissistic modes of experience and behaviour. From narcissistic relations to objects the moral standards of the superego orientated by ideals take shape, while from the Oedipal relationships are derived the moral demands which are turned more towards reality. Through this the different contents of the demands of the superego can be explained. In a sketch of the genetic development of the conscience, this phase, according to J.M. Hollenbach, represents the first stage, the so-called habituation-conscience of early childhood. Typical of this stage is the guidance of decision from outside, from which any spontaneous self-expression is lacking. This phase also shows the original incompleteness of man, his need first to learn what is right and proper for himself and others. Furthermore the dialogue character of conscience is already apparent, its dependence on social contact for its formation. A second phase from about the fourth to the tenth year of life, brings the development of the ambivalent habituation-conscience. Here the child has to learn to bring its demands into harmony with the various needs of the reference persons and social groups. It has to learn to distinguish between persons entitled to give instructions and those who are not. At the same time the self-utterance of conscience has also to be deployed. For this, the knowledge of criteria of action and their correct application to the particular concrete case is indispensable.

A further phase is represented by the pre-critical responsibility conscience. This coincides more or less with puberty, and brings with it an unsparing scrutiny of the norms previously held valid. This often involves a rigorist elaboration of moral claims which are held with inexorable severity and logic. This one-sidedness can be explained by the lack of personal experience of the world.

The self-critical responsible conscience represents as it were the final phase of conscience formation. It is very closely linked with the experience of and orientation towards *value* (*q.v.*) of a mature personality, and is able to distinguish between rigorist fulfilment of norms and truly moral decision. This kind of outline of the development of conscience makes it clear that conscience cannot be regarded as an innate human drive which has reached its full development, having, as it were, unfolded of itself according to its own laws and without the cooperation of the environment. But neither can conscience be understood as a set of rules of moral duty lying dormant in man, which only need to be brought into consciousness. The psychological view of the development of conscience, however, does indicate that in man there is something like a disposition for conscience, though of course it requires for its development a complicated interplay of ego and value discovery. Further light on the phenomenon of conscience is made possible by considering what is specific to its various strata. This directs attention to three basic aspects.

The intra-individual aspect of conscience centres on everything concerned with human self-realization. The philosopher Martin Heidegger made a significant contribution in this field in *Being and Time*. For him, conscience discloses itself in human existence as care, as a summons to human beings to leave inauthenticity, where they are victims of impersonal anonymity, into authenticity, the self. This human existence or reality which has to be protected from succumbing to anonymity, is the whole human being with his corporeal structure, any injury to which announces itself in the biological awareness of health, with his psychological structure, injury to which gives rise to phenomena such as oppression, inhibition and neuroses, and with his intellectual or spiritual structure, on which conscience likewise has great influence. At the same time the intra-individual aspect of conscience points to an ego-relation, to the awareness that one's own person is at stake, but at the same time to a relation to value, which makes man capable of decision even in this personal domain.

The intersubjective aspect of conscience, in agreement with psychoanalytic and even theological considerations (Aquinas), emphasizes the dialogue structure of conscience, as is shown in the 'guilty conscience' of having harmed another human being. In the verdict of conscience, however, both domains, the self-judgment and that emanating from the partner, form an inseparable unity and condition one another.

The meta-empirical aspect of conscience follows from the

impossibility of adequate explaining conscience by immanent categories; a circumstance which even in Antiquity led to the assumption that God reveals himself in conscience. In the course of time this led to the idea that conscience is the voice of God. Even if one does not want to accept this view, the judgment of conscience nevertheless manifests a clear tendency to feel oneself responsible not only *for* someone, but also in a radical way *to* someone, who is identical neither with one's own ego, nor with another human being, nor with society as such. This awareness of responsibility to someone is so unconditional that it goes beyond knowing oneself responsible in regard to an abstract principle, and points to an absolute personality.

5. *Manifestations of conscience.* Four different categories can be distinguished here. In the first place, according to the kind of declaration in which conscience is expressed. A distinction must be drawn here between an attitude of rejection and one of approval. In regard to past or present decisions, we speak of a guilty conscience accusing or condemning, or of a good or quiet conscience. However, conscience does not express itself only after certain actions in the sense of the 'inner judge' (Kant) who reproaches the accused with his guilt, but also before an action, in which case its attitude may once again be favourable or unfavourable. So we speak of a warning or guiding and directing conscience in regard to the future. These forms of conscientious judgment are of great practical importance for human action, for they affect actions directly by their influence.

From the fact that conscience develops through various phases, which, moreover, exhibit a tendency from external guidance to inner control, its development may be disturbed. This gives rise to the well-known defective forms of conscience. The over-conscientious or scrupulous conscience is a faulty attitude, often due to excessive strict moral demands imposed in early childhood. The opposite attitude, lack of conscience or lax conscience, represents a deviation downwards. Its basis can be lack of guidance in childhood. This defective form may range from underdevelopment of sensitivity to movements of conscience to complete moral insensibility in the form of a blunted conscience. For the conscience dominated by law, and out of touch with real life, the movement of conscience has become a stencil which is applied without regard for human considerations (what has been called the penitent's catalogue-of-sins conscience). Another variant is the pharisaical conscience in which small duties are magnified, while great and decisive ones are neglected. Unscrupulousness is often used to mean the actual behaviour of a man who behaves as if he had no conscience at all. Total absence of conscience, however, probably cannot be shown to exist. Certainly the voice of conscience can be so faint that one might suspect a lack of conscience in general. On the other hand, an absence of even considerable spheres of activity of conscience can come about.

6. *The moral importance of conscience.* For concrete human action and its ethical quality, conscience plays a rôle that is not to be underestimated. For a decision often does not involve a question of the application of a law or a norm to a concrete situation, but rather means discovering and recognizing with the help of conscience what is right, where duty lies. Tradition took this fact into account by regarding the judgment of conscience as the final and authoritative norm for the individual decision (*regula proxima moralitatis*), even if the judgment were later to turn out to have been objectively wrong. It is assumed here, of course, that the conscience in question is what is called 'certain', that is to say, that there is no known reason to doubt the appreciation of the situation, circumstances and values. If this certainty (*certitudo*), which of course can never be mathematical, but always a moral one, is lacking, there is either theoretical or a practical conscientious doubt. A theoretical doubt does not make action illicit, but in case of practical doubt, action must be postponed and every effort first be made to remove the doubt. This can be achieved by fuller information, through the application of general axioms or of a general reflex principle. Another requisite is that the judgment of conscience must be correct. This correctness (*rectitudo*) is attained if the judgment corresponds to the objective moral *norm* (*q.v.*), otherwise a superable or an insuperable error of conscience is present; the first has to be removed, but in the second the

conscience is binding. The certain conscience is always decisive for subjective action. The importance of conscience is also rightly shown by reference to freedom of conscience, a right which is inseparably bound up with human dignity, which transcends time and the State, and from which the right to the free practice of religion also derives (cf. Vatican II, *Decree on Religious Freedom*). For the exercise of this right man is dependent to a high degree on the virtues of *prudence* (*q.v.*) and *toleration* (*q.v.*), because they mark out the frame within which a meaningful and socially beneficial realization of the right to freedom of conscience is possible.

For the Christian, the significance of conscience goes beyond the mere possibility of development of the personality and self-realization. He knows that the voice of conscience does not confront him with an anonymous principle; he recognizes in it the summons and exhortation of the personal God who by this call really individualizes the human being and gives him a freedom which, far from being in any way arbitrary, enables him to achieve his authentic being.

Bibliography: **Aronfreed, J.:** Conduct and Conscience. New York & London, 1968. **Bandura, A. & Walters, R.H.:** Social Learning and Personality Development. New York, 1963. **Berkowicz, L.:** The Development of Motives and Values in the Child. New York, 1964. **D'Arcy, E.:** Conscience and its Right to Freedom. London, 1961. **Erikson, E.H.:** Childhood and Society London, 1963[2]. **Greet, K.:** The Art of Moral Judgment. London, 1976. **Hartshorne, H & May, M.A.:** Studies in Deceit. New York, 1928. **Heidegger, M.:** Being and Time. London, 1962. **Janssens, L.:** Freedom of Conscience and Religious Freedom. London, 1966. **Kohlberg, L.:** Development of Moral Character and Moral Ideology. In: **Hoffman, M. & Hoffman, L.W. (Eds):** Review of Child Development Research, Vol. 1. New York, 1964. **Mowrer, O.H.:** Learning Theory and the Symbolic Processes. New York, 1960. **Peters, R.S.:** Freud's Theory of Moral Development in Relation to that of Piaget. Brit. J. Educ. Psychol., 1960, *30*, 250-8. **Piaget, J.:** The Moral Judgment of the Child. London, 1932. **Pierce, C.:** Conscience in the New Testament. London, 1955. **Ramsey, I.T. (Ed.):** Christian Ethics and Contemporary Philosophy.

London, 1973. **Sears, R.R., Maccoby, E.E. & Levin, H.**: Patterns of Child Rearing. Evanston, 1957.

W. Hesse

Contraception. See *Birth control*.

Conversion. See *Biblical ethics; Forgiveness*.

COURAGE

One of the main virtues. The human ability to remain true to convictions and awareness of responsibility despite all risks, whatever the risk to social recognition, health and even life. Spiritual courage is due striving for an maintenance or defence of truth. Like all virtues, courage is learned. This occurs through the repetition of courageous behaviour but depends on other factors such as a lively sense of social awareness and criticism, and an individual sense of responsibility which does not flinch at consequences or avoid decisions. Education is essential in the process of inculcating courageous action and must avoid all tendencies to inculcate instead any obedience to authority without due criticism. It must promote self-determination.

V. Eid

Cowardice. See *Hope*.

D

Death. See *Aging; Guilt; Suicide*.

Death of God. See *Godlessness*.

Decalogue. See *Biblical ethics*.

DECISION

An active moment of the human impulse to self-realization. Also the process of sensory discrimination.

Despair. See *Hope*.

DEVELOPMENT AID

1. Scope: Development aid comprises the various forms of capital aid (credit), charitable aid (such as food and medical supplies), technical aid (for example in the form of advice) and educational aid, which as well as providing emergency relief, ensure and promote the physical and spiritual welfare of the so-called under-developed countries, namely the needy areas of the Third World.

Development aid may be effected through private or official, national or international channels and not least through religious organizations such as Justitia et Pax and Caritas International. They aim not merely to eliminate or alleviate material need and distress but to promote and ensure a truly human standard of living, stability, prosperity and world peace. Above all development aid is simply the first step to self help; the recipient is throughout capable of independence and self-supporting progress and development. Neither 'alms' nor the simple distribution of charity can therefore suffice for development aid is a question not of distribution but of production. But nor is economic aid alone sufficient. Church documents give especial prominence to this point, in view of the present economic situation which they regard not only as deplorable in itself but a potential threat to world peace. Indeed they insist that the primary object of economic aid is the promotion of the welfare of those receiving it; more specifically in the view of the encyclical *Populorum Progressio* (PP) aid must be directed toward human progress and development in the widest sense and must ensure the participation of all peoples in a culture that is at once ethnically, nationally and regionally differentiated, and totally human (a new humanism) (see II Vat. GS 63-65; 83; PP 14; 20; 34). This demands an expanded aid programme particularly in the fields of educational and social reform (for example a campaign against illiteracy) so as to further widespread participation in political life, cultural and structural reform and an ambitious and practicable development policy. See *Alms*.

2. Moral responsibility: The concept of development aid is morally grounded in the humanitarian concern of the countries with more advanced economies and a higher standard of living for those peoples in greater economic need. Church documents relating to ethical and political questions see all men's participation in the material and spiritual goods of the earth as a God-given right; they demand responsibility and care for the whole human community and base their concern on the notion of the natural and supernatural brotherhood of man which must be realized through supportive solidarity, social justice and universal love (GS 84; 86; PP 44). The difficult question of whether and how far development aid may stem from motives of profit or of altruism (or from a mixture of both) cannot be answered here. But in view of the entanglement of all aid programmes with massive economic interests and the consequent dependence of developing countries—with the effect that the poor become progressively poorer—attention should be paid to the repeated warnings against all forms of abuse and exploitation whether in the form of an exagerated seeking after profit, national prestige, political and military supremacy, ideological indoctrination or neo-imperialism. All this contradicts the basic principle that development aid should meet the needs and aspirations of the recipient, and above all that there should be an effective partnership between giver and receiver encouraging the maximum independence and involvement on the part of the latter.

3. *The Christian mission*: The Church's own work in the field of development aid stems from her conception of herself as a 'Church of the poor', 'a Church bound to service in the spirit of love' (Völkl). 'The spirit of poverty' which she assumes in response to Christ's command and example both commits her to the service and protection of the poor and prohibits her identification with the rich. Her political and cultural neutrality guarantees her detachment from colonialism, 'Europeanism' and all attempts to impose control, and assures her disinterested commitment to the ideal of service. Her central concern is with justice and with the elimination of the *scandal* (*q.v.*) of the unequal distribution of goods among Christians (for example in the Latifundian economies of the so-called Catholic countries) and the consequent cultural inferiority of the native population. But the driving force behind this concern is universal love—the fundamental principle of the 'transformation of the world' (GS 38). Christ called his followers to love the poor, with a love, that transcending good intentions, takes the form of effective action. Christians are called to more than the traditional giving of alms; they are asked to share the 'substance of their wealth' rather than merely donating a part of their 'surplus'. In this way 'the spirit of love' is translated into a world-wide programme of aid and an

effective campaign to serve the needy (GS 88). But in view of the undeniable difficulties and economic problems, which can impair the readiness to give aid, it is the Church's duty, through its preaching and influence on public opinion, continually to clarify, reinforce and preserve this ideal of service to man and humanity.

Bibliography: **Assmann, H.**: Practical Theology of Liberation. London, 1974. **Gollwitzer, H.**: The Rich Christians and Poor Lazarus. London, 1970. **Gutierrez, G.**: A Theology of Liberation. New York & London, 1973. **Preston, R.H. (Ed.)**: Technology and Social Justice. London, 1971. **Vaughan, B.N.Y.**: The Expectation of the Poor. London, 1972.

R. Völkl

Dignity. See *Human dignity*.

Dispossession. See *Liberation*.

Domination. See *Conflict*.

Doubt. See *Faith*; *Hope*.

Drug Addiction. See *Addiction*.

E

Ecology. See *Environment*.

Economy. See *Capitalism; Development aid; Social ethics; Socialism*.

EDUCATION

There is no generally accepted definition of the term. It refers to a human activity which is always socially and historically determined, but which is subject to change and requires a form of legitimation which is not directly derivable from its historical and social determination. The notion of education as formation in its modern acceptation goes back to the ideas of the French Enlightenment and its realization of the bourgeois ideals of each individual as representing the idea of humanity.

In general, however, education is taken as referring to all those processes by means of which the 'coming generation' is enabled to undertake the tasks laid down within the framework of a pre-existing social situation. Education as formation demands critical insight into such social tasks as well as their accomplishment. The norms, means and institutionalization of education depend on the particular self-understanding (extent of consensus about values and tasks) and on the economic structure of a society (complexity, division of labour, the development of productive forces). On the other hand, society is also dependent on education in regard to the handing on of its *status quo*, further development, and the possibility of change.

Education may be understood as a process of goal-directed effects, and educational measures may be judged according to whether they impart the results (behaviour patterns) intended in each case. Hence education may be interpreted as a social sub-system and the question of the legitimation of educational processes is either excluded from the area of scientific reflection (Karl Popper) or reduced to the cybernetic principle of the maintenance of stability in the system (Talcott Parsons).

In the practical behavioural understanding, education is a process in which the person to be educated is enabled to enter into critical confrontation with the social demands he encounters and is fitted for co-operation in the human-ization of society. Educational measures and institutions are judged according to whether they promote or hinder such learning processes, and analyze both the social conditions which reduce the possibilities of education or promote them, and the educational actions and forms of interaction which could contribute to a change in social conditions.

A theological ethics which is not prepared to sacrifice the profound dimensions of human existence to the purposive technical interests of society would have to opt for the second more practical notion of education. The various social groupings (family, youth groups, schools, Christian parishes) are duty-bound to establish the possibilities of learning so that convincing models and a climate of love are available. See *Family; Moral Education*.

Bibliography: Allport, G.W.: Personality. New York, 1937. Id.: Pattern and Growth in Personality. New York, 1961. Backman, S.W. & Second,P.F.: A Social Psychological view of Education. New York, 1968. Bantock, G.H.: Education and Values. London, 1965. Id.: Education, Culture and the Emotions. London, 1967. Bernstein, B.: Social Class and Linguistic Development: A Theory of Social Learning. In: Halsey, A.H. et al. (Eds): Education, Economy and Society. New York, 1961, 288-314. Id.: A Socio-Linguistic Approach to Social Learning. In: Gould, J. (Ed.): Social Science Survey, Harmondsworth, 1965. Bloom, B.S. (Ed.): Tax-onomy of Educational Objectives. The Classification of Educational Goals, 2 vols. New York, 1956-64. Bruner, J.S.:

The Process of Education. New York, 1960. **Id.**: Toward a Theory of Instruction. New York, 1966. **Id.**: Learning About Learning. Washington, 1966. **Cox, E.**: Changing Aims in Religious Education. London, 1963. **Deutsch, M., Katz, I. & Jensen, A.R. (Eds)**: Social Class, Race and Psychological Development. New York, 1968. **Freire, P.**: Education for Critical Consciousness. New York & London, 1968. **Id.**: The Pedagogy of the Oppressed. New York & London, 1969. **Gage, N.L. (Ed.)**: Handbook of Research on Teaching. Chicago, 1963. **Gagne, R.M.**: Learning and Individual Differences. Columbus. 1967. **Goldman, R.**: Readiness for Religion. London, 1966. **Halsey, A.H., Floud, J.E. & Anderson, C.A. (Eds)**: Education, Economy and Society, New York, 1961. **Kay, W.F.**: Moral Development. London, 1968. **Loukes, H.**: Teenage Religion, London, 1968. **Id.**: Teenage Morality. London, 1968. **Peters, R.S.**: Authority, Responsibility and Education. London, 1963. **Id.**: Ethics and Education. London, 1966. **Rogers, C.R.**: The Clinical Treatment of the Problem Child. Boston, 1939. **Sluckin, W.**: Imprinting and Early Learning. London, 1964. **Stenhouse, L.**: Culture and Education. London, 1967. **Tanner, J.M. & Inhelder, B.**: Discussions on Child Development, Vols 1-4. London, 1971. **Tibble, J.W. (Ed.)**: The Study of Education. London, 1966. **Wilson, J., Williams, N. & Sugarman, B.**: Introduction to Moral Education. Harmondsworth, 1967. **Wiseman, S.**: Education and Environment. Manchester, 1964.

D. Benner

Education, Moral. See *Moral education*.

ENVIRONMENT

1. Terminology and state of the question. Environment is used for the whole set of domains of reality which act on an organism (from outside) and of which the organism itself forms part. Two particular domains are especially important, namely the sociologically determined social environment (personal contemporaries, milieu) and the ecologically determined environment, which is what we are more particularly concerned with here. This comprises the linked ecosystems in a region of living beings (plants and animals) and inorganic substances (air, water, rocks, soils, mineral wealth), which are interwoven in cycles (of oxygen, carbon etc.; photosynthesis) and food chains, which are interdependent and are able to ensure their survival by natural balanced flows. Human life is integrated into these ecosystems and has always felt their effects both as animate and as inanimate nature.

Although a healthy human social life is dependent on proper functioning of the ecosphere, scientific technological interventions in the environment have become increasingly drastic in modern times. At present there are many domains in which serious types of pollution of the environment have occurred (smog, as a danger to health and even sometimes to life in dense industrial areas, pollution of air, land and water by industrial and domestic refuse, poisonous effluent etc.), so that there is talk of a 'suicide programme' already in operation (G. R. Taylor), of the 'creation on the edge of the abyss' (G. Altmer). A. M. K. Müller speaks of the mortal threat to our future; this, he says, is not an inexplicable fate, but the result of scientific and technical endeavours, in which an unparalleled increase of human power over nature is being achieved without any reliable awareness of the right use of this power.

2. Chief desiderata. Since damage to the environment is the result of one-sided human decisions or omissions, human beings are responsible for it. Before it is too late, individual and social behaviour as a whole must be directed towards responsibility for the environment. Re-thinking and a change of outlook must accompany conversion from the kind of narrow, one-sided thinking in terms of progress, growth and power which has gone on too long. Every day now the 'limits of growth' are more plainly evident (Club of Rome 1972). Human behaviour in the industrially developed countries must cease to reflect the attitudes of societies of superabundance and waste, and achieve a reasonable production and consumption with due concern for how the limited resources can in a socially just way benefit all, including the economically underdeveloped countries. Out of solidarity with all men, the waste of resources (foodstuffs, raw materials, energy) must cease, as well as all avoidable damage to the environment, starting with individual behaviour (an end to disposing of litter in woods or water instead of in communally regulated ways, switching off engines that poison the air) and extending to the social problems of reducing or stopping industrial effluents into air and water, of salvaging certain materials for repeated use (recycling), and of finding political ways of preserving natural landscapes (town and country planning). Nowadays these are morally relevant problems, equally with that of a responsible growth of population. Since human life depends on the use of mineral wealth and raw materials and, for agricultural products on natural growth, mankind's claim to take the environment into service cannot be questioned. Nevertheless, its ruthless exploitation is irresponsible and unworthy of man. Here, too, some methods of feeding or keeping animals must be critically examined, as well as various fertilizers and methods of pest control (DDT and its derivatives). One-sidedly scientific, technological and economic efforts have led to the environmental crisis; cautious efforts taking account of the whole pattern of living things must seek a way of escape from it and change men's behaviour accordingly.

An ecological ethos is based above all on insight into the interdependence of living things, and must be guided by what is really capable of serving human life in its relation to its environment now and in the long run. A new relation to nature will respect the environment as a common possession (cf. GS 69,1), which should contribute to making men's vital activities good and healthy. Good behaviour in regard to the environment will reject any arbitrary disregard for pollution or poisoning of the environment as inhuman and immoral.

3. *Contribution of faith*. People who endeavour to solve their vital problems by Christian faith, must consider the fact that the full meaning of the accounts of creation (Gen 1 and 2) does not signify irresponsible conquest or domination of the creation, but rather a caring and protective attitude similar to a shepherd's. God himself is the Lord and shepherd, who rules with forbearance. The love (agape) which Jesus entrusts to Christians as God's encour-

agement and as their task (1 Jn 4), will strive to know and fulfill God's will for the environment. The Church's teaching (cf. Paul VI in *Octogesima adveniens*, 1971) points to responsibility for the environment as based on a comprehensive view of man and of humane conduct (cf. AAS 59 B1967] 264) (see *World*).

Bibliography: Schaeffer, F.A.: Pollution and the Death of man: the Christian View of Ecology. London, 1970.

F. Beutter

EPIEIKEIA

This Greek word in itself means mildness, fairness (Latin *aequitas*), and was used to denote the appropriate interpretation of a law. Epieikeia is taken from Aristotle's Nichomachean Ethics, and Scholasticism made it indispensable in theological reflection on the extent to which a law applies.

1. Epieikeia in tradition. Because laws as norms of human conduct are necessarily stated in general terms, they cannot always prescribe the conduct to be followed in a particular situation. This discrepancy between the general law and the actual requirement of action can be bridged by epieikeia. According to Aquinas, equity is to be applied wherever the literal following of a positive law would go against its intention and consequently against the spirit of justice and the common good. That state of affairs lifts the obligation to follow the law. So equity does not judge a law, but the validity of the law is in fact actually confirmed, because what the legislator intended by it is regarded as what is ultimately binding. Aquinas accordingly regarded epieikeia as part of the virtue of justice.

From Suárez onwards, epieikeia was regarded more as a prudential rule (see *Prudence*) by which the individual can free himself from the onus of a law. Epieikeia stands in the service of all the virtues in any case where their intrinsic meaning is threatened by the purely external fulfilment of a law. Moral theology avoids the danger of intellectualist narrowness by declaring epieikeia a fundamental Christian attitude, as the 'virtue of freedom' (A. Adam) which is in a better position to meet the requirements of reality as a whole than purely formal adherence to law.

2. Conditions. Without reliable knowledge of a moral value (see *Value*), and mature decision in its favour, epieikeia would merely be a sign of lack of moral earnestness. The spontaneous feeling for values (sensitivity to value) renders the decision emotionally justifiable, but it needs to be rationally confirmed by further information, anthropological and theological argumentation and honest self-reflection.

Epieikeia is also presupposed to practical wisdom, prudence; it provides the handhold for disregarding a law for the sake of a higher moral good (the greater good rule). Well-considered judgment of that kind may even make epieikeia a moral duty.

Epieikeia only applies in the domain of human law, because the divine will is ultimately binding on the Christian. The more concrete a legal provision as derivative from the divine will, the more relative it is and the greater the duty to examine closely whether the law really expresses the divine will, and, if need be, to apply epieikeia.

Epieikeia is therefore never at the service of a laxer morality, and is more than a rule of interpretation; it is rather the Christian's awareness that over every legal fixation stands the will of god. Epieikeia expresses his habitual readiness (see *Virtue*) to give that will absolute priority in everything, in accordance with biblical ethics.

3. Epieikeia demands maturity. All kinds of lines of thought, for instance the Reformation, the Enlightenment, reflection on biblical origins, psychology etc., make it clear that laws, even moral laws, are not absolute normas but only derive meaning from their intrinsic purposefulness. It is this purpose that the individual must follow (and not the law); in other words, he must act not because of pressure from outside but from inner maturity, which means the degree of maturity that gives the awareness of being able and of having to take in hand one's own moral life freely and responsibly.

Consequently epieikeia is a plea against heteronomy and

external domination by law. It ensures that the norm always remains in contact with conscience and therefore humane. Personal responsibility as a fundamental moral attitude, cannot do without epieikeia in the dialogue between conscience and norm if it is to escape unfreedom in bondage to law and self-dissipation in hedonism. This shows that epieikeia is not aimed at getting round the moral norm, but rather preserves the personal character of moral action. To an over-anxious person, epieikeia looks like a justification of a lax attitude. But epieikeia brings out the meaning of moral obligation by deciding for the better (as opposed to the merely good) and thereby makes it clear that moral action comes about only through the use of personal faculties. Cultivation of epieikeia as the 'virtue of freedom' can also show that the aim of Christian ethics is not a morality of drill and domination, but a summons to personality and freedom.

F.J. Illhardt

Error. See *Truth*.

ESCHATOLOGY

Eschatology, from the Greek for 'end', is an understanding of the ultimate fulfilment of all things in Christ. All Christians accept that this takes place in one form or another, but the content of their belief, as so often, can vary enormously. Such a fulfilment is known only by revelation; indeed it is one of the important ways in which Christian thinking differs from secular. (Marxism is sometimes called 'eschatological', but only by those who have failed to understand it.) Thus it derives from the Bible. But though there has always been some recognition of eschatology in 'traditional' Christianity (seen in such expressions as 'the four Last Things', 'the end of the world', 'the Second Coming') it is only in the present century, mainly through the classic study by Albert Schweitzer, that we have realized how it dominates the New Testament writings.

Christianity inherited this strong sense of eschatology from the Old Testament. The 'Day of Yahweh', 'Day of

Visitation', or simply 'that Day' all express Israel's growing belief in a future judgment by God that would end the present age and inaugurate a new one. This was collective; individuals were judged as part of Israel or the other nations. Moreover it was strongly materialist: the earth and its inhabitants were to be renewed, not spiritualized away.

With Christianity came a sense that this judgment was entrusted to Jesus, who by his 'Coming' (the qualifier 'Second' is not used) would judge the present age and begin the new one. This was felt to be so close that reasons had to be found for its delay, from the earliest writings (Thessalonians) to the last (2 Peter). Nevertheless a certain slackening of expectation inevitably occurred, affecting the outlook of the New Testament authors in varying ways. What is common to them all, despite increasing influence of Greek thought, is the collective and materialist character of their eschatology, so foreign to our reading of it.

Obviously these eschatological emphases influence the ethical notions of the various writers; behaviour is affected by our expectations of its future consequences. Paul's understanding of this is characteristically subtle. The coming of Christ would, he believed. inaugurate the new age: but the resurrection had already brought that new age partly into the world. The pledge of this was the Holy Spirit, bringing the 'first-fruits' of that new time. Thus the Church lives in tension between resurrection and fulfilment, and Paul's practical judgment about morally correct behaviour in this period varies according as he looks more to beginning or end. Sometimes he judges by criteria such as relationship within the risen body of Christ, relevant at any period; sometimes he thinks of the Church as already in the time of fulfilment, so that ordinary moral considerations (like the goodness of marriage) are not operative.

Mark's thought is also strongly dominated by the expected end, so that beyond his general emphasis on living under the rule of God he pays little detailed attention to the solution of moral dilemmas. The fall of Jerusalem in 70 AD no doubt acted as a watershed. The Church for which Matthew wrote accepted that the world would struggle on a while, and needed detailed guidance on the problems raised by property, sex and so on. Though he uses eschatological

73

ideas it is in a much cruder way (most of the hell-fire passages come from this gospel). Luke by contrast has almost eliminated eschatology, and ethics has become in consequence a matter of human concern, especially about justice for the poor and helpless.

John, later still, approaches the matter quite differently. He presses on one side of the present-future relationship held in tension by Paul. For John the Christian community seems to be living wholly in the future age, starkly contrasted with a world given over to evil. Thus no moral teaching is needed beyond the demand to love one's brother.

The eschatological element in Christian moral thinking undoubtedly helped to give it a characteristic tone different from secular ethics. No doubt neglect of that element over so many centuries helped in the atrophy of moral theology so that it became scarcely distinguishable from idealist or, later on, existentialist moral philosophy. The revival of interest in eschatology has not yet resulted in a revival of Christian ethics; all the work remains to be done.

Bibliography: Houlden, J.L.: Ethics in the New Testament. London, 1973. **Moltmann, J.:** The Theology of Hope. London 1969.

L. Bright

ETHICS

Ethics, which western tradition since Aristotle has treated as a philosophical discipline in its own right, is distinct from morality, when morality is taken as morally derived behaviour: this is, behaviour controlled by the consciousness (conscious mind) and qualified as good or evil. The distinction is that ethics reflects morally significant supra-individual behavioural norms within a systematic frame of reference. Both terms derive from the etynom or primary word *ethos* (originally the 'usual domicile', and later: character, genius, prevalent tone or sentiment, custom, use, usage). In the moral theology which prevailed from the sixteenth century onwards, the Catholic version of ethics prevailed insofar as that was distinct from the

Protestant ('Christian moral teaching' or 'theological ethics') and philosophical moral doctrine.

1. Object of ethics. The present fundamental problem of every ethics, including theological ethics, is the delineation of the range of application which might be considered specific to it. In addition to the clarification of cognitive and scientific questions in the realm of theory, that demands the elucidation of socio-culturally based anthropological constants or norms of human behaviour which, as analytical guidelines or variables, enable us to comprehend the cultural plurality and the historical transformation of 'morally' responsible behaviour (*Sich-Verhalten*). Both mere recourse to the notion of morality and to the *a priori* postulation of a 'natural moral law' (see *Norm*) can do no more than open out the universality of the problem and cannot offer a direct explanation of it.

The western tradition of ethics saw man as acting in a naturally constituted world as a being which comes into his own in the open dynamics of freedom and social union (society) according to absolutely incumbent criteria of meaning (see *Value*), which he recognizes thanks to the discernment of his own rationality. Ethics enables such reflections to be systematized, even though the actual contents of ideas of applicability and necessity, and even their logical structures, vary. The mode of deciding the 'ought' in ethics and the conscious discrimination of usage, custom, morality and justice, and the competition between ethics and the empirical theories of human behaviour which nowadays are proposed as independent disciplines, are themselves to be seen as the expression of actual, objective behavioural situations in which the actors find themselves.

Ethics has always to answer three central questions: that of the categorical structure, that of the origin of the notion of duty in human conduct and that of free decision about behaviour, and that of the determination and legitimation of the contents of moral norms. That shows the close connexion of ethics with metaphysics, theology, the theory of creation and the theory of knowledge. As such attempts to interpret the world vary and change, so the importance and relevance of a specific ethics change in the system of knowledge of a particular culture; the necessary reformulation of the problem under the conditions of a modern secular culture can only ensure the historical identity of a *Christian* theory of morality if it succeeds in a new practical demonstration of its essential nature.

2. *Historical typology*. The necessity in apologetics to set something adequately Christian against pagan philosophy and science, caused Christian theologians in the late classical, early Christian period to have recourse to so-called parenetic (see *Biblical ethics*) ethics in regard to purely practical evidences on topics arising in the confrontation with the pagan state. Systematical ethical reflections are found for the first time in Augustine, in his confrontations with the Manichaeans and Pelagians. Like the apologeticists and especially the Alexandrists, Augustine was heavily indebted to the Stoics (especially Cicero and Seneca) and Neo-Platonism. The fundamental principle of a just life is accordingly Nature as the all-inclusive, unchangeable cosmos personally posited by God as the 'eternal law' and therefore independent of all human subjective influence, and known in the conscience of the individual (knowledge as perception), and therefore the norm for the conduct of the human being who is himself located within this universal order. Hence the moral law is legitimated by the demonstration of its ontological and cognitive association with the divine nature or order of being. Augustine resolves the theodicy problem (which in view of the existence of moral evil became increasingly relevant and pressing in relation to the Christian personal notion of God) by means of the doctrine of free will. The associated antagonism between freedom and the law is avoided by previously deriving all concrete norms as from the absolute goal of moral striving, the highest Good (God and the kingdom of God). This determination of goals includes from the start a strong tendency to internalization. Salvific revelation is adduced so that reference is made to the essential moral inadequacy of mankind (original sin) which is set against redemption, and this then becomes essential for the establishment of true morality.

The scholastic theology of the Middle Ages saw itself as entirely speculative in this regard. It left the solution of direct behavioural problems of everyday life to the pastoral practice of the Church. Early scholasticism was confined to a great extent to the systematic treatment of the interpretation of Scripture, exegesis, the received doctrine of the Fathers of the Church and the discussion of theological questions. Moral and ethical problems were more or less arbitrarily attached to the dogmatic treatises. According to one of the most widely known schemata (after Abelard and Peter Lombard) the redeemed life of a Christian, in other words, grace, virtue and the law, are to be treated in association with the doctrine of creation and sin, Christology and soteriology. This method of presentation remained dominant throughout the Middle Ages. In addition, right into the thirteenth century, philosophical ethics (especially as the theory of virtue, following Cicero and Seneca) was practised almost exclusively in faculties of arts. On the other hand confession books and penitential manuals concerned themselves with practical moral questions, and from the time of Tancred and St Raymond of Penafort, closely followed the casuistic approach of ecclesiastical or canon law.

The great significance of the theological ethics of Thomas Aquinas in the second part of the *Summa Theologica* (which oes its actual theologico-historical relevance mainly to the revivalist movements in Spanish late scholasticism, and Neo-Scholasticism) is that for the first time since the rediscovery of Aristotle's *Nicomachean Ethics* the traditional ethical topics are presented systematically together with the 'secular' or 'civil' virtues (*virtutes politicae*) as problems of the order of creation. Here Thomas uses as a model the analogical presentation of God (already to be found in Albert the Great) as the principle and goal of salvation history, on the teleological principle of the Aristotelian concept of practice (*praxis*). For Thomas the threatened dichotomy of nature and grace, law and freedom, knowledge and faith, is still sublated in the one, universal order of things derived from God himself. For Thomas the contents of the natural moral law (see *Norm*) and of the positive divine law are one and the same thing in the writings of the Old and New Testaments. Their accordance is grounded neither in voluntarist acts of God nor in the power of spiritual or worldly forces, but in the purely given order of being itself.

The crisis of metaphysics already evident in nominalism, with its heavy emphasis on the individualistic-voluntarist morality of conduct, the Reformation, the establishment of natural states, the development of new technologies, the discovery of hitherto 'unknown' worlds and the consequent revisions of the old cosmology and the revolutionization of economic structure by early forms of finance capitalism, were faced with the conservative reaction of Spanish late scholasticism. It had a threefold interest: immunization against Protestantism, refutation of rationalist philosophy (the postulation of quasi-scientific evidence of the metaphysical order), and justification of the power claims of the Spanish throne ('colonialism'). The recourse to the Thomist 'system' practised by the Italian Cajetan, and after Vitoria by the Salamanca theological school, together with the use of the later moral handbooks, produced the legitimation of an enclosed Catholic part-culture with claims to universal validity. Moral theology now separated from the rest as an independent discipline and obtained a central function in the system. Whereas G. Vasquez and F. Suárez were still concerned with a general theory of the law, and especially with the connexion between 'natural law' and the law of nations, the authors of the handbooks of *Institutiones morales* from Azor to Busenbaum avoided the justification of the morality of dogmatic theology, and restricted their efforts to a wide-ranging casuistry. In so doing they laid the foundations of the debate on 'moral systems'. Moral theology was therefore from the start forced to play the part of a reflex instrument of the individual external control institutionalized in the sacrament of penance and exercised by authorities which established themselves systematically and in permanent contradiction to the demands for freedom characteristic of the modern age.

Modern ethics up to C. Wolff, on the other hand, starts from the incongruence of the order of being and the order of knowledge. Irrespective of whether the knowledge questioned was secured by the certainty of the self-conscious subject (rationalism), or in the criterion of sense experience (the empirical tradition), the question of human scope and access became paramount. Accordingly norms were discerned either in the cognizing subject, or that subject had artificially to produce order. The metaphysical teleology of nature was replaced by the force-fields of natural phenomena ('interests'). Consequently most modern theories of ethics have a utilitarian tinge. Both traditions in the period mentioned were supplemented with three ideal-typical forms of natural law ethics. They referred to reason posited as the fundamental substance of the individual (in any case accepted as common to all subjects), and oriented to the perfection of the individual (so-called 'rationalist natural law' for Descartes, Spinoza, Leibniz, Wolff, and others); to the acceptance of a 'moral sense' specific to the subject (Shaftesbury, Hutcheson; and, in a modified version, Hume); to the antagonism of individual interests contained in nature as the pre-historical and pre-social primal condition of man; when the use of force could be excluded only by an artificial ordinance (a contract). In this context an autonomous, explicit and systematic theory of law and the state was developed for the first time, one to which ethics was subordinated (Hobbes, Locke). This process of the dissolution of knowledge (and action) from being, which sees in the God of revelation only a *superadditum* of nature, and presents itself in terms of Grotius' formula *Et si Deus non daretur*, finally had its most radical result in the rational law of the French materialists who saw the whole of reality in the empirical, physical order and raised egotism to the status of an ethical principle.

In the foreground of interest in moral theology during the Enlightenment was the dispute about probabilism (the difficulty of deciding one's certainty on the binding nature of a moral law in a specific case). Under the leadership of Spanish and Italian theologians there developed the minimalist equation of Christian morality with the recognition of a legalist, canon-law positivism. The *Theologia moralis* of Liguori went into over seventy editions and was the most influential of the manuals directed exclusively to pastoral, in fact penintential, ends. There was no reference to a total ethical consideration of the entire moral horizon of human behaviour. The political and cultural changes following on the French Revolution nevertheless took the ground from under this theology, in Central Europe at least. J. M. Sailer and J. B. Hirscher once again focussed moral-theological thought—in contradistinction to casuistry

and taking into account the philosophy of the Enlightenment—on the problems of the establishment of Christian
morality which they based on the Gospel in terms of a
'theology of proclamation' (Häring), or conceived as a
'theory of the realization of the divine kingdom in mankind'
(Hirscher). Yet the moral theology of the Tübingen School
in its indebtedness to Hirscher (cf. especially Jocham and
Linsenmann), like that of the spiritually akin Deutinger,
could not prevail against many-sided intrigues, canon-law
regulations and the rising Neo-Scholasticism.

In the context of modern ethics we find Kant's attempt at
a 'pure' grounding of practical philosophy both conservative and critical. Kant opposed to any empirico-
natural derivation the absolute nature of moral demands
which he also asserted against the deduction of a divine
order of being. This occasioned an analytical process, the
approach of the cognizing subject and the formal character
of the reason and will of the subject. Since reason for
established by moral action did not accordingly find its
matrix in any order of things, but solely in the autonomy
of the reason and will of the subject. Since reason for
Kant was still universally posited, morality (in strict
distinction from legality) was exclusively dependent on the
universalizability of subjective maxims. For Kant, the still
present recourse to the theologico-ontological order was
postulative.

Fichte discovered the unity of theoretical and practical
reason missing from Kant in the individual subjectivity
understood absolutely. Because this was exclusively 'a
tendency to determine oneself absolutely, without any
external impulse', and was not a fact but a factual action,
there was no access to an objective world of being in itself.
Consequently all philosophy, moral theory and being were
to be deduced from action. The moral world order in which
every subject and all action had their function in promoting
the universal purpose, that is, 'God', was a pure postulate,
not of something substantial but as predictive of practice.
This radicalized notion of the modern problem of autonomy
enabled Fichte, in contradistinction to Kant, to perceive the
waning of all concrete content in consciousness in favour of
the formal universality of the law. In both Kant and Fichte
the state and law countered as purely external measures to

ensure the self-determination of their members.

Hegel posited the realized moral will, that is, 'real' action, as the object of ethics. The dissolution finally carried out by Kant of objective morals, institutions, politics and society ('legality') from a 'morality' restricted wholly to the inwardness of the subject was sublated by Hegel in the reintroduced (with reference to Aristotle) institutional notion of morality. It consisted of family, civil society, and the state. Beyond the Aristotelian position of a politics grounded in ethics, the Kantian position was not destroyed but criticaly integrated by Hegel when he made subjectivity and morality (as the transition to modern times) the subject of objective institutions and laws themselves. The state was the 'reality of concrete freedom', the 'self-conscious moral substance' which enabled 'objective spirit' to develop and in which law and morality, individual and society reached synthesis, so that ethics was sublated in the philosophy of right as the 'science of the state'.

Neo-scholasticism, which arose in the context of a reawakened ecclesiastical centralism and integralism, meant a return to the morality of the manuals. But there was a new attempt to associate penitential casuistics with a 'systematic thought' that would legitimate it (P. Hadrossek), for instance the conception of a systematic, natural-law papal social teaching. Thomism was defined by Leo XIII in 1879 as universally binding and it has had a considerable influence until now, at least on 'special morality'. Its difficulty lies however in the problematical nature of the association between grounding (according to Augustine, Thomas and Suárez) and casuistry (according to the model of Alfonso de Liguori). Here it seems to find its specific function: the decisionist positivity of the concrete remains subject to authoritative interpretations of the magisterium, not however to the speculative reflection of moral theology. Hence all Neo-scholastic authors from Probst to Schilling share a tendency to apologetical criticism of post-Kantian philosophy and modern science. Even before the second world war Tilmann, Steinbüchel, Müncker, Schöllgen and others tried to overcome the consequent isolation from modern culture—especially in the area of pastoral practice—by a renewal of biblical and especially Christological and personalist principles, exactly

81

like Sailer, Hirscher and Linsenmann. That did not mean
that the crisis in modern theology was removed, any more
than it had been by the newly conceived autonomous
morals.

Hegel's 'sublation' of the opposition of subjective free
activity and legal state force typical of the modern era,
provoked on the one hand the ethical approaches of
Kierkegaard and the Schopenhauer with their decisive
reference back to the individual; on the other hand, they
were at one extreme descended from the materialistic social
theories of Feuerbach and Marx. For Marx, morals and
ethics were purely epiphenomenal components of the
ideological superstructure determined by the organization
of the economic basis.

In the subsequent period, with only a few incon-
sequential exceptions, the tradition of philsophical ethics
came to a halt. There remained only material value ethics
(Scheler, N. Hartmann) which started from the postulate of
a hierarchy of non-existent but effective values, and
existential philosophy according to which human existence
and being were constituted only in action on the basis of
individual free decision (Heidegger, Jaspers, Sartre); :in
association with this trend, ecclesiastical 'situation' or
existential ethics tried to find a connexion between existence and norm); and the analytical ethics which has
recently spread beyond the English-speaking world, enabl-
ing ethical questions to win social relevance.

With the downfall of traditional philsophical ethics, its
object is increasingly transferred to the competence of the
sciences. Morality and law are no longer considered
insubstantialist but in functionalist terms as dependent
variables in a 'behavioural system', or are considered as
derived from interests. As such they are the object of an
autonomous social anthropology in the form of history
(Nietzsche, Dilthey), an evolutionary biology (Darwin,
Spencer), psychoanalysis (Freud), or political economy
(Marx, Engels), and recently comparative psychology or
ethology (Lorenz and others) and sociology (Comte, Durkheim, M. Weber; see *Norm*) are especially important in this
regard.

In contradistinction to the foregoing, in the English-
speaking world the tradition of philosophical ethics has

persisted, though to the point of its substitution by science (by logics and mathematics in this instance). This has occurred as a naturalist reduction (by so-called non-cognitivists), or, as in most cases, as a self-restriction to that form of meta-ethics concerned with the analysis of moral discourse (analytical ethics).

Since the beginning of the nineteen-sixties a protest against the technological ideologization of all areas of life has formed outside existential philosophy and Neo-positivism in a number of approaches to a 'rehabilitation of practical philosophy' (M. Riedel), which all aim at the restoration of normative competence for the formation of social reality. The most powerful impulse in this direction was provided by so-called 'critical theory' (especially J. Habermas), yet the approach is also shared by other philosophical emphases, above all the historico-hermeneutical (Gadamer, Ritter, Spaemann, Lübbe, Oel-müller), the Erlanger school (Lorenzen, Schwemmer, Kambartel), 'critical rationalism', and recently the responsibility ethics of W. Schulz and the humanism 'without God and Marx' mentioned by G. Szczesnys.

3. *Moral theology as Christian ethics.* The detachment of an independent philosophical ethics from theology is the result of varying reactions to the crisis of order since the late Middle Ages. Whereas modern philosophy as a whole saw its most important task as the establishment of a theory of knowledge, moral theology held to the inherited ontology. reality is then taken as given, even when it is to be divided into a natural and a grace-bearing. For modern philosophy, on the other hand, reality means initially accessibility, and later constitution, by the subject. The radicalization of this understanding ends in atheistic positivism and materialism. Both strands of ethical reflection are planted as it were in a different institutional context. Moral theology develops its concept and self-understanding within the framework of post-Tridentine priestly formation and the associated means of social control intended for it and exercised by means of the instrumentally operated mechanisms of social control by church authorities. The ethical philosophers were able to escape their sanctions at first only in Protestant countries, and then in France. Only 'humanist' (in part very

anti-ecclesiastical) groups, especially Freemasons, the state universities and the eventually legally guaranteed autonomy of the sciences ensured the appropriate freedom of thought. The concentration on the institutional sacrament of penance, immunization against the Reformation, modern science and philosophy and the thoroughgoing retention of traditional social structures by the moral theologians were opposed to the adoption of modern philosophical ethics by various emancipatory and revolutionary movements. The final suppression of ethics by science and the associated 'demetaphysicization' of law and politics was the most obvious expression of the process of theoretical dissociation between order and application introduced by the separation of theological and philosophical ethics at the beginning of the modern period.

Factors affecting human action may now be conceived as social and factual without their structures being any less 'binding' in nature. They may be plannable and organizable factors such as the system of social domination and the economic system, but no less the irrationality of institutional processes, the limits of the learning capacity of the individual, and above all the readiness to fall victim to crises of human experience and action.

4. *Christian ethics now*. Neither political consensus theories nor individualistic ethical systems whose tautological starting-point is to be found on some '*a priori* of the communications society' (Apel) determining whatever is to be constituted, may validly be offered as solutions for the establishment, legitimation and stabilization of norms for the direction of individual behaviour, if that behaviour is to serve social integration as well as the meaningfulness of the individual as a human being. Any theological ethics can escape this dilemma only by knowledge of the historical unity of faith and action. Ethics has to avoid any insistence on abstract theological theories. The true nature of ethical demands remains closely bound up with the structure of social and personal relations between those of whom the demands are made. The mere morality of command and obedience as conceived explicitly in traditional moral theology does not fit that situation. We need a new *Christian* ethics which unites the varied contributions of theological

ethical propositions, ecumenical traditions, the human sciences, the magisterium of the church and, not least of all, the lived and as such conscious ethos of the individual Christian, so that Christian morality may be appropriately composed.

Bibliography: Anderson, J. N. D.: Morality, Law and Grace. London, 1972. **Aquinas, Thomas**: Summa Theologica, I, q. 5; I/II. **Aristotle**: Nicomachean Ethics. **Barclay, W.**: The Plain Man's Guide to Ethics. London 1973. **Barnsley, J. H.**: The Social Reality of Ethics: The Comparative Analysis of Moral Codes. London, 1972. **Barr, O. S.**: The Christian New Morality. New York, 1969. **Barth, K.**: Church Dogmatics. I/2, London, 1956. II/2, London, 1957; III/4, London, 1961. **Berman, H. J.**: The interaction of Law and Religion. London 1976. **Böckle, F.**: Law and Conscience. London, 1966. **Id.**: Moral Problems and the Christian Conscience. London, 1966. **Id.**: Understanding the Signs of the Times. London, 1967. **Bonhoeffer, D.**: Ethics. London, 1971. **Bourke, V. J.**: History of Ethics. New York, 1970. **Broad, C. D.**: Five Types of Ethical Theory. London, 1971. **Culpitt, Don**: The Crisis of Moral Authority. London, 1972. **Curran, C.**: A New Look at Christian Morality. Notre Dame, Ind., 1968. **Davies, J. G.**: Christians, Politics and Violent Revolution. London, 1976. **Duncan, A. S, Dunstan, G. R. & Welbourn, R. B.**: Dictionary of Medical Ethics. London, 1977; **Dunstan, G. R.**: The Artifice of Ethics. London, 1974. **Dunstan, G. R., Ed.**: Duty and Discernment. London, 1976. **Flew, A. G. N.**: Evolutionary Ethics. London, 1967. **Fuchs, J.**: Natural Law. London, 1965. **Greet, K.**: The Art of Moral Judgment. London, 1976. **Griffiths, B., Ed.**: Is Revolution Change? London, 1972. **Gustafson, J. M.**: Can Ethics be Christian? London, 1976. **Häring, B.**: The Christian Existentialist. London, 1968. **Id.**: Faith and Morality in a Secular Age. London, 1972. **Id.**: The Law of Christ, 3 vols. London, 1966. **Id.**: Medical Ethics. London, 1972. **Id.**: Sin in a Secular Age. London, 1974. **Id.**: Towards a Christian Moral Theology. London, 1966. **Hengel, M.**: Property and Riches in the Early Church. London, 1975. **Kant, I.**: Critique of Practical Reason and other Works on the Theory of Ethics. Trans. by T. Kingsmill Abbott. London, 1909[6]. **Id.**: Fundamental

Principles of the Metaphysics of Ethics. Trans. by T. Kingsmill Abbott. London, 1955[10]. **Keeling, M.**: Morals in a Free Society. London, 1970. **Id.**: What is Right? London, 1968. **Leclerq, J.**: Christ and the Modern Conscience. London, 1956. **Lehmann, P. L.**: Ethics in a Christian Context. London, 1963. **Lewy, G.**: Religion and Revolution. London, 1976. **Long, E. le Roy, Jr.**: Survey of Christian Ethics. London, 1976. **MacIntyre, A.**: A Short History of Ethics. London, 1976. **Mackinnon, D. M., (Ed.)**: Making Moral Decisions. London, 1969. **Maclagen, W.**: The Theological Frontier of Ethics. London, 1961. **Maritain, J.**: Moral Philosophy. London, 1964. **McCloskey, H. J.**: Metaethics and Normative Ethics. The Hague, 1969. **Milhaven, J. G.**: Towards a Christian Theology of Morality. Garden City, 1970. **Mitchell, B.**: Law, Morality and Religion. London, 1976. **Murdoch, I.**: The Sovereignty of Good. London, 1970. **Niebuhr, R.**: An Interpretation of Christian Ethics. London, 1935. **Nielsen, K.**: Ethics Without God. London, 1973. **Oppenheimer, H.**: The Character of Christian Morality. London, 1965. **Osborn, E.**: Ethical Patterns in Early Christian Thought. London, 1975. **Ramsey, I. T., (Ed.)**: Christian Ethics and Contemporary Philosophy. London, 1973. **Ramsey, P.**: Basic Christian Ethics. London, 1953. **Roubiczek, P.**: Ethical Values in the Age of Science. Cambridge, 1969. **Saddhatissa, H.**: Buddhist Ethics. London, 1970. **Schnackenburg, R.**: The Moral Teaching of the New Testament. London, 1965. **Shotter, E. F., (Ed.)**: Matters of Life and Death. London, 1970. **Sleeman, J. F.**: Economic Crisis: A Christian Perspective. London, 1975. **Taylor, J. V.**: Enough is Enough. London, 1975. **Thakur, S. C.**: Christian and Hindu Ethics. London, 1969. **Theilicke, H.**: Ethics of Sex. London, 1975. **Id.**: Theological Ethics. London, 1966. **Tillich, P.**: Morality and Beyond. London, 1964. **Vann, G.**: Morals and Man. London, 1960. **Waddams, H. A.**: A New Introduction to Moral Theology. London, 1972. **Warnock, G. J.**: Contemporary Moral Philosophy. Oxford, 1967. **Warnock, M.**: Ethics since 1900. London, 1975. **Id.**: Existentialist Ethics. London, 1967. **Winch, P.**: Ethics and Action. London, 1972.

K. Hilpert & H. Oberhem

ETHOS

In contradistinction to ethics as the theoretical and scientific exposition and establishment of that which is moral, *ethos* is in general the actual-historical structure of an ethically determined existence, the entire complex of the ordinances of the moral consciousness, the dominant viewpoints and attitudes of the evaluative mind, and actually applied behaviour patterns and attitudes; in short, the binding practice of moral life. In this sense ethos is a predetermined factor which critically questions, but as such is not to be referred back to any other factor.

As a direct datum of the human aspect of a human being, ethos is not independent of the other areas of the seriously human. It is inwardly affected by socio-cultural factors, economic conditions, customs, habits, cultures and time-conditioning, and not least of all by religious and generally philosophical and similar attitudes (see *Humanity*). It is subject to change. But the evolution of ethos is not to be simply equated with development towards a better human existence. As history shows, a change in ethos is only meaningful if it does not destroy in the name of revolution or restoration, but acts conservatively; that is, when it remains oriented to a future determined on an evaluative basis, and remains in continuity with history. Whatever the basis and changeability of ethos it is always of a binding nature. It always has to do with the decision-taking aspect of an individual; with what should and should not be done; and choice between good and evil. Ethos also contradicts that state of being in which a man finds himself and which would dictate how a man should behave in future. Ethos is affected by an essential antagonism. Those tendencies which lead man to higher things are also opposed by destructive tendencies, and in certain periods the trend to degeneration can win the upper hand. On the other hand, all humanly significant aspects of ethos never win through in the same degree.

Ethos can take several forms. There is the ethos of a group, a tribe, family or organization, a specific social class, and so on, and then ethos can be institutionally secured. A man is necessarily inserted into a context in which a certain ethos, or a mixture of ethoses, tell him one does this or

87

does not do that. This means that a person's possibility of independent ethical judgment is always restricted by the group ethos. But, with due awareness of pressures and group conformity, ethos can also be an instrument of increased utility for the individual able to set suasion against suasion.

There is also the ethos of a particular extraordinary individual who has shown such creative freedom in the exercise of ethos, in combination with natural and environmental possibilities, that he has produced new possibilities of human ethical achievement against which others may now measure themselves. These can act in various ways, offering models but also counter-models and counter-utopias to the ruling social ethos, which we must continually remind ourselves must be enlivened or opposed by the new.

The recognition, analysis and establishment of norms are the tasks of any scientific ethics and occur initially through the action of human perception on the basis of the actual life-experiences of ethos. The human perceptive faculties show what injury may be expected, for instance, if this or that course of action is followed; for instance, ethos informing perception will make the human being aware of what is missing but ought to be there in a specific situation of ethical choice. Ethics must remain critically distant from such movements of ethos so that they are kept under continual check.

In view of the present dangerous state of the world, it is essential that all nations work towards a fundamental ethos which is universally acceptable and accepted. The minimum demands of a universal ethos would have to be: unconditional respect of human dignity, the guaranteed right of all to life, the will to make human history worthy of man, freedom as a negation of force, and the prevention or reduction of suffering (see *Humanity*).

B. Stoeckle

Ethics, Social. See *Social ethics*.

Ethology. See *Behaviourism*.

EUDAEMONISM

The theory of ethics that would define moral obligation in terms of personal happiness or well-being, but under the rule or reason not pleasure in a hedonistic sense.

EUTHANASIA

The literal interpretation of the word euthanasia is 'happy death'. In practice it has come to mean the right to choose the means and the timing of the conclusion of one's life. It is to be distinguished from suicide by the intervention of another person who provides, co-operates and facilitates the termination of life, and often by the presence of a painful, incapacitating or terminal disease.

Christian teaching has always upheld that the author of life is God and that man holds it in trust without the right to determine its span other than for exceptional reasons. Another fundamental issue is the meaning of pain and suffering. The life, death and resurrection of Jesus Christ have added a dimension to the meaning of suffering which does not form part of the philosophy of the agnostic or the atheist, who do not see any intrinsic value in suffering, cannot conceptualize its transformation in and through Christ, and reach the natural conclusion that any undue prolongation of meaningless suffering should cease. The advocates of euthanisia favour a legalized alliance between patient and doctor which, with certain safeguards, would permit the latter to terminate life at the request of the former.

When they are presented in the traditional form of a polemical dialogue, there appears to be a large gap between the two views. This is not the case. Christian teaching distinguishes between the use of ordinary and extra-ordinary means of prolonging life. Whereas the former are obligatory, the latter are not; and in no sense does Christianity insist on the unnecessary prolongation of life. Furthermore, ordinary and extraordinary means will vary in different parts of the world depending on medical resources. It is only in advanced societies that the technical facilities of extraordinary prolongation of life exist and even

89

here there is no obligation to use these simply to prolong life in a physiological sense. There is also a greater affinity between the two aspects when it comes to the presence of pain. Christianity advocates the use of every possible means to relieve pain so that the ensuing life is still able to reflect the image of god in man. Pain and suffering have an intrinsic value only when they are used to enhance this image by being meaningfully integrated and transformed in the whole person.

Ultimately, the philosophical debate will focus on the nature of man. Christians wish to prolong life as long as it can reflect the image of God in man. Agnostic or atheistic humanism sees no intrinsic value in a life beleaguered by pain and suffering since there is no ultimate link with the ability to transform human limitations into a God-given meaning. These basic differences will remain to influence the retrospective views of pain, suffering and death.

In practice, however, a third view is emerging; it is reflected in the practice of helping the dying to live their lives fully in the sense of a fulness that reflects whatever ultimate values the person holds.

Bibliography: **Boros, l.**: The Moment of Truth. London, 1965. **Church Information Office**: Decisions about Life and Death. London, 1976. **Häring, B.**: Medical Ethics. London, 1972. **Shotter, E.F. (Ed.)**: Matters of Life and Death. London. 1970.

J. Dominian

EVIDENCE

1. Evidence as integrating moral obligation. There is no doubt that morally good action can take place without ethics in the sense of rational justification of the moral duty to do good and avoid evil. Nevertheless, to establish the rational evidence of that duty is an indispensable element of morality. For if morality is to assert its essentially imperative character, and fully vindicate its radical claim to binding force, it must be *certain*; there must be adequate warranty that it is well-founded and unconditional. No demand that seriously claims to be essentially moral and therefore binding in character, can afford to be unsure of the grounds of its legitimacy. If we also take into consideration the necessity, in the widest interests of present and future human living, to work towards a rationally communicable and therefore universally binding ethics, a solution to the problem of evidence would appear to be particularly pressing.

2. *Ethics and rational discourse*. But what source is there for the evidence which morality indispensably requires to manifest its validity? What can we appeal to? In the past, people were of the opinion that the degree of certainty required for the affirmation of moral norms and for moral action, could be obtained in the ethical domain itself, and that human reason was therefore quite able to establish convincingly the ultimate ground and consequently the evidence of moral truth. Just as in regard to the natural knowledge of God (see *Godlessness*) people acted as if reason rightly used could not but support all the fundamental morally important requirements. Recently, of course, this assumption has met with widespread scepticism. H. R. Schlette, for example, points out that any attempt to provide a rational basis for ethics and so make it certain, is affected by the dispute about the possibility of metaphysics. As, however, metaphysics itself suffers from uncertainty as to its foundations, and as it is hardly likely that existing metaphysical disagreements will be cleared up, every attempt at a rationally compelling justification of ethics breaks down. What remains, is simply the possibility of an option in favour of concrete *humanity* (*q.v.*) based on probability. In this view, then, moral concensus, if achieved at all, springs purely from will: it can only be built on agreement. Such an agreement, however, is always liable to be retracted, and consequently morality itself is laid open to doubt. Similarly, W. Stegmüller regards the problem of moral evidence as insoluble on the rational plane. The attempt to find an ultimate foundation for morality, ends in a blind alley. If evidence can be hard, it will only be by a 'pre-rational basic decision'. H. Albert agrees with this. Since the endeavour to find an ultimate ground leads either to an infinite regress or to a vicious circle or to interrupting the process of justification by giving preference on dog-

matic grounds to some premiss, he considers that there is only one course left—to decide by a pre-rational moral choice for the principle of permanent rational criticism. This has to take the place of an ultimate rational foundation (This is also Popper's view, and, on a modified form, that of Monod). In recent theological opinion, too, the endeavour to establish the rational evidence of moral obligation has been judged to be more or less vain. W. Pannenberg, for instance, maintains that from the human situation, even taking in social considerations, no universally valid ethical certainty can be drawn: 'The relativity of ethical contents cannot be overcome in the ethical field itself.' Similarly, K. Petes has argued that any attempt to definite morality on the human basis alone, leaves hidden not only the origin but also the breadth and depth of the content of morality, as well as the gravity of moral obligation. Furthermore, the doctrine of values threatens to disintegrate into an endless and contradictory pluralism of merely partial viewpoints. There is then no answer to the question why, for instance, freedom, justice, kindness and helpfulness are unconditionally to be preferred to injustice, greed for gain and cruelty.

3. *Evidence based on faith*. These views that it is impossible to establish ethics on evident rational principles, are supported by two anthropologically significant facts. The first is the recognition of the existential confusion of human beings. According to D. Wyss, while it is true that man is orientated towards absolute values, both reason and drives and instincts, by their historically broken conditions, are not able to give man certainty about binding moral decisions. Secondly, it must be admitted that man by his very ontological constitution is 'homo absconditus', that is, inaccessible to observation by his own subjective reason as regards origin and goal; man is consequently unfathomable and inexpressible (cf. the suggestion by U. Sonnemann and J. Splett that what is needed is a 'negative anthropology'). For the purpose of moral knowledge, the reference to man's radically hidden character is decisively important, for what constitutes a moral action cannot simply be read off from the regular processes of nature or from biological, psychological intersubjective or social wants (the so-called

anthropological necessities). It is rather most decisively determined by the question of what man recognizes as the ultimate meaning of his life and therefore as the ultimate goal of his action (see *Norm*). Since, however, precisely these two natural 'eschata' fall in the domain which coincides with that of the concept of 'homo absconditus', and since human reason can say nothing absolutely binding about them, a decision of faith is necessary for their perception (Rotter). This means that ethics cannot establish the data of ultimate meaning and goal necessary for its own evidence, and can only draw them from the total understanding of human reality which is not accessible to reason alone, but only to faith.

4. *Function of Christian faith*. From this point of view, Christian ethics has to realize that constant and insistent demands are made on it. It should come to realize that the function of theological faith for moral life cannot consist solely in providing a supplementary motive for the so-called universally self-evident principles of the human order. Certainly it must be maintained that human reason is quite capable of knowing and formulating moral norms. Nevertheless that is not so when it comes to justifying and establishing rational certainty for what has been grasped. In this respect, reason left to itself would probably meet with no small difficulties. Consequently, what faith has to do as regards a well-founded Christian ethics, is above all to point out man's origin and goal, which is the indispensable foundation of moral obligation as well as the justification of the central precept of unconditional brotherhood and love of the neighbour. For ultimately only faith can furnish an evident explanation 'why, despite all the often terrible differences between them, no individual is more or less a human being than another, and why each individual is infinitely important' (Kaltenbrunner). Not without reason, Horkheimer himself noted that without appeal to something divine, the good action, 'the saving of the unjustly persecuted', loses its 'splendour'.

B. Stoeckle

93

EXPERIENCE

1. An ambiguous term. Experience is a special mode of knowledge or apprehension of reality; in contradistinction to discursive or projective thinking which proceeds from the subject alone, experience is based in *direct* encounter with what is objectively given, with what offers irrefutable testimony of its presence (*evidence*).

Hence experience is defined both in terms of that which is experienced (objectively) and the experiencing subject. From the standpoint of that which is experienced, it is seen as evidently based in events and objects available to sense-perception (the natural-scientific concept of experience, neo-Kantianism), as the apprehension of reality dependent on the historical dimension (Dilthey), as dialogical experience (Martin Buber and others), as critical or limit experience (Karl Jaspers), as real experience (J.H. Newman), as transcendental or religious experience (Pascal) and as the experience of faith. From the viewpoint of the subject, experience is co-constituted insofar as that makes it active: on the one hand reflectively and cognitively by the arrangement of percepts in a meaningful context, on the other hand affectively and existentially in that the subject allows itself to be concerned and affected by what is apparent.

2. Analysis. Experience as becoming directly concerned with an affective something results in the transformation of the subject and may be described as learning.

The process of experience may be described psychologically as direct sensing and perception of existents in the human world, whether external or internal: primary experience which becomes experience proper only by resolution into significant contexts (reflection). By means of such experience processes a child (interacting with the structures of reality) constructs a cultural or intellectual structure (Jean Piaget) and the association of thing and expression or term or learnt (conditioning).

Sociologically, language is the sediment of social experience (Peter Berger, Thomas Luckman). The individual is to a great extent linguistically pre-structured as far as his possibilities of experience are concerned (see *Com-*

munication). At the same time an individual is essentially capable of transcending socialization and experiencing reality anew, so that that individual has something new to say (in art, for example). Nevertheless new experiences have to be integrated linguistically or the individual will run the risk of social disorientation.

3. *Moral implications*. The infant is capable of thinking and acting only by participating in adult reference-persons' thinking and acting. Such people pre-form him or her by means of preliminary experiences (John Dewey). Only the process of becoming a self, together with the experience of normative distance and the possibility of choice, makes it possible to enjoy moral responsibility in any real sense. Moral responsibility is based on the experience of the exercise of *conscience* (*q.v.*) in the sense of the experience of the uniqueness of the ego and its unconditional sense of obligation for good and against evil. Conscience is experienced with especial clarity in a situation involving a difference or contrast to practices which are socially predominant.

4. *Contrast experience* (see *Ethos*) has the same basis; it is made by individuals and/or an entire social group in regard to morally unjustifiable behaviour (for instance, the establishment and running of the concentration camps in Nazi Germany). Morally positive personal experiences becomes ethical experiences which strengthen the inheritance of an experienced norm (for example, the struggle for freedom led by Martin Luther King).

As human behaviour, ethos is handed on primarily through experience (imitation of models). Its legitimization is the concern of ethics which is intellectually responsible reflection on and for the practice of morally responsible living. Ethics legitimizes by reinforcements or criticizes by correctives the positive exercise of ethical experience.

G. Biemer

F

FAITH

1. *Fundamental moral meaning*. Faith is primarily a free gift of God, who has lovingly revealed and communicated himself, who in Jesus Christ has entered personally into the world and history, and whose word and promise, action and work live on and remain present in the Church as the community of believers. Faith is, however, in a secondary sense, also a human moral activity insofar as man with the help of grace responds freely by *love* (*q.v.*) to God's saving call, not simply by rational assent (*fides quod*, belief that so and so) to what God has revealed and presents through the Church for belief (orthodoxy), but also by total existential self-giving to God (faith as commitment to a person(and a life based on personal commitment to God (ortho-praxis).

Faith is therefore also a matter for ethical reflection. But whereas dogmatic theology is mainly concerned with the nature and content of faith, and fundamental theology with its presuppositions, theological ethics is interested more in the meaning of faith for human life in its personal and social dimension, in the moral integrity of the act of faith, and in the dangers it runs from the world around and from personal failure. The relevance of faith lies in the light it throws on the meaning of human life and history; it offers man no ready-made solutions to all the particular questions of life, but gives an answer to the question of meaning, the question of man's origin and goal, the why and wherefore of what he does. According to the testimony of faith, mankind and the world are not self-originated, but created and redeemed by God through Christ, and will one day be

96

brought to fulfilment by him. For the believer, the history of mankind and the world is a sacred history of redemption, and its goal will be reached when Christ gives over the kingdom to the Father so that God may be all in all. Faith also testifies, however, that God does not will to carry out his plan of salvation without man. He has called man to be a partner, that is, a co-creator, co-redeemer and co-fulfiller of his creation, so that he may bring his own potentialities to fruition through objective and appropriate organization and conduct of life, society and the world. By fulfilling this (wordly) vocation in free responsibility before God (theonomy—*autonomy*) and in imitation of Christ (see *World*), he comes to know his own dignity and works out his God-given salvation. The man-made world of truth and life, justice, love and peace, will one day become the kingdom of grace when Christ raises up man together with the values he has created, frees them from all egotism and confers on them a new and enduring form.

This vista of meaning which faith opens out becomes, for the human being who affirms it in faith, a project for existence or life, and gives his concrete *action* (*q.v.*, and also see *Value*) decisive fundamental oriental towards God, with consequent deeper motivation and a more radical character.

The decision for faith (*fides qua creditur*) is made as a response to God's revelation; it therefore presupposes not only the knowledge and acceptance of the revealed truths of faith transmitted by Scripture and Tradition (*fides quae creditur*), but also the constant endeavour to achieve a deeper understanding of them appropriate to the present time. And for this, of course, the individual again needs the supporting solidarity of a believing and confessing community (Church) as well as of definite formulae as protection against any mistaken interpretation of the essential content of saving truths and redemptive history (dogmas).

2. Faith in temptation and trial. The necessity and value of this support cannot be overestimated. Faith as the individual's response to God's offer of salvation is essentially a matter of decision and venture. It is therefore at all times exposed to temptation. The difficulty of harmonizing faith and knowledge always involves the possibility of doubts about faith, while the attempt inspired by lack of trust, to bring God under human control by means of magical manipulation, or to make oneself safe from him, leads to all kinds of superstition. Typical of the present time, however, is the great danger of unbelief as a result of the individual's vulnerability and uncertainty. Whereas formerly the believer as a matter of course, as it were, was received into the bosom of a national church and a closed Christian society, at the present time he stands to a large extent alone in an open, pluralist world characterized by technology, industry, belief in science and progress. Everywhere a rapid decline in the practice of faith and growing indifference to the Church and to questions of belief is apparent. Even among nominal Christians (those who at least were baptized) consumer atheism is spreading—the kind which claims to be satisfied with the superficial satisfaction of desire for a higher standard of living and excludes the deeper question of the meaning of life. There is a continual increase of religious indifference and practical atheism, which makes people decide and act as though there were no God. In fact, the changed experience of the *world* (*q.v.*) and the new attitude to life, seem also to be a clear barrier to faith as a help to orientation in life, as though many problems can be solved without faith, often even better without it. Finally, the fact that too many religious, ethical and philosophical fundamental problems connected with faith receive different, sometimes to some extent contradictory answers, produces far-reaching disorientation which can undermine the certainty of faith and lead to unbelief, which may even be culpable, to the extent that the individual must be held responsible for his lack of interest in educating and critically discussing his faith, or for giving up and emigrating from the community of believers to which he belonged.

In view of this common temptation that afflicts all who are willing to believe, the scandal of denominational differences or the separation of the churches is very painfully felt. Nothing is gained, however, by mere refusal to consider, or by even trying to hush up, the differences that for so long have been emphasized by both sides. Increased readiness to understand on the part not only of church authorities but of all Christians, will be needed to reduce such differences by personal contacts, joint discussion and prayer, and so promote the success of the ecumenical movement.

Unity of Christians in faith is all the more urgent because modern atheism (humanism, existentialism, Marxism) totally calls that faith in question as a possible explanation of the meaning of life, or as a real help to actual living. The representatives of modern atheism contest the fundamental capacity of faith to make an independent and above all positive contribution to the humanization of man and his world (see *Humanity*). They argue from the undeniable facts that in the course of history non-believing people have often shown more sensitive feeling for and commitment to humane causes, and that many problems (peace, social justice, scientific and technological progress, education, etc.) were approached and mastered not by Christianity but without it, and frequently in the teeth of bitter opposition from Christians. Consequently these modern atheists regard faith as a downright hindrance to human fulfilment, because the fundamental statement of faith about God's authority (theonomy) appears to them merely to be regulation from outside (heteronomy) and consequently man's alienation from himself. They allege that by faith man does not become himself, but is led to seek the guarantee for the success of his personal life outside himself and his own history. This again is said to give him a false sense of security and above all totally to stifle rather than to promote and fulfil his inherent vitality. The declared aim of modern atheism is therefore to liberate man from all divine and god-like tutelage and domination. This is a logical continuation of philosophical and scientific atheism and its demands for absolute freedom for man (see *Freedom*) and of the absolutely worldly character of the world (secularism). Only when this is attained, its advocates say, will man have achieved his true dignity (see *Human dignity*), and only then will there by any possibility of realizing the humane aspirations of present-day and future mankind.

3. Debate with atheism. The view taken of modern atheism by the Catholic Church and theology has become more discriminating and more open since the First Vatican Council. The rejection of atheism on principle of course remains, but atheism is no longer viewed one-sidedly as it used to be, solely as a phenomenon of cognition and

99

knowledge in the sense of a false doctrine, or simply dismissed out of hand as the work of the devil. It is admitted that we must ask what exactly those who profess atheism are denying, and listen to them without any ready-made answer learnt off pat beforehand. It is recognized that 'some seem more inclined to affirm man than to deny God', though they 'laud man so extravagantly, that their faith in God lapses into a kind of anaemia' (GS 19). It is admitted, in self-criticism, that believers themselves as well as religious bodies, 'frequently bear some responsibility', because some are 'dificient in their religious, moral and social life' and 'conceal rather than reveal the authentic face of God' (*ibid.*), while others in the past often claimed God as the guarantor of conditions and ideologies, presented God and his kingdom to the poor and disinherited as an other-wordly con-solation, and thereby hindered the liberation of man from enslavement as well as the alteration of inhuman social and economic conditions. Modern atheism is therefore ac-knowledged to represent a well-founded challenge to Chris-tians, and to perform for the Christian faith itself a purifying and clarifying service. Some go as far as to speak of atheists as 'anonymous Christians' (K. Rahner) and to number them with the 'People of God' (cf. LG 16), if their attitude is an expression of their conscientious conviction or even of a protest against a distorted conception of faith.

As a result of its open attitude, the Catholic Church and theology have now entered into a dialogue with atheists. This may certainly contribute to further clarification of the various standpoints and aims, and perhaps even lead to mutual enrichment, for Christians will become more explicitly aware of the relevance of faith for the specifically human sphere and the world, while atheists for their part may come to realize the need for man and the world to be open to a transcendence. No doubt it can also deepen common concern for the future of mankind and lead to united effort in view of the world-wide threat of hunger, over-population, indifference and total self-destruction. A definitive solution of the question of principle cannot, however, be looked for from dialogue alone, for ultimately what is under discussion is not the validity of particular theoretical doctrines, but the question of which scheme for reality and human life stands the test better, the Christian or the atheist. It is therefore the responsibility of the individual Christian as well as of the believing community, to attest the efficacy of their faith by their life and dedication in the world (see *Godlessness*).

Bibliography;: **Kasper, W.**: An Introduction to Faith. London & New York, 1979. **Küng, H.**: Being a Christian. New York & London, 1977. **Rahner, K.**: Christian at the Crossroads. London & New York, 1976. **Ratzinger, J.**: Introduction to Christianity. London & New York, 1968. **Feiner, K.**: The Common Catechism. London & New York, 1975.

A. Elsässer

FAMILY

1. Basic form(s). Franz Böckle has described the family as a 'fundamental institution of human society' and as such it has legal protection in most countries. As a 'primary group', it situates the individual within a network of social relationships and through the education (*q.v.*) that takes place in the family, makes an essential contribution to the process by which the child becomes human. It also fosters the development of society as a whole by helping it to reproduce and renew its structures. At the same time, it operates as a necessary balance to the claims of public life by providing a space of freedom. In the freedom of the family, relationships are private and personal rather than functional and the members of the family can recover their souls, after public life has threatened to destroy them.

The structure of the family differs according to the culture within which it is found and its basic form has changed in the course of history. Despite this, however, a certain fundamental pattern is discernible in all societies and at all time. The industrialization of western society has led to a reduction of family size and to a change in the function of the family. Unlike the earlier extended family of several generations, this nuclear family usually consists only of the parents and their children who are not yet of age or who cannot provide for themselves.

In many western countries, two or three children are now

regarded as the 'ideal' number and this voluntary limitation has been brought about in various ways by responsible family planning. It has also unfortunately been caused by a certain hostility towards children, a shortage of homes suitable for families or a reluctance to accept personal restrictions. Closely connected with the spread of the small nuclear family pattern is the movement from a patriarchal family structure to a fuller form of partnership. This type of family relationship is characterized by the members' mutual trust and responsibility for each other.

The change in the function of the family cannot be regarded as a loss, since the productive, educational and other tasks that are now undertaken within other structures in society were previously the responsibility of the large, extended family. The functions performed by the family are different now. The modern family has above all to satisfy the increasing demands made by contemporary society for the education of young children and for a psychological balance between the tensions caused by society. The supporting social checks previously provided by the neighbourhood or the environment in which the family was placed have now to a great extent disappeared.

2. *Tasks.* The family has the fundamental task of building up the social and cultural personality of the children who are born into it. After it has been born physically, the child has to learn, in the educational processes of becoming a member of society, how to find its way in its environment and its rules of behaviour. It would seem that this second social and cultural birth can only take place satisfactorily within the family, because the group solidarity and intimacy is so great there that it penetrates to depths that are usually inaccessible in other social groups (R. König).

Through the constant presence and sympathetic attention of the parents—during the first months of the child's life, it is the mother above all who fulfils this rôle—the infant develops a fundamental attitude of trust and social confidence. Without this attitude, the child may never become sufficiently conscious of himself to make the values and norms of society (including the sexual values) his own and will thus not be able to play a full and balanced part in that society. The function of various social organs outside the family as factors in the process of socialization which takes place as the child becomes increasingly autonomous rests almost entirely on the foundation built up in the early years of the child's life within the family.

When the parents are responsible, children cannot be regarded simply as objects determined by their parents alone, because so many of their needs can only be satisfied by the social system of the whole family. If this task is not undertaken by the family (as, for instance, in the case of a mother of very young children working away from home), the social relationship can be disturbed by a psychosomatic retardation of the child's development (of the kind that often occurs when the child is hospitalized at an early age). In such cases, it is not absolutely essential that this task should be carried out by the physical parents. 'Social' parenthood (and 'natural' parenthood must always, of course, become 'social' in this sense) is more important to the child than the rights he has acquired through a blood-relationship. If the natural family is unable to carry out this process of socialization (because it rejects the child, for example, or because of the death of the parents), the child should be adopted or fostered by another suitable family as soon as possible after birth, rather than be placed in a home.

Religious values and modes of behaviour are also imparted mainly through the family. Parents, who, according to Vatican II, co-operate with God's grace and bear witness to faith, are responsible for introducing their children to faith (q.v.) The interpersonal relationships in the family are a precondition for the child's personal relationship with God. The family enables the child to experience faith by the interpersonal experiences within the family itself and by speaking about and with God. The children's response in trust to their parents' turning towards them forms the basis for their response in faith to God's turning towards them. It is in the family that they have to learn their rôle as God's partners.

3. *The family and contemporary society.* The family is frequently criticized nowadays because it seems to reproduce and perpetuate the existing social relationships and

103

because of its apparently authoritarian structure and its norms, which are the product of the education acquired within the family and which are believed to frustrate the happiness and full development of the child. The nuclear family is 'pathogenous', according to this common view, because it destroys the self-identity (*q.v.*) of the child by its norms, taboos and sanctions. The political dimension of this view is important in that the family is perhaps the best medium of all for handing on norms, it is often quite hostile to society as a whole and it is to a great extent protected from outside influences. Any criticism of the values transmitted by the family is therefore bound to lead to a criticism of the structure and institution of the family itself. Various counter-models or counter-balances to the nuclear family have been suggested and even tried out. These include the earlier extended family, the commune or community, the kibbutz and schooling or education of the young child on a totally social basis. None of these have, however, so far shown themselves to be really viable alternatives.

There are nonetheless a few possibilities open to the family, which is placed nowadays in such difficult conditions, to help it to overcome its isolation and to do justice to the demands made on it as an educative structure (see *Education*). There is an urgent need for a longer period of preparation for the tasks of education and a more secure financial and legal framework. In the case of family conflicts and difficult educational situations, a counselling service is also very valuable. Common patterns of life can emerge in family groups without any claims to universal validity and these circles can also help families to achieve freedom (*q.v.*) by discussion and mutual support. Family groups can also help to integrate families more completely into the Church community. The community experience within such groups can play an important part in overcoming traditional individualistic piety and—if the introduction to the sacramental and social life of the community is transferred to the family at the same time—the Church community itself can also be built up again from below.'

Bibliography: **Bowlby, J.**: Maternal Care and Mental Health. London, 1951. **Dominian, J.**: Authority. London,

1976. **Id.**: Proposals for a New Sexual Ethic. London, 1977. **Nye, F.I.**: Family Relationships and Delinquent Behaviour. New York, 1958. **Parsons, T. & Bales, R.F.**: Family, Socialisation and Interaction Process. Glencoe, Ill., 1955. **Toman, W.**: Family Constellations. New York, ²1969.

K. H. Mengedodt

Fixation. See *Addiction*.

Flesh. See *Body; Celibacy*.

Force. See *Liberation*.

FORGIVENESS

1. Fundamentals. Christians live in the presence of divine forgiveness, which develops into historically accessible form in the saving encounter with Jesus Christ (Mt 5. 45b; Lk 6. 36): They are accepted by God as sinners and justified through his grace (1 Cor 6. 11). Every form of legalistic self-justification is now definitively swept away, and the division of obedience to the Law is replaced by radical reconciliation deriving from the obedience of faith which means letting oneself be taken over by the new experience of God which has appeared in Christ (Rom 7). Since in him God has become the neighbour of human beings, a new form of human neighbourliness has become possible which is summed up programmatically in the radical commandment to love, which includes love of enemies (Mt 22. 37). The relationship with one's neighbour is no longer dominated by self-assertion mitigated by nervousness or worldly-wise calculation in strict mutuality, which simply reinforces the vicious circle of *guilt* (*q.v.*) and *retribution* (*q.v.*). The positive formulation of the Golden Rule also shows that evangelical love of neighbour goes beyond the art of external accomodation; the power given to us to overcome evil with good (Rom 12. 21) knows no limits or restrictions (Lk 6. 32; 10. 29) (*Biblical ethics [NT]*, *q.v.*).

2. *The shape of Christian forgiveness.* In the light of this, Christian forgiveness is more than a forgetting and passing over the guilt of others. Just as the believer knows that God has taken the first step in loving him, he goes out to meet his neighbour in limitless love (Mt 18. 21-22). He possesses the power to endure and creatively transmute first of all the conflict which exists in himself, and he is able at the same time to create the external conditions for a better future. For him there is ultimately no such thing as a hopeless situation, and this means that his initial decision is based on measured confidence. The presence of *salvation* (*q.v.*) frees people for reconciliation in the present. Because the believer relies on God's descent into history, human community is healed at its roots. The gift of forgiveness is the first sign of all-inclusive solidarity in salvation. It leaves one's neighbour to his own experience of God and thereby transforms the Jesus-event into a human reality (Mt 18. 32ff; Eph 5. 1). Injuries done by one's neighbour are accepted calmly in the active consciousness of one's own poverty and need for forgiveness; the final judgment on history is left to God (1 Cor 4. 5).

3. *Conflict and forgiveness.* Totally sincere forgiveness does not remove the need for intelligent foresight. It does not mean unbalanced blind confidence, which tries to undermine the right and duty of possible *resistance* (*q.v.*) with utopian ideas and so obscure the persistence of *conflict* (*q.v.*) in existence. Disruptive resistance must always be in the service of a wider reconciliation: this is the crucial rule of priorities. The limitlessness of the desire for reconcilation must increasingly be brought to coincide with the limits of its possibility. The painful tension between desire and capacity must be gradually reduced. It is by its awareness of this responsibility that the genuineness of forgiveness is measured. It does not remain in the interiority of a mere attitude, but boldly sets out to transform the conditions in which all decisions are made. The underlying impulse comes from the folly of the Cross, which can be seen through the radical demands of Jesus' preaching and is a permanent mark of his desciples (Mt 10. 38) (*Mercy, q.v., Retribution, q.v.*).

K. Demmer

FREEDOM

In general, the possibility of undisturbed self-development and realization. Freedom is never unconditioned and unconditional. In addition to suasions of time and space, individual and social factors ineluctably affect human volition. Therefore freedom may be defined as the ability to affirm one's own being in spite of all personal and material states and occurrences. In this sense freedom is characteristic of a number of aspects of life (for instance, artistic freedom, freedom of opinion of information, freedom of choice of human conditions of life), without any particular emphasis on its moral relevance, which nevertheless comes into play whenever freedom is endangered in any area of life. Freedom is of ethical significance as a condition of human existence as a whole in each of its actual manifestations.

1. Distinctions. Traditionally freedom was considered as freedom of will or volition and action. It represented the essential condition for the possibility of the very phenomenon of morality (responsibility, accountability). Where freedom of action means the possibility of making unfettered free decisions, then freedom of will or volitional freedom is understood as the capability and ability of the will to act freely in an actual situation in regard to several possible motives or values or possibilities of action, or in other words, self-determination without compulsion from without.

Man can become fully conscious of his freedom of choice, in contradistinction to any notion of total determinism which holds that the human will is necessarily and compulsorily psycho-physically and causally determined. Freedom of choice which is so to speak self-aware and oriented to free insight and the free adoption of a certain position is also to be set against the older kind of totalitarian behavioural theory which asserted that man was no more than a growing, increasingly complex yet fixed stimulus-response mechanism, a creature indeed of habits. Personality would then be ultimately no more than a highly complex system of such associations. It is hardly possible however to assume a unilateral position in the ancient determinism-indeterminism debate. In all decisions of the will, biological or inherited behaviour patterns play a part together with accumulated habits, as do characteristics affected and learned in the course of time and conditioned by situation and environment, as well as similarly acquired conditions and attitudes. To these effective factors must be added the particular psychological type or constitution, which plays an essential rôle. Therefore, in any responsible moral theological understanding of human freedom, we must speak of a *relative indeterminism*.

Freedom does not disappear in the process of volitional self-determination. It is cancelled yet preserved in the Hegelian sense of sublation, in that the determination of the will persists as conscious self-determination in regard to reasons and aims.

2. Freedom as personal responsibility. Freedom of action is grounded in freedom of will, and thus brings into question the total personal and existential freedom of the human being. Self-determination of the will is self-determination of the person. Freedom of the person does not consist solely of behaving in this or that situation in this or that way, in regard to the demands of that situation, but also of behaving in this or that way towards oneself in that situation. Free decisions are also decisions about one's own nature and existence in the sense of a personally responsible and conscious direction to what has been recognized as being morally valuable and appropriate, and what is therefore striven for as such. In this way, the individual always attains to a new existential stance: free decisions are among the prerequisites of any future decisions. Self-determination comes in here. But it is also a question of the surrender of freedom in the very pursuit of freedom. This kind of free self-determination enables the individual to attain increasingly to a total freedom by growing in self-possession and reducing alien influences and susceptibility. This is anthropologically significant, since in the course of his personal history man forms himself: man is open to self and is not there, readymade from the start. The history of man's self-formation is the history of his freedom. It is the history of a freedom which is open to self and which realizes self.

In the complexity of many individual free decisions, a form of pre-decision (see *Guilt*) is discernible which is made once and for all, but is so to speak constructed from the human moral decisions which are oriented towards the point of complete identity. Freedom represents the human possibility of self-choice and self-formation. That includes the possibility of correcting earlier decisions on the basis of new insights. Freedom is not only the never entirely evident presupposition of the possibility of guilt *(q.v.)*, but also the presupposition of the possibility of free self-alteration (metanoia).

3. Social reference. But freedom is not purely individualistic. It must have a basic social dimension, since man is always a neighbour and always has a neighbour. This is true in education, work, language, sex, and so on). In order to gain and preserve individual freedom, man needs in all stages of his life a basic orientation to others. Freedom is also socially determined in that the moral values and norms by which it operates are essentially intersubjectively structured. Egotistical and arbitrary freedom is not only contradictory but in fact un-freedom. True freedom always refers man to the need of his neighbour, and to the value of his and his neighbour's human dignity (see *Love; Virtue*). Individual freedom is truly present where a man frees himself from self in order to exist wholly for others.

Because of its social dimension, freedom also has a major political function. This consists above all of the fact that freedom is not restricted to the realm of thought (when it would become ineffective in the real world), but has to exercise an emancipatory and critical form of control in regard to all human alienation, and all forms of unfreedom (see *Conscience*). True freedom is also against the use of (a quite feasible) technology of behaviour intended on the basis of subtle knowledge of the laws governing behaviour to programme and in the end repressively to control that behaviour. Freedom also has a politically corrective rôle, for man is subject to a number of social rôles and institutions in public and in private life. The requirement of freedom is nowadays a demand too for a certain distance—critical distance—in regard to rôles and institutions (on the presupposition of full awareness, of course, of the tasks they imply).

4. *Education to freedom*. Since freedom is fundamentally characteristic of man as a person, yet is not something to which he has automatic access in a readymade state, man needs to be educated to it. That means becoming aware of one's own potential, drives and so on, and of external influences, their possibilities and one's ability to change them. This form of education includes practice and learning, and indeed lifelong learning. The ability to discern and acknowledge moral values has to be acquired, as has the ability to behave appropriately. This form of education to freedom is opposed to all authoritarianism and is one of the prerequisites of human maturity.

Training for freedom also includes awareness of those laws which govern group training and group behaviour.

5. *Restrictions of freedom*. These can be individual and social. The personal difficulties include psychological deficits and defects, anxiety, depression, scrupulosity, excessive guilt, loneliness and drug or other forms of addiction, and all those compulsions and impulses which lie in the human psyche or can be traced to social causation: environmental imprinting, uncaring and unloving upbringing, and so on. Social restrictions of freedom include any external compulsion, whether direct (threat, punishment, aggression, repression of opinion, the use of subtle means of repression whether in the media or elsewhere, dependence, and so on—see *Manipulation*—) or indirect, structural and so on (for instance, compulsion at work, any demands in regard to performance, fashionable behavioural trends, political prejudice, suppression or disadvantage of minorities). In all these instances what is in question is either insufficiency resulting from illness, or an alien influence, or both simultaneously.

Medical aid as far as it is available and competent can be called on to help the psychologically sick attain to due freedom. Political means should also be used against direct or structurally indirect pressures if that is necessary to remove any existing inequality or immaturity and to establish the opportunity or courage to make individual decisions (see *Resistance*).

110

Among restrictions on freedom we may also count moral norms and values representing ancient presuppositions which are no longer scientifically or otherwise tenable. They have to be changed or removed (see *Ethos*). If they persist, *Epieikeia (q.v.)* is permissible in regard to them.

6. Theological significance. The access to self-determination which determines the history of human existence is not a human creation but experience by man as given. Man sees his history from the start as a history of freedom, and one referred constantly to God. Human freedom is guaranteed by God. But that includes the knowledge of failure and guilt: that is, of the partial and possible total failure of one's own history of freedom. In Jewish belief this awareness led to the aetiological determination of a general subjection of all men to original guilt, or original sin, which disturbs if not destroys the human capability of freedom. The essence of all guilt is that corrupting misuse of freedom which draws man egotistically back into himself, where he loses his freedom. Hence Paul says (Romans, Galatians), that as against man's enslavement by egotism and therefore guilt and future death, the OT divine law offered him true help. Through Jesus faith became the existential medium of ultimate freedom, for faith meant above all a new and absolute binding orientation to God's acceptance of man. Guilt is not final but retractable.

Faith *(q.v.)* is the decisive dimension of bestowed freedom, for it is the dedication of human life to God. Love is the specific presupposition and realization of freedom and includes both a man's relationship with God and his relationship with his fellow man. The truth of God is inseparable from grace and love. The more the faithful Christian surrenders to Jesus and experiences God through Jesus, the more he is able to experience the liberating, clarifying, anxiety-dispelling effect of God's truth (Jn 8. 32)..

The fulfilment of this love is not the tedious and anxious fulfilment of laborious duty but is identical with that action of belief that continues the operation of love as begun by Jesus. It is the turning of man to his suffering, dominated neighbour and the establishment of justice here on earth. The freedom obtained from Jesus is not devoid of actual content. It is the committed freedom of faithful decision. It is expressed in all moral concern that accords with the spirit of Jesus. Hence it is also evident as that maturity by means of which a man can prove himself without compulsion before God and with his neighbour (the freedom of the children of God).

In Catholic circles this freedom was poorly developed until recently as a result partly of a defensive attitude to Luther and the Enlightenment tradition, excessive anti-Modernism, casuistic ethics, and so on. The opportunities for Christian freedom were not readily perceived. But nowadays the Christian community, the parish, should be precisely the place where the freedom of Jesus is lived, practised and exercised without compulsion and in an communual effort and commitment, above all in the removal of alienating pressures, by the establishment and assurance of free communication (*q.v.*), by counteracting false prejudice, and by unconditional mutual forgiveness and hep. This exercise of freedom received from Jesus and permeated by faith in God makes possible an initial but certain real experience of salvation (*q.v.*) and happiness (*q.v.*).

Bibliography: Barth, K.: Church Dogmatics, IV/3. 1962. **Rahner, K.:** Theological Investigations. II, 1964; IV, 1967. **Rondet, H.:** Gratia Christi. 1948. **Rzadkiewicz, A.:** Philosophical Bases of Human Liberty According to St Thomas. London, 1949.

V. Eid

Freudian Psychology. See *Drive; Psyche*.

Future. See *Faith; Memory; Promise; Technology; Time*.

G

GODLESSNESS

1. *Biblical position and modern problem.* In biblical terms
godlessness ranges from pious nameless veneration of the
'unknown God' (Acts 17. 22ff in the light of Eph. 2. 12) to
the inexcusable refusal to acknowledge what is known for
certain but the truth of which is 'suppressed' in daily life
(Rom. 1. 18ff.). There is no trace in the Bible of a theoretical
denial of the existence of God, such as is presented by
modern atheism (materialism, positivism, etc.). The 'fool'
who does not know God (cp. Ps. 10. 4; 14, 1.) denies the
efficacy of God's power, in particular its relevance in the
practical and moral conduct of man's life. Godlessness as a
worldwide, social mass phenomenon is something new. It
is less an explicit and anti-religious negation of God, than
determined by an areligious plan of existence, in which
Godlessness is more a condition that is taken for granted
than an explicit concern.

2. *Doctrinal tradition.* Since a 'natural' knowledge of God
was considered easy, indeed almost inevitable, *traditional
theology* taught the doctrine that it is 'in itself' unthinkable
(that is, in normal circumstances) for a negative atheism
which does not recognise God, or reserves judgment about
him, to be without fault. A positive atheism, which
explicitly denies the existence of God directly or indirectly,
is seen as possible (even in the long term) but is termed
culpable on principle. In this context the main causes of
godlessness so defined are regarded as spiritual incapacity
or fundamental lack of moral attitude.

113

3. *Essential distinctions*. In contrast to this type of judgment, a differentiated understanding of the many different forms of godlessness is a primary necessity today. It depends less on a prior theoretical concept than on orientation towards the actual phenomenon of godlessness (e.g., despair and indifference, *q.v.*, as causes, militant atheism, etc.). Far more weight must be given now than in previous times to the fact that, over and above his free personally committed attitude, the individual is more strongly dependent on the opinion of the society in which he lives. Equally important, however, is the point of view that it is possible for the individual to misinterpret what he is actually doing in his life in the objectivizing conceptuality of the subjective consciousness. So a 'godless' individual who conforms to the claims of morality, may be affirming God incidentally in a way hidden from us, while denying Him in conceptually objectivising formulae. Conversely, pious talk of God is not certain proof of God's living and powerful presence in an individual's daily life (this is nominal theism, which is basically godless). True godlessness exists only when the individual shuts himself off radically from the free, ever greater transcendence (in fact, the ultimate good) which is revealed in its final truth as the personal God. When the autonomy of the individual is thus total, any and every invitation or offer of divine grace is rejected.

4. *The Church's teaching*. Every theoretical and practical judgment of godlessness today must be guided by the pronouncements of the Second Vatican Council, which constitute a considerable advance. The most important text (from *Lumen Gentium* 16) runs as follows: 'Nor does divine Providence deny the help necessary for salvation to those who, without blame on their part, have not yet arrived at an explicit knowledge of God, but who strive to live a good life, thanks to his grace' (cp. the texts *Lumen Gentium* 16 and *Gaudium et Spes* 19-21).

5. *Morality and godlessness*. On this contentious subject the relationship between moral experience and 'good' is central. It is not disputed that an atheistic ethic can find and recognise valid norms and values for interpersonal com-

munal life. Here there are possibilities for a better under-standing in dialogue with atheism (human dignity, *q.v.*). If the establishment of these values is not to remain bogged down at the level of instinct, convention and utility, the *absolute* validity and binding nature of these norms must be legitimised—or at least recognised pragmatically in daily life. The moral sphere includes absolute certainty and unqualified fulfilment of what is obligatory in an especially intensive way. For this reason, too, Christian belief is convinced that the full and developed awareness of these norms and values can only be recognised and observed in the long term, if the absolute validity of morals is based and affirmed in the personal God. For this reason it should be made clear to the atheist in what way he may meet 'God' in his daily life. Ethics and moral theology today have a missionary task of particular importance (faith, *q.v.*) in demonstrating that the ultimate basis of the ethos lies in a free, and merciful God.

Bibliography: **K. Rahner,** 'Atheism,' in *Encyclopaedia of Theology*, London & New York, 1975.

K. *Lehmann*

GOOD, the

1. Terminology. 'Good' in a quite general sense signifies a judgment that something is desirable and worthy of approval. Consequently, the good means either the object so designated (*bonum*) as an object of evaluation, or the reason for the favourable judgment (*bonitas, ratio boni*) in a person or a thing. Since the good as a most general term cannot in itself be defined, attempts have been made at various times to define it in terms of an idea of the good, of a highest good (*summum bonum*), of perceptible effects, or, as in Aristotle, in relation to the dynamism of a teleological order (see *World*) which rules the whole of nature (*quod omnes appetunt*). In view of the multiplicity of its aspects, distinctions were drawn beween the various relationships of serviceability or utility (*bonum utile*), of satisfaction of a need (*bonum delectabile*) and of what is intrinsically valuable (*bonum honestum*); overlapping was

115

inevitable. As a value word (see *Value*), the good, even in the sense of what is intrinsically good, does not simply express an attribute of the existing object, but in that object as it stands in relation to human experience, aspiration and action. What is designated is not some ontological characteristic in itself, but a value content which affects the will as a motive, and in the fullest sense in respect of man's free activity. The traditional account of the good as ontological perfection must be interpreted in this sense because of its particular metaphysical assumptions, but without abandoning its objective view.

2. *Moral good: its value-character*. On account of this reference (to the human will), the good for the most part makes a direct value statement about human experience and action, about its foundations, contents and effects, as long as free self-determination is involved in some way. Consequently the good includes an element of claim or demand, which modern value ethics in particular seeks to grasp with the help of the concept of value, and which is embodied in various ways in practical maxims or norms (normative function). In content, the good in human activity generally can be distinguished according to the various domains of meaning and value of individual and social life among which the moral domain has central and comprehensive importance. As specific factors of personal self-determination, good and bad motives, decisions, actions and attitudes are subject to moral judgment. To be distinguished though not separated from these, is the distinction between moral right and wrong which concerns the relevant epistemological foundations.

Moral meaning and function. Whereas evaluation as good in the various domains of human activity derives in each case from considerations of goal, meaning and importance for the unfolding of human life in some particular respect (e.g. conservation of physical and psychological life of body and soul, professional, economic, social, artistic activity), moral good relates essentially to the totality of personal life, to the responsible, free self-realization of personal being itself in essential humanity and life with others. Consequently it is the ultimate and highest guiding concept of free action. In *conscience* (*q.v.*) it is experienced as an unconditional claim on behalf of the right realization of human reality. Consequently the determining ground and content, criterion and standard, possibilities and exigencies of moral good must be seen in relation to personal life in the deepest and widest sense. Various attempts at a single uniform definition that have been made in the history of philosophy and theology, in most cases in terms of individual social or natural teleology, tend to be one-sided and restricted. Moral good is to be understood in the perspective of the whole dynamic human structure of free personal life in personal relationships and intercourse with other people in human society. We have to stop thinking in terms of purely static order, and take into account as far as possible the whole context of life with the ever new potentialities that it offers. Positive and negative values of human action in the experience of conscience and the experience of life in past and present, are probably the richest source of moral knowledge, providing that careful historical criticism is brought to bear on it. Because of the obvious variety of opinions and their mutability, the contrasting experience of evil, which destroys, impairs or impedes the order of human reality, its conditions, fundamental values and data in past, present and future is of special importance for knowledge of the good (see *Ethos, Experience*). Evil is a conscious deviation from the ordered pattern of human life in favour of the superficial, facile egotism of a one-sided, selfish attitude or action. Concrete particular *norms* (*q.v.*) of moral good cannot be obtained by rational deduction from ethical axioms. One-sidedly deontological argument cannot do justice to reality as a whole. The main contribution of teleological argument consists in the clarification of basic realities and largely concerns moral rectitude; it therefore needs to be placed in the wider, comprehensive perspective of moral value.

3. *Theological aspect*. Revelation throughout sees the personal God as the ground, force and goal of the good, in the world and for man. Extending beyond the moral realm, good preserves and frees from the world's contraditions, and is perfected in *salvation*. For his action man is shown what is good (Mic 6.8).

This applies to the law and ordinances of the Old

117

Testament as well as to the example and instructions of Jesus, which are not to be understood as primarily or exclusively moral in character. Moral achievement takes place in the obedience of faith and in discipleship. That is what gives rise to a clear conscience. The moral distinctions between good and evil undergo radical interiorization and deepening. In *faith* (*q.v.*) the good receives a fundamentally new potentiality, is given its centre in the love of which the Christian is made capable. The claim which moral good makes, the absolute character of moral obligation, are seen as directly personal and take on a deeper concretely individual sense. It is this specifically religious ground and the general consequences it entails, and not any special particular norms of moral action, that characterizes the good in revelation. See *Biblical ethics*.

R. Hofmann

GUILT

1. Limits to rational understanding. Guilt is one of the central themes of man's history, but it is essentially a secondary phenomenon in relation to the primary phenomena of *salvation*, redemption, grace and the search for happiness. This is the 'logical groundwork' for an understanding of guilt, valid from a humanist as well as a specifically Christian standpoint; only on that basis should one assert that guilt is the 'greatest evil', which in origin and in its consequences is a barrier to man becoming what he was created to be. This disruptive process is endemic in mankind though 'unnatural' and hard to explain; it becomes even more of a mystery when seen against a background of Christian belief in a benevolent creator God. Like mortality, guilt is one of the defining boundaries of human experience and reflection. The dismay it brings receives its rightful expression in mankind's sacred writings, in personal discourse and, sometimes, in literature and the plastic arts. But systematic thinkers do in fact address themselves to the question of guilt, so it must be accepted as a legitimate subject for their consideration, provided the 'logical groundwork' of the problem is remembered.

2. The need for a theology of guilt. The fact of guilt is a matter of experience; guilt-feelings, a consciousness of guilt, a need for punishment, pangs of *conscience (q.v.),* and remorse all arise from our psychological make-up; but the actual nature of guilt is a matter for faith, for in the last analysis, as Karl Rahner says, there can only be guilt where God has been sinned against. So for Christian ethics guilt and sin are identical concepts: it is not the case that guilt is the result of a breakdown in human relations while sin is to be seen as a specific breaking of God's law. But God is not, strictly speaking, an object of our experience: so when we say: 'Against Thee, thee only, have I sinned' (Ps 51.6), we are in the realm of *faith (q.v.)* because we pre-suppose a relationship between God and man. Nietzsche sensed this when he said that radical atheism and a kind of second innocence belong together.

But this does not imply that the *capacity* for guilt depends on a personal belief in God. The ethical person becomes aware that a deed is guilty and so can recognize his guilt; the believer thinks of this guilt as being also sin. Christians believe, quite correctly, that god will ask an account of believers and unbelievers alike for their good and bad deeds (which includes, of course, their thoughts). It is the least important function of guilt in religious belief to provide a basis for moral behaviour. The God of Christian faith is not a blind judicial authority, but the all-knowing creator; to him the unique potential of each person is transparent (Kierkegaard), and that person alone is called to fulfil that potential in the concrete circumstances of his life. The term 'debt' should apply only to this calling. If man is to be freed from his 'essential indebtedness' (Nicolai Hartmann) and yet keep his dignity, it can only be through an ethic which sees the debt in terms of a personal relationship between God and man. But if the debt-guilt is measured in terms of values, of damage to one's own or another's life, then conflict situations often arise in which there is no arbiter who can settle the debt: one is irredeemably guilty. On purely anthropological grounds it might be insisted that people should not be free from guilt, because that would make them irresponsible infants. But if guilt is understood in ultimately religious terms, then it is disobedience to and refusal of the will of God—the 'debt'—

which is *written into our being*. The guilty person has failed to become the person he could have become in God's plan. So any liberation from guilt must be experienced as renewal, restoration and enrichment of personal worth (*love q.v.*).

Nor is it clear how renewal can take place through contrition, conversion and expiation unless there is belief in God. The purely psychological experience of release may echo Christian renewal when it is preceded by deeply oppressive guilt-feelings. But not every instance of guilt is accompanied by such feelings. The more abstract one's consciousness of guilt, the less likelihood there is of a sense of emotional release. If guilt is seen in relation to God it is 'spiritualized' in principle; so the spiritual joy in the God-given grace of conversion and subsequent forgiveness is largely independent of physical or psychological accompaniments. Ideally, of course, there should be no split beween experience and belief. But sadly Christians are not in practice more integrated, relaxed and 'redeemed' than non-believers. This cannot be blamed on the doctrine of guilt and forgiveness, but on the fact that religions can, as many psychologists complain, increase people's sense of guilt.

Christians with pastoral responsibilities must take this reproach seriously, because the final goal of a Christian ethic must be, not to provide a foolproof system of morality, but to help redeemed sinners to reach in practice their full *humanity (q.v.)* through *love (q.v.* and *happiness (q.v.).* So the theoretical definition of guilt as sin in God's sight is not enough. We must also reflect on experience and analyze the different kinds of guilt, and the different attitudes of people to the fact that they can become guilty and to the possible ways of shedding guilt.

3. Distinctions. Franz Scholz would define the traditional mortal sins as decisions in the depth of our being against God. These are sins as decisions in the depth of our being against God. These are sins properly so called, real guilt. If we wish to form a concept of the nature of guilt, it seems sensible to derive it primarily from mortal sin, since that alone throws light on the shattering theological mystery of lawlessness (2 Thess. 2.7), which defies facile analysis. On the other hand it is precisely the 'venial sins', arising from our weak and wounded nature, which pose the anthropological riddle: why, when someone's basic commitment is toward the good, is his hard-won portion of peace and contentment upset time and again in so many ways? One is tempted to agree with Freud's dictum that the scheme of things is not designed to make men happy. Our nature is such that however much good will we have in general, we find opposing forces at work within us. This is not a matter of fated inability to do otherwise, but of ethically wrong decisions which are experienced as sin, not merely as a dull pain induced by lack of fulfilment in the personal and interpersonal sphere (cf. Rom. 7.14ff).

4. *Freedom and guilt*. Sin is a free personal act, not a thing; so we can define its contents only in very general terms. Our prime concern is with the nature of the decision, not with the so-called 'grave matter', even if 'grave matter' does presuppose a corresponding commitment of the will. The problem is less simply with seemingly minor failures: the outward appearance gives one fewer clues about the inner disposition. In either case the basic impossibility of guessing the inside from the outside gives point to the scriptural injunction not to judge (Mt. 7.1) So if we come across someone whose apparently minor failings are accompanied by oppressive guilt-feelings, we have no right in principle to dismiss them as the expression of a hyper-sensitive, neurotic super-ego. Nevertheless the experience of psychologists would suggest that there is more likelihood of someone having an over-anxious conscience than of the opposite possibility—namely that estrangement from God will be expressed in trifling sins.

On the concrete situation of dealing with our own and other people's guilt, it proves helpful to consider the different types of possible decision. First it might be advisable to distinguish between immature and mature decisions. The former may be normal for a particular stage of development (e.g. that of a child); but they may indicate blockages in development, normally characterized as infantile regression or neurotic fixation. In both cases the capacity for guilt is diminished, because guilt is in its full sense presupposes a mature personality.

121

A fully humanized person makes his decisions on the basis of a developed conscience; these decisions may be fundamental or peripheral (Scholz), and the latter would relate to failures through weakness. Only the fundamental decisions form the basis for a completely moral or immoral act; in the nature of things they are not very common. In life as it is lived, all types of decision rub shoulders with each other. But experience, especially in the realm of psychopathology, indicates that individuals have clearly dominant traits. So for example mature moral decisions are highly unlikely from an over-scrupulous person, especially in view of his compulsively harsh verdicts on his own failings. Yet even here moral theology cannot rule out the possibility of a fundamental decision: for moral acts are, ultimately, a secret of the heart which can never be told.

5. Guilt-feelings and capacity for guilt. It is now clear that there is a particularly close connexion between pathological types of conscience and decision-making on the one hand, and a deeply tormenting experience of guilt on the other; and between the quite speficic 'contents' of sin, and a correspondingly severe self-reproach. This is the area of those basic forces in human history which Freud characterized as eros and aggression. Now, the 'spiritualized' Christian understanding of guilt proclaims a goal for ethical development; but it does not harm Christian ethics to search out the primordial sources of guilt-feelings with the help of depth-psychology and its hypothesis: 'The leap (*Sprung*) from murder to guilt is the origin (*Ur-Sprung*) of conscience' (Szondi); or, as Freud says: 'We cannot dispense with the premise that mankind's guilt-feeling comes from the Oedipus complex and was acquired through the slaying of the father by the alliance of brothers.' The meaning of this hypothesis is to be sought in the realm of cultural anthropology rather than of possible historical truth; at the point where men, torn between eros and lust for destruction, respond to their destructiveness with guilt, there is cultural advance. So guilt-feelings protect the individual and society, and help a culture to advance. The more nuanced viewpoint of Christian ethics need not discount this pre-religious function of guilt-feelings. Capacity for guilt is a friend of life, though guilt itself is its enemy. The traditional Christian connexion between guilt and death (which has some support in linguistics) retains, on its higher plane, some primordial echoes. Since guilt is in the world—its only proper place—there is death. But guilt, as sin in God's eyes, refers beyond the world; and from God comes our hope that we will be freed from guilt, and that death will be destroyed. 'In the world you have tribulation; but be of good cheer, I have overcome the world.' (Jn. 16.33)

Bibliography: Eysenck, H.J.: Crime and Personality. London, 1970. **Freud, S.**: Civilisation and its Discontents. Complete Psychological Works Vol. XXI, London, 1964; Articles by **K.Rahner** in Theological Investigations, London: Guilt and its remission: the borderland between theology and psychotherapy. Vol 11, 1967; Guilt—Responsibility— Punishment within the view of Catholic Theology. Vol VI, 1969; Traditional Theology and Guilt. Vol XIII, 1975. **Monden, L.**: Sin, Liberty and Law. London, 1969. **France, M.**: The Paradox of Guilt, London, 1967. **Vann, G.**: Moral Dilemmas. London, 1975.

W. Lauer

H

Habituation. See *Addiction*.

HAPPINESS

1. Happiness as a moral principle
Although everyone wants to live and be happy (Seneca, Pascal), there is considerable disagreement on how to interpret the term. Depending on where one's interests lie, it can be used to refer to the satisfaction of the more material and superficial desires and needs of Man ('lower' pleasures) or to the state of being in all respects a complete and successful human being ('higher' pleasures). Aristotle had already awarded happiness in this second sense, a central significance: in the quest for happiness, this unity of virtuous life and an adequate supply of exterior pleasurers, he recognizes the ultimate motive of moral action as well as the true object of ethics. Seen from this point of view, morals bear a large eudaemonistic mark. Even Christian doctrine (especially Augustine and Thomas Aquinas) had adopted this eudaemonistic foundation of ethics, although it tried to deify it, i.e. to anchor it in 'summum bonum'—in God itself. This idealization was, however, unable to conceal convincingly the typically hedonistic character of a system based primarily on personal interests such as self-preservation and self-love. It was just this aspect of eudaemonism that prompted Kant to declare happiness as being contradictory to duty and to eliminate it as an unsuitable, even inferior method of establishing moral rights. See *Endaemonism*.

Even if one does not share this opinion, the question still

remains open whether happiness is capable of being a constant, ethical principle. What exactly happiness on a human level is supposed to be, is in each case determined before hand, for instance, by the table of values that have previously been decided on. History shows (cf. Bentham: 'The greatest happiness for the greatest number') what a crucial part subject-immanent and superficial factors play (eg. preferences, pleasure, satisfaction of needs). The inclination to interpret happiness on hedonistic lines, that is, in terms of *pleasure (q.v.)* cannot simply be ignored. Hence the difficulty of making it clear that happiness, and what is good and right for Man cannot be equated without further ado.

2. *The Bible and happiness.* That the New Testament completely ignores the contemporary theory of eudaemonism and does not even use the term to describe inner satisfaction, can be traced back to the scale which can be observed leading up to this category of subjective welfare in the definition of happiness. This is further aggravated by the fact that just those people are deemed 'blissful' whom common-sense would call unhappy: the poor, weak, mournful and hungry. The term 'makarios' (meaning 'fortunate) used here does not, therefore, denote a sum of worldly virtues and even less the state of subjective welfare, rather it denotes the salvation promised by God, which of course must be understood not as a consolation or a reward for later on, but as a pledge for a future which produces radical alternations in the present.

3. *Neo-eudaemonism.* To what extent reservations about happiness as an ethical principle are justified, is made apparent by a look at the ethos of the present day. It is strongly influenced by a neo-eudaemonistic feeling of life and futher supported by the relevant theories (cf. Marcuse). Happiness here seems chiefly concerned with the attempt to satisfy, completely and unhindered, the need for the useful, enjoyable and comfortable things of life, and the guarantee that as many people as possible should enjoy the *pleasures (q.v.)* they seek.

Narrowed down thus, 'The happiness of life' undergoes an ethical process resulting in the 'moral disqualification of those forces which prevent the maximum happiness'. The readiness to put up with aversions, drive-deferment, frustrations and *renunciations (q.v.)* is the first to be effected. Then comes the fading out of borderline situations in human existence (sorrow, illness, death) and a lack of interest in people once they have crossed one of these repressed borderline situations. To the Christian idea of humanity, Neo-eudaemonism must seem unrealistically optimistic and therefore inhuman and cruel.

4. *The need to experience happiness.* Unaffected by these misgivings about using happiness as a basic moral principle and equally binding for Christians is the realization that the experience of huamn happiness constitutes a necessary integral of the complete person *(joy, q.v.)*, and that it is a truly human task to make life worth living and thus to ensure that people live happily with each oher. It must be remembered that the happiness of the individual is best achieved when as many people as possible, and ideally the whole of society, are happy. Finally it should not be forgotten that moral action itself is one of the main sources of happiness: the satisfaction arising from the feeling of having behaved responsibly makes for the real happiness worthy of a human being. Regardless of the type of happiness meant, a calm approach when dealing with pleasure is in any case decisive. (cf. Augustine, *uti non frui*).

Bibliography: Adams, R.M.: 'Motive Utilitarianism' in The Journal of Philosophy, vol. LXX, 111 Nr. 14 (12 August 1976), pp. 467-481. Kurtz, P. (Ed.): Moral Problems in Contemporary Society. Essays in Humanistic Ethics. New Jersey, 1969. Norwell-Smith, P.H.: Ethics. London, 1954. Sidwick, H.: The Methods of Ethics (1st ed. 1974; 7th ed. 1907). Smart, J.C.C. & Williams, J.: Utilitarianism, For and Against. New York & Cambridge, 1975.

B. Stoeckle

HEDONISM

The ethical doctrine that pleasure or happiness in a personal sense is the main and ultimate end of human life.

HERMENEUTICS

The principles by which propositions of any kind are to be interpreted. Ideally, the reconciliation of the traditional principles of interpreting Scripture and ecclesiastical dogma, in the light of the findings of modern and particularly the physical and psychological sciences.

Bibliography: **Gadamer, H.G.**: Truth and Method. London & New York, 1975.

HONOUR

1. *Human aspects*: Giving another his due place, acknowledging his dignity, respecting him: these are some of the effective basic forms of Christian fellowship. Honour is given to a person when his fellow men acknowledge his worth in practice, when they award him his position in society. Honour in the sense of appreciation of a human being is determined by two factors. The subjective factor is the quality, worthiness and honourableness of that person: his intrinsically justified claim to honour. The objective factor is the recognition and the respect, expressed in a sign, of the worthiness of a person, of his *human dignity* (*q.v.*). Since honourableness is based on both moral and social grounds, two fields of reality and value overlap in the question of honour. Ethical and social problems emerge when intrinsic honourableness and extrinsic honour do not correspond.

Desire for recognition and honour, which is one of man's basic aspirations, must be seen in terms of individual and social psychology as the anthropological basis for the ethical and social phenomenon of honour. When he is honoured man is able to find independence and social effectiveness in a community and also to develop a positive self-consciousness. Being together becomes organized and established. To be wholly without honour is the biographical negation of a person. Ostracism and isolation deprive him of the opportunity of making his justified claims and fulfilling his duties in accordance with his orientation to the community.

HONOUR

2. Christian mandate: In Christian ethics, as a result of a prior emphasis on "intrinsic honour", there is always a danger of false humility, leading to a depreciation of extrinsic honour. All pietistic life-styles tend to this sort of inwardness, to the cultivation of individualism and inter-subjectivism. Hence asocial and apolitical tendencies emerge. Aquinas on the other hand, as representative of a healthy Christian tradition, declares that honour is quite simply the greatest of the external things at man's disposal (S.T.II II q.129 a.l).

Christ and Christianity adopt a dialectical attitude to honour. Seeking merely external honour before men is strongly condemned (Mt 6.1-18; 23.5-7). In imitation of the Lord, the disciple must endure external dishonour alongside inward honourableness which is unsought (Mt 16.24; 10.25f). The honour of serving is that which is appropriate for the Christian (Mk 10.42ff; Jn 13.1–16:feet washing). On the other hand Christ withstands insult, abasement and unjust treatment. Dialectic is possible because love for God and men counts for more than honour. Among Christians honour is regarded as a relative factor. But it is never irrelevant.

3. Concretizations: The modern attitude of reserve in regard to traditional forms of paying honour, if it is not motivated by envy, should be seen as a justified attempt to give honour only where there is intrinsic honourableness. It must be observed however that honour is often a kind of advance assurance of society's confidence.

Further questions on acceptability, repute, fame, prestige, must be approached in the light of a clearer understanding of honour. Vanity, pride, arrogance, craving for honour, as also unjustified suspicion, rash judgment, calumny and slander, should always be considered attentively in the light of social psychology and ethics, in order to avoid injustice and to resist tendencies both to exteriorize honour and also completely to level out interpersonal and social relationships.

H. Kramer

HOPE

For Kant the two most important questions for man concern what we can know and what we should do; the question of hope ranks third and last. This is because he places hope within the sphere of religion and therefore, strictly speaking, outside the sphere of philosophy. Only in the more recent past has this formerly neglected topic been treated comprehensively. Philosophy, human sciences and theology are all equally involved in the enterprise (Bloch, Pieper, Plügge, Moltmann, Metz). Although they take up very different standpoints, all contributors to the discussion agree on one thing: they see hope as the decisive and fundamental motive-force in human striving, and conceive of it in strongly ethical and practical terms. However, a rapid loss of confidence in the future and a neurotic concern with apocalyptic have for the moment considerably lessened interest in the subject of hope.

1. The anthropology of hope. Undoubtedly the strongest impulse to the new thinking about hope has come from Ernst Bloch. His thought is centred on that which gives man his primary motivation: the 'topos ahead', the Utopia which stands for the real possibility of a space and place which have not yet achieved a present realization. Hope corresponds to this kind of future as wishful thinking corresponds to utopian fantasy. It reaches out to the 'kingdom', the 'commonwealth of identity', to the man who has achieved oneness with himself, with humanity and with nature. So the underlying theme of every philosophy is seen as the quest for the commonwealth which is still to be, the onward dream (cf. Richard Schäffler: 'Saving goodness is the theme of the First Philosophy'). But for Bloch this goal for which man strives in hope will be realized within the realm of a purely earthly evolution. This-worldly reality has the potential to lead hope to its fulfilment *(Time, q.v.).*

Ludwig Binswanger agrees with Bloch when he says that what a self-aware person is thrusting towards in hope when he is involved in loving relationships is to be understood in terms of coming home to one's native land. Similarly H. Plügge says that what man is fundamentally hoping for it nothing other than personal wholeness, becoming one's true self. But he and Josef Pieper differ from Bloch in this, that for them there is no question but that the goal of that great hope which can survive unscathed the collapse of life's little hopes lies beyond a purely earthly future; this is because there is nothing which could serve as that goal within the processes of historical, this-worldly forces. For since hope reaches out for *salvation*, it bears the hallmark of a transcendence which is not at man's command, and without which it would not make complete sense. Seen in this light, hope can be distinguished from the humanly attainable.

This analysis of hope and its goal seems unquestionably more realistic than Bloch's concept, which substitutes for transcendence a creative power immanent within the world, but thereby mythologizes the natural evolutionary process, and robs hope of its value in spite of a forced attempt to give it moral status. When man's future is proclaimed as an uninterrupted extension of the present and a continuation and ratification of the past, then hope has no significance. 'If hope does not reach beyond death, then we ought only to use the word with inverted commas, knowing that it is not really hope at all' (Emil Brunner).

2. The theology of hope. Church tradition was thoroughly competent at expounding hope as one of the three theological virtues, but the existential dimension of hope in relation to *faith* and *love* (q.v.) was insufficiently devloped; this was because dogmatic theology paid little attention to eschatology and, in its teaching on the Last Things, concentrated on the immortality of man's created soul; while moral theology gave precedence to casuistry and situation ethics—'a morality of short perspectives'—and limited the discussion of behaviour to the dimensions of the immediate present (*Time, q.v.*).

The theology of hope is only given convincing form when the fully-rounded New Testament concept of man's future is brought to bear on the subject. The New Testament has many evocative expressions for that to which hope is directed, and in which it is consummated: the 'commonwealth' of God who changes our present 'lowly body' into a 'glorious body' (Phil. 3.20f) (*body*, q.v.); a 'house not made with hands' for which we will, once and for all, exchange our 'earthly tent' when we are 'further clothed' (2 Cor. 5.1ff); a transformed cosmos, for the created order shares with man in redemption as well as in fall (Rom. 8. 19).

So this final condition will not be an ethereal Beyond, but a 'new heaven' on a 'new earth', that city where there will be no more crying or pain, where, to quote Herbert Marcuse, man's 'unreal Utopias' (freedom from suffering, death and conflict) have become reality. And there is no question but that this new future is brought about by the power of God rather than the arm of man.

3. Hope and ethics. The purpose of Christian hope would be radically misunderstood if one thought of it as mere promise without actual ethical import. Rather, it is the summons of God to our present, which, in the direct light his future, becomes the moment of decision. It is this profoundly imperative element in hope which gives the Christian's ethical life its distinctive onward-thrusting dynamism (see Is. 40.31). Such an understanding of hope ensures that ethical behaviour is not distorted by dualistic considerations: the Christian is called to renewed bodily existence; his purpose is not to free spirit from matter. His response to the promised future is a full-blooded Yes to his embodied self, and a determination to develop fully as a man (*body, q.v.*).

Moreover, hope gives three determinative and specific tendencies to ethical commitment. Seeing man as destined for happiness under God's care, it gives us firm assurance of a final, irreversible liberation; but it sees the present order of creation as merely relative (*salvation, q.v.*). So those who are humanly speaking in a hopeless plight are offered a real future, and hope contradicts the counsels of absolute pessimism. This consciousness of freedom is reflected in a deep-seated joy which is expressed in festival, ceremony, worship and play (*leisure, q.v.*), in the liberating laughter which Harvey Cox sees as hope's last and best weapon, and in the buoyant readiness to live with *patience*, through the sufferings of this age, which are merely the 'travail' which heralds the coming redemption (Rom 8.22–25).

131

Furthermore, hope gives Christians the capacity to take a truly human perspective on their contemporary world, because they know that there is no longer any human institution, plan for the future, or earthly Utopia which can claim to be the last word in human happiness. This might well require opposition to the constant threat of absolutist demands entailed by blueprints for the future, and resistance to the compulsions of naked determination and intolerant moral stances. In this sense hope means having a passion for the relative; it does not commit the Christian to any specific goals of a purely earthly kind, but inclines him to prefer the patchwork provisional to even the most impressive schemes for the improvement of conditions.

Only through such calm detachment will the man of hope be able to involve himself without bitterness, and therefore fruitfully, in the pressing problems which surround him, as he breathes life into each day's small hopes. Hope teaches us to 'gird up our loins', bids us step into the arena of history, and calls forth the will to change things. It attempts a twofold operation: it protests against all that is alien to God's future, such as discord, hatred, enmity, force and oppression; such enemies of man's dignity must be exposed and as far as possible removed. At the same time it tries to make present such concepts as brotherhood, sympathy, caring, closeness and personal relationship, for these are anticipations of the life of the 'great commonwealth'.

Since, as is plain, hope is a vital element in all human striving towards goodness and self-realization, we must ask whether it should be thought of as a moral principle in its own right, at least from the Christian viewpoint. Augustine and, even more strongly, Zeno of Verona, would seem to say we should. The former says: 'sublata fide resurrectionis mortuorum, omnis intercidit doctrina christiana'* (Sermo 361 PL 38/39, 1599). And the latter: 'tolle spem, artes virtutesque cessabunt. Tolle et interrempta sunt omnia'** (PL 11, 270).

Bibliography: Moltmann, J.: The Theology of Hope. London & New York, 1967. **Cox, H.**: The Feast of Fools. Cambridge, Mass., 1969. **Graef, H.**: Modern Gloom and Christian Hope. Chicago, 1959. **Marcel, G.**: Homo Viator:

Introduction to a Metaphysic of Hope. London, 1951.
Rahner, K.: articles in Theological Investigations: 'Christianity and the "New Man"', vol. V. London, 1966; 'Marxist Utopia and the Christian Future of Man', vol. VI, 1969; articles on 'Eschatology', vol. X, 1973.

* Once faith in the resurrection of the dead is taken away, all of Christian doctrine lies in ruins.

** Take away hope, and culture and virtues will cease. Take it away, and everything is wrecked.

B. Stoeckle

HUMAN DIGNITY

This is a term often cited today and sometimes passionately affirmed. It is also a notorious fact that human dignity is not always pursued most earnestly by the people who talk about it most loudly. Scepticism is called for.

It is worth pondering on the fact that an essentially uncompromising humanitarian ethic can serve extremely one-sided political agitators as a camouflage and weapon in a bid to attain the total domination and levelling of mankind.

1. Basis of human dignity: Of special importance is the question of what the dignity of man implies, on what it is based and from what premises it may be deduced.

It is true that reference to the constitution of man as a rational being and a freely responsible person is just as inadequate for a justification of human dignity as is recalling the special position of man in relation to the sphere of other living beings (cf. Hegel's ethnology of mankind as a 'spiritual animal kingdom').

Recognition of human dignity is based in the first instance more on an admission of man's person-ness.

That is to say, that man not only possesses individuality and self-determination in a unique and peculiar way, but that he also infinitely transcends himself. This is ultimately due not to his own power but to an Otherness which trancends him, so that he is not completely absorbed in his

133

inner world (*Love, q.v.*).

As a person, man as *homo absconditus* is hidden and withdrawn at the same time. It is just that which assures him an insurpassable position and a non-disposability which is beyond question.

It is here significant that the classical concept of the person and the concept of the personal did not grow from the soil of philosophical speculation but entered western thinking from the Judaeo-Christian experience of faith.

Indeed the person-ness of man is not all as obvious as is widely assumed. Consequently, what the humanist tradition regards as man's indisputable dignity may not be so inherently unquestionable that it can be simply overlooked and bypassed.

Nor is anything altered by Heidegger's attempt to get round the baselessness of the modern outline of man by declaring man's origin to lie in an unimaginable fate (destiny?)

Man's person-ness as a guarantee of his dignity is more in the nature of an article of faith than an isolated demonstrable element of anthropological discovery (Pannenberg).

There is in fact no better or more convincing basis for human dignity than the reference to the "infinite intendedness" of every individual, as affirmed in the biblical teaching of man being made in God's image and the involvement of the human element in the Christ event.

Only in this way is a final proof possible that every man without exception, because he is affected by God's radical love for man, has a right to personal dignity and may consequently be neither a God nor a wolf to other men (Moltmann). Even the weakest or most repulsive human existence—indeed precisely these—should not fear for their unencroachable worth.

2. *The basic demand*: Reverence is the only appropriate attitude towards human dignity ultimately guaranteed by God. This will manifest itself as an unconditional willingness to treat every human existence as non-disposable and to protect it.

Thus reverence will resist all the actions which 'prostitute' man, violate him, make inconsiderate use of him or debase him merely as a means of achieving objective goals (whether economic, social or political).

To that extent the attitude of reverence contrasts with all scientific theories which purport to be able to take complete account of man by reason alone and plan for his needs. Without such reverence there would after all be no binding criterion at all (G. H. Schwabe).

Bibliography: Cranston, M.: What Are Human Rights. London, 1974. **International Commission of Jurists**: Human Rights in the One-Party State. London & Geneva, 1978. **Melden, A.I.**: Human Rights. Belmont, Calif., 1969.

B. Stoeckle

HUMANITY

1. Programmatic survey. Humanity is a word—now becoming a cliché—which recurs with increasing frequency in the mass media. The term 'humanity' has certain overtones of the concept of humanism, a word which reflects the ideal of the ancient world, but the former seems likely to replace it. When the old feudal structures disintegrated at the end of the eighteenth century, the problem of man's humanity appeared for the first time (in Germany) in the works of Lessing, Kant and Fichte. It is clear that today the concept refers to the central, normative moral determination of human conduct and, as a consequence, no ethical project, no socio-political programme which relies on solidarity can afford not to present humanity convincingly as its direct concern. The way in which this theme is developed points to a conception of humanity which is no longer bound up with a religious or ideological position and which some-times even takes up a position entirely hostile to any theological justification of itself (see *Faith*). So Albert Camus, for instance, argues for a humanity without God ('atheistic humanism'). The underlying factor here is that in spite of disagreement and dissension as regards what humanity means or requires, it provides a common basis for understanding and debate in the modern world and that, therefore, an appeal can be made in the name of humanity to those of conflicting views. Because of this assumption there is widespread unanimity on the reasons for concern for humanity: the predominance of scientific and technical thinking (cp. the talk about the arrogance of man), the oppressive weight of the anonymous *apparat*, institutions and ideologies of the modern world, the degradation of man into a readily expendable object, the functionalization of many aspects of life. All those phenomena are widely seen as inhuman. Consequently there is widespread agreement on the measures to be adopted for a humanization of man. These are basically: an affirmation of the right to live, which includes men's recognizing one another and refusing to degrade one another as objects, as well as being ready to lessen suffering and increase the welfare of all men. In practical terms this means: ensuring the right to live for every man, raising the general standard of life, the humanization of working life, social provision for our society's disadvantaged groups, in particular extension of the health service, abolition of the death penalty and torture, humanization of the penal system and increasing opportunities for resocialization.

2. *Christian faith and humanity.* In questions concerning humanity, there are three main considerations for Christian ethics, arising from Christian principles. Since ethics is given to man to make him more human and the moral precepts of revelation are intended for the preservation of what is human, Christians should do all in their power to work with non-Christians in harmony on moral matters and to show their readiness to co-operate in carrying out the commonly acknowledged primary and indispensable fundamentals of humanity. Secondly, humanizing can never mean the politicizing and socializing of all spheres of life but must be related to the idea of the integrity of personal identity, the 'person identical with himself' (Jürgen Habermas). Such a hypothesis is only convincing if there is a corresponding unqualified respect for the unique nature of human existence, which is at the heart of the doctrine of man's creation in the image of God. A purely secular view is saddled in contrast with an impenetrable and insuperable ambivalence, with a lack of clarity (virtue, *q.v.*, world, *q.v.*, human dignity, *q.v.*,). Finally it is worth realizing that in spite of every conceivable progress, humanity will never be

fully achieved within human history; that there are limits to humanitarian evolution; and that to exceed these limits is equivalent to a reversal of humanity into inhumanity. If every increase in personal and social security is only to be gained at the cost of new regulations, of restrictions on individual freedom, then an inner core of inhumanity exists. It is, moreover, a characteristic of all secularist aspirations in this sphere that they deviate into a humanitarianism (Arnold Gehlen) which, while claiming to eliminate man's pain and suffering, in fact concedes everything to everyone, avoids any demands of a decisive kind and tends towards an uncritical acceptance of the current view. The inevitable failure of this sort of humanizing is clear, for example, in the views which represent abortion on demand and euthanasia as humanitarian necessities. A Christian has to present as an alternative the humanity of his God, which is revealed in Jesus' divesting himself of everything even unto death. This viewpoint sees man's misery in the world as coming from guilt and sin and finds true freedom and humanization in reconciliation with God. Christian humanity instructs Christians very specifically in caring for all who suffer pain or misfortune or who live in fear because their personal existence as individuals is threatened.

B. Stoeckle

Human science. See *Anthropology*.

Humanization. See *Humanity; Moral education*.

Humour. See *Joy*.

I

IDENTITY

As a central concept for the healthy personality, 'identity' was introduced by E. H. Erikson, who linked in it the findings of psychoanalysis, social psychology and cultural anthropology. It has also recently become an important concept of sociology, and in educational theory has been postulated by H. v. Hentig as a goal for education. Modern literature has treated it as a fundamental human problem (M. Frisch).

1. Concept. According to Erikson, identity is a lasting inner sameness and continuity, as well as a lasting participation in certain specific group character traits; it therefore includes a reciprocal relation between the core of the individual and membership of a group. Identity is therefore felt as a sense of being oneself, of self-realization, of living in inner sameness and continuity, confirmed by the environment important to the individual. Within historical reality, identity shows itself as the sum of all images, ideas and forces which influence into a person or a nation the feeling of being and acting as they really are. The value of identity is mostly only perceived when it becomes confused or is even lost, because felt as alienation from self, infidelity to one's own core, loss of grip on one's own time.

2. Epigenesis. The quest of identity as a way to self-discovery begins at the latest at a child's birth. For personality develops, of course, in a series of stages, which is predetermined in the readiness of the human organism to

138

be impelled towards a widening range of significant individuals and institutions, to become conscious of itself and to enter into mutual interaction with them. Each step of the development involves a potential crisis because of the radical change of perspective. The personality emerges from each stage with a growth of identity, or, if this is not achieved, it will repeatedly experience regression to earlier stages until the specifically necessary growth of identitity takes place. Erikson divides identity discovery into six stages: 1. Baby stage or oral phase. The child lives through the crisis between basic trust in its own existence and in the world, and basic mistrust. If the infant does not become aware of the meaningfulness of existence through the loving devotion of a reference person, it falls into depression and mistrust. A successful infant period brings the identity gain: 'I am what hope I have and give'. 2. Early childhood or anal phase, decisive for future loving goodwill or hateful self-insistence; autonomy takes shape through struggle against shame and doubt. If successful, the child leaves this state with the identity gain: 'I am what I can will freely'. 3. The age of play. At play the child develops purposefulness and personal initiative in conflict with guilt feelings. The identity gain striven for is that 'I am what I can imagine I will be'. 4. School age. The child experiences the value of industry and of its own achievement and struggles with feelings of inferiority. If it comes to realize that it can do something right, it has achieved the identity gain that 'I am what I can learn to make work' and moves into 5. adolescence. In search of continuity the young person once again has to come to grips with the crises of earlier years, and now consciously seeks identity with himself because he senses his inner confusion. Childhood identifications are subordinated to a new kind of identification. The *model* (*q.v.*) increases in importance for the discovery of a personal ideal of the self. Various rôles are tried out in order to get the feel of an identity. In view of the vast range of possible choices presented nowadays in views of life, careers, life-styles, it is more difficult to find identity than it ever was. Escape into subcultures, star cults, drugs, extremist ideologies, is often the expression of a desperate search for identity. The young person, after all, regards a negative identity as better than none at all. If he passes through adolescence successfully, the young person enters into 6. adulthood with the feeling that, 'I am the one I take myself to be and whom others think I am'. The ego-syntheses from childhood stages and youth are contained in the adult's personality structure. Even if he repeatedly suffers regressions to earlier phases, he possesses identity as a basis in order as a mature personality to become capable of intimacy in struggle against a sense of isolation, of generativity and care against selfishness, and of integrity against disgust with life and despair.

3. *Moral theological outlook.* Erikson speaks of these stages of adulthood as 'beyond identity'. The mature personality places itself at the disposal of others, which is possible where it has experienced the love of others as the condition and source of its own strength. Love is therefore the enduring bond of the various ego-syntheses. Identity is gift and task. The highest self-realization is found in loving devotion to the beloved partner, which for the Christian has its ultimate motive in the promise of God's love, from which all human love takes its origin (see *Love*). Yet the cross teaches that Christian identity is also possible in suffering, even where no harmony exists any more with a visible environment, but only with God. Erikson's statements about identity raise other important problems for moral theology e.g. the morality proper to different ages (especially ethics for adolescence), ethics in *education* (*q.v.*).

Bibliography: **E. H. Erikson**: Childhood and Society. London & New York, 1963; Identity, Youth and Crisis. London & New York, 1968.

L. Fleischer

Immigrant workers. See *Racism*.

Independence. See *Freedom*.

INDIFFERENCE

In everyday usage indifference is an attitude which

indicates emotional apathy. Things, values, people sink into insignificance for the indifferent person (in colloquial terms: it's all the same to me, it doesn't matter—and similar terms of assessment). Indifference is occasionally necessary to protect the individual's emotional life from an excess of affection: but such affective selection presupposes a fundamental choice and is therefore not indifference in the true sense of the word.

1. Analysis. Indifference is related to not wanting to know (*ignorantia affectata*) (*abstinence,* q.v.), an attitude which enables a person to ward off any claims which might demand committed participation from him; for example, moral norms, values, or even such things as the experience of social injustice. In contrast to this not wanting to know, this rejection of clear involvement, is the attitude of conscious solidarity, which results from Jesus' commandment of love: 'But if anyone . . . sees his brother in need, yet closes his heart against him, how does God's love abide in him?' (1 Jn. 3.17). Thus the Christian view of man prohibits closing one's eyes to the moral imperative ultimately inherent in existence and to its normative value.

Indifference lies also in abandoning the *discerning of spirits* (as a Christian charisma: 1 Cor. 12. 10; in moral theology: *discretio* (criticism q.v.)). In this case a person refuses to evaluate the different possibilities of moral action and its worth and so acquiesces in the failure of what is good.

The attitude of indifference becomes a threat to man's self-realization, where it means total resignation in face of the mystery of life and man's access to what is infinite. In monastic spirituality this was termed *acedeia* (literally not wanting to be concerned), and represented symbolically in the noon demon of *sloth*. As one of the seven deadly sins it stands for the end of any mental and spiritual awareness and activity, the giving up of man's restless striving towards what is better, what is divine: in the final analysis it was 'sadness about the divine goods' (Thomas Aquinas). Kierkegaard recognized it, therefore, as the 'sickness unto death', the original sin of shutting oneself away from one's own greater self, from the intimacy of man and God. H. G. Cox has shown well that for modern man 'the time-honoured word 'sloth' describes our spiritual weakness better than the concept of pride. Sloth describes our tired lack of will to enjoy the festival of earth or to share in full measure the suffering in life and the responsibility for it'.

2. *The ethical importance of indifference.* Indifference is, therefore, far more than an insignificant episodic cessation of a man's vital intellectual and spiritual interests. It is the attitude of the person who no longer wants to be a human being, whose own greater self is as unimportant as his fellow human beings' right to see the development of his personal and social potentialities. He also abandons any thought of looking above and beyond himself and of realising the transcendental character of his relationship to God in the unending nature of his deeply disturbing (and far from indifferent) questioning. Indifference touches both the secular and religious figure of man and is, therefore, rightly placed among the fundamentally wrong attitudes (deadly sins), a place accorded it by early theologians (on this point cp. Hermann Broch, Albert Camus).

3. *Present trends.* Because of the technocratic pre-programming of human activity, a readiness to share responsibility, to share decisions or make them independently is not valued highly and the chances for the survival of this readiness are threatened. P. E. Tillinghast has given a warning about the 'cult of melancholy': 'One of the less pleasing aspects of our post-industrial society lies in this way that *acedeia* is once more on the increase . . . The signs are there among young people . . . boredom, restlessness, aimlessness.' Among the consequences of this growing indifference is the inhumanity of our plans for the future.

When transcendence, man's reaching out beyond himself, is being phased out an existential frustration inevitably sets in, which shows all the signs of a 'sadness of life which it is now difficult to control' (Stoeckle). Certain attitudes are clearly typical: aimless activity, fear of loneliness (q.v.), escape from the creation of a strong self, retreat from social commitment, fatal boredom, rejection of both direct and indirect religious questions. All this reveals an agonized humanity.

In so far as a diseased, melancholic-depressive state is

not responsible for indifference and its phenomena, a Christian ethic should open up a human approach to the world, one which takes the tasks of life seriously and radically. It must innovate the motivation for a new *recognition of values* and through meditation (spirituality q.v.) prepare man's mind on the meaning and scope of self-fulfilment and through awakening the sensibilities to the depths of experience inherent in cult and festival (leisure q.v.) prepare for joy in man's own transcendental and divine nature.

Bibliography: Cox, H. G.: The Secular City. New York & London, 1964. **Kierkegaard, S.:** The Sickness unto Death. London, 1941.

Interest. See *Social ethics; Truth.*

J

Jealousy. A state of hostile rivalry in attitude or feeling towards one's neighbour.

JOY

1. *The human dimension.* The term 'joy' has become debased, like the terms 'love' and 'happiness'. Freud once called man a 'tireless pleasure-seeker', because he tries by every imaginable means to wrest love, happiness and joy to himself; but by that very effort he misses what truly characterizes these states: they are *gifts* (and it is not only a religious viewpoint which sees them as such). It has been said of joy: 'It is an access of feeling when something in the world—a thing, a being, an event—comes straight into our life so that we experience it as a gift, radiant with light'. Unlike cheerfulness, which is an expression of a person's inner temperament, and therefore subjective, joy is governed by its objects. For a child they will often be material objects (e.g. a new bicycle); as one gets older the experience of joy becomes more markedly spiritual and moral. But an adult must avoid killing the child in him if he is to be capable of true joy. The capacity for spontaneous joy is sadly lacking in many adults who, misunderstanding the meaning of maturity, have developed onesidedly and spoiled the immediacy of the child's responses.

There is another source of joy: the child's self-assertion, a certain 'triumphal narcissism', to use the language of psychology; for joy is not only the serene acceptance of a gift, but a spontaneous exultation in conquering and possessing. This element sometimes comes to the surface in that profoundly human reaction: joy at another's misfortune. But joy is not merely a spontaneous feeling: inasmuch as it is a specifically human attitude, it need not and must not be independent of a person's conscious moral will. So joy at another's misfortune, if it is given a completely free rein, becomes an evil. The same must be said of commercialized pleasure: whatever the degree of joyful feeling it involves, our assessment of it cannot be value-free; we must ask after its moral justification.

We can weep for joy, and there is much evidence that this kind of joy touches a deeper human nerve than is touched when we laugh for joy. However, people usually connect their experiences of joy with happy laughter, with fun and games, and with all the manifestations of the 'kingdom of comedy'. Within this 'kingdom', with its boundaries extending from harmless jokes to biting cynicism, pride of place must go to the sense of humour: through humour one becomes aware of life both as gift and as burden; it is never completely free of sadness, but does not therefore follow cynicism in renouncing joy. The specific mood of a person with a sense of humour is not so much joy as what Hugo Rahner calls 'grave mirth'. His whimsical joy in life always carries traces of a sorrow at earth's incompleteness. Sorrow is joy's counterpart: in sorrow, life loses meaning; in joy, it gains and possesses meaning as a gift. In the actual human condition, 'joy and woe are woven fine'; and in a life whose dominant tone is its sense of humour, they achieve a unique synthesis. But the person who cannot live, within this synthesis, the extremes of jubilation and desolation; or who can be only sad or only joyful—this person is lacking a dimension. The person who cannot rejoice uninhibitedly in the delight of a moment is as stunted as the one who dare not face a moment's dejection. It might, however, be worth noting that it is not necessarily good-will alone which governs our emotions; psychological fixations, as well as happy or unhappy outward circumstances, materially affect our ability to run the gamut of life's experiences in an emotionally mature manner.

2. *The Christian dimension.* But at this point we could well

take account of the *hope (q.v.)* which comes from believing the 'good news': such hope is experienced in the manner appropriate to a person's psychological make-up, but can sometimes, through its intellectual content and its spiritual dynamic, provide a fresh structure for human experiencing. Paul tells the Philippians more than once to rejoice in the Lord (Phil 3.1, 4.4.). This kind of joy travels beyond the bounds of this world: those who believe in the Lord who is to come have a gift of infinite greatness, and in receiving it become children again—but at the higher level of the 'children of God'. This joy, or, better, gaiety of heart, is something more than earthly joy as expressed through a sense of humour; it is no longer a question of being thankful that one may live in an incomplete world, but of sharing in advance, through faith, in the 'glorious liberty of the children of God' (Rom 8.21). As long as faith is faith, these words are true: 'I will see you again and your hearts will rejoice, and no-one will take your joy from you.' (Jn 16.22)

Bibliography: **St Thomas Aquinas**: Summa Theologiae 1a 2ae 69: Eyre & Spottiswoode edition, vol. XXIV. London, 1974; **Lewis, C.S.**: Surprised by Joy. London, 1955. **Rahner, H.**: Man at Play. London & New York, 1965; **Rahner, K.**: 'Thoughts on the Theology of Christmas' in Theological Investigations, vol. III. London, 1967.

W. Lauer

JUSTICE

1. Concept and essential nature. Justice may be considered from four aspects: as a virtue, as the basis of law, as the principle of man's social existence and as a religious conception. All these aspects are inter-related: the basis of law and the principle of social life are conditioned by one another (politics, *q.v.*); the virtue of justice, although it exists in an individual sense, refers in general to a social responsibility; the religious conception has to be considered as the basis which enables a man to achieve justice. Behind the various external forms of justice is the unity of the idea of the 'recognition of the other person in his otherness' (F.

Böckle) (*toleration, q.v.*). Therefore the conditions necessary for subjective justice—justice as a constant disposition of the will—and also for objective justice—justice as a foundation for social order—must be examined. It is important to distinguish between this general idea of justice and the historical form of justice, which is found in the constant process of elucidation of man's moral sense from facts and propositions. To this extent justice relates to the essence of morals: it defines morality in the communal and social sphere.

2. Theological aspect. Christian ethics must always put the dual question: how can a man be just and how should he act justly? The question of whether an individual is just is put even though the impossibility is recognized of either attaining or exhausting the idea of justice, in the various historical forms of just standards or just social orders. In the christian doctrine of justification, justice as an achievement comes second to justice as a virtue. Even in the Old Testament man had first to be accepted into God's justice, before he could himself act with justice. For Paul man does not achieve justice in his life until he has achieved justice towards God by his participation in salvation (q.v.). This does not mean that once a man has achieved justice, there is no possibility of his failing to practise justice, but that divine justice always anticipates, or rather outstrips, human justice, which our experience tells us is defective.

3. Basis and scope of justice. Justice can be conceived as the objective point of comparison of a relationship (proportional justice) or as the best possibility of development for that relationship (productive justice). In so far as justice characterizes only the relationship between individuals and these are never susceptible of calculation proportionally, the final basis of justice can only be social love. The measure of proportional justice is the constant will to give each man his due (*ius suum unicuique tribuere*); the measure of productive justice is the will to give that sort of love, in which the other person is more than the sum of his actions (*velle alicui caritatem*—H. Rotter). Neither aspect should be considered in isolation or played off one against the other. When justice is considered as a principle of

147

order, then various distinctions have been made (since Aristotle): between corrective or commutative justice (*iustitia commutativa*) among the parts of any social entity (balance of interests, agreement, exchange); distributive justice (*iustitia distributiva*) in the relationship of the whole neitity to its parts (guarantee of a just share in the common good) and legal justice (*iustitia legalis*) in the relationship of the individual to the community. Social justice seems to be the sum of all these various aspects (social ethics, q.v.) and at the same time its dynamic structural driving force, since on the basis of proportionality and productivity it aims at the development of the social order by concentrating on the development of the individual person.

Bibliography: **Tillich, P.**: Love, Power and Justice. London, 1954. **Pieper, J.**: Justice. New York, 1955.

D. Mieth

L

Language. See *Communication; Experience; Truth; Value.*

LEISURE

1. *The place and importance of leisure*: Leisure can be seen in the context of temporality (see *Time*) or of the lifespan as a whole. This determines the demand for leisure and at the same time defines its limits. On the one hand, leisure is simply the antithesis of *work (q.v.)*: a period of mental and physical relaxation to ensure the consistent performance and productivity of the working force. But equally it is something essential to man's nature: it gives him pause for self-examination, self-knowledge and the ordering of his life. In his leisure time he can distance himself from work and all its pressures and find value in himself and other people, irrespective of their achievements or productivity. The alternation of periods of work and leisure preserves men from monotony and creates a rhythm symbolic of man's domination of time. Today this rhythm is threatened on two fronts. Firstly through the persistent idolization of achievement and activity and the development of a way of life so dominated by work that man's capacity to order his leisure time in a constructive way is progressively blunted and destroyed. Because of increasing mechanization and the dual and often barely distinguishable pressures to produce and to consume, leisure ceases to be something qualitively distinct. This is particularly serious (and herein lies the second part of the threat) for, in most professions the amount of free time is becoming quantitively greater,

149

bringing with it a whole series of problems. Questions about the meaning of human existence are being therefore continually reformulated. Because fewer and fewer working hours are needed to secure a reasonable standard of living, and the majority of professions offer so little in terms of satisfaction and involvement, leisure is looked to with feelings of longing and expectation—attitudes that intensify under the pressure to succeed. In addition the private sector where such success is usually sought, is over-subscribed and the consequent passivity and resignation is reflected in an equally unconstructive approach to the spending of leisure time. Dissatisfaction and alienation increase and the possibility of some kind of change becomes daily remoter.

2. *The task*: Christian ethical teaching has a duty to give some sort of guidance as to the constructive use of leisure. If our leisure time (evenings, weekends, holidays and periods of rest) was treated with the seriousness and organization that we devote to our work, all the talent and potential that are dormant during working hours, could be fruitfully mobilised. Leisure is a time for *creativity* (q.v.), communication and liberation, and provides an opportunity to improve unsatisfactory working conditions. The creation of more human working conditions is a possible aim here, but perhaps only at the expense of shorter working hours or even a reduction in leisure time. But the most desirable solution is to make work itself something enjoyable and fulfilling. But even as things stand, leisure both offers opportunities and presents a challenge. It is a time for the individual to use for himself, for others and for God. A way of life that is perpetually hectic and distracting, lacks the balance and regularity that bring a measure of autonomy, a fairness and integrity founded in an understanding of men and an openness to perceive the love and eternity of God.

Bibliography: **Brightbill, C.**: Educating for leisure-centred Living. London, 1966. **Raliner, H.**: Man at Play. London & New York, 1968.

M. Meesters

Liberty. See *Freedom*.

LIBERATION

Since the term 'liberation' (which is but old 'freedom' writ large) became fashionable with the movements to liberate women, gay people, and school students from the oppressions that constrain them, it was inevitable that Christians would cash in with theologies of liberation. These, so far, have emanated from Latin America, and have therefore mainly been concerned with freedom from the economic and political stranglehold of the West.

But in seeking to be theological, finding their roots, that is, in the Bible, they have depended to some extent on ambiguities. 'Liberation' can be used in an absolute sense, but more specifically it is followed by the word 'from', and not enough care has been taken to see that the modern movements are concerned with liberation from anything comparable to the objectives of liberation in scripture. This is much more than a verbal quibble; where we are dealing with moral, that is to say practical questions, their material context is crucial.

The freedom of which the Old Testament prototypically speaks is freedom from foreign domination, the main image being provided by the exodus from Egypt. In the New Testament more abstract notions appear; Paul speaks of freedom from sin, from the Jewish law and commandments, from death itself. Similar themes, though very differently treated, appear in John. But there is no real concern for social and political freedom. The Greek notion of the free citizen in the free state (though the majority of inhabitants were slaves) finds no echo. Paul can state the theological principle magnificently in Gal 3.28 that no distinction can be made on political, racial or gender grounds between one person and another, but when he comes to practice he counsels subservience to the state (Rom 13) or writes the disastrous letter to Philemon.

This is why contemporary theologies of liberation, in seeking biblical justification for their thoroughly commendable moral positions, are on the whole unconvincing. Injustice in a political sense is far from being the main

151

object of condemnation even in the Old Testament, let alone the New. The mistake is methodological. By starting not with the oppressions of their political situation (however much they claim to do this) but with the academic biblical exegesis of their German mentors, these authors fix themselves at an abstract, idealist level.

The moral arguments for liberation from oppression in all the sectors mentioned, when based on analysis of the socio-economic factors producing it, are compelling. The biblical responses to different forms of oppression and liberation in totally different material situations are equally authentic. Nothing is gained by trying to force one into the mould of the other. The Christian who engages in whatever sector of the liberation struggle he finds appropriate need only understand this as a contemporary expression of the action of the Holy Spirit, inspiring people throughout history to a similar but different work.

In this connexion the special question of the use of force always arises. Here too we need to avoid a fundamentalist approach. Maybe Jesus was more politically involved than the New Testmament authors were prepared to make explicit (if they knew) in the different political conditions under which they wrote, but we can hardly create a theology of violence, any more than one of non-violence, from the record. Throughout history the Church has more often accepted the need to use force than not, more usually in the modern world, it must be said, in wars brought about by capitalist struggles for markets than in liberation struggles against the exploiters. Once more it should be clear that we cannot import solutions from the New Testament even if we had any warrant to choose one rather than another; we have to decide in each particular case from the objective nature of the conflict, the results to be achieved, and so on.

Bibliography: Assmann, H.: A Practical Theology of Liberation. London & New York, 1974. Gutierrez, G.: A Theology of Liberation. London, 1974. Windass, S.: Christianity versus Violence. London, 1964.

L. Bright

Libido. See *Pleasure; Sex.*

Lie. See *Truth.*

LONELINESS

1. Terminology. Loneliness is one of several words relating to being alone: solitude, solitariness, lonesomeness, isolation, abandonment, desertion; their range of meaning is considerable. In Christian mysticism, solitude bore a favourable meaning, which was denounced by the Enlightenment as a result of morbid melancholy, only to be rehabilitated in the nineteenth century as a pseudo-religious romantic feeling for Nature. Both tendencies have persisted till this day: rejection of solitude as contrary to human nature, and demand for solitude as a means to achievement of self-awareness and identity, and self-transcendence. Comparison of German 'Einsamkeit' and English 'loneliness' or American 'lonesomeness', shows that the German word includes the positive and negative aspects of solitude and loneliness, which English and American tend to keep apart, 'loneliness' tending to suggest weakness and anxiety.

2. Loneliness in modern anthropology. The significance of loneliness is studied particularly in psychology and sociology. *Loneliness as inability to make contact with others* is investigated more especially by psychology. According to the psychology of development, all 'object relationships' (R. A. Spitz) of the child are based on contact with its mother. In the 'sense of basic trust' (Erikson) between mother and child, the social optimism of the young human being is built up together with his ego-*identity* (*q.v.*). He develops his ego and his capacity for interpersonal relations first of all in family relationships and then in wider contacts with the world around him, and so turns relations with fellow human beings into his own personal moral act. In cases where the foundations of this development process are disturbed, there is a partial or total absence of human contacts, or else what relationships there are, are felt to be unsatisfying and broken. The feeling of being forsaken, of dereliction, leads through the experience of loneliness to an impairment of identity. In this respect, loneliness cuts right into the essence of the human being, who can only live in the duality of the I–You–We. It is therefore a basic problem of the moral personality (see *Anthropology*).

Loneliness as loss of rôles is a theme of sociology. From the sociological point of view, loneliness is 'always a reduction of the individual rôle economy and consequently a limitation of the relevant domains of social activity open to the individual' (Dreitzel). The sociologist regards as grounds for this loss of contact: deprivation, discrimination, stigmatization and withdrawal from the group milieu, and also the loss of contact due to circumstances such as separation (divorce), old age, sickness, death. Loneliness figures here as a real situation, and raises for social interaction patterns and for institutions the problem of the extent to which these deprivation mechanisms can be understood and reduced by a humanization of the structures of *communication* (*q.v.*).

3. *Loneliness and existential discovery of meaning*. This is studied by philosophy and theology. In existentialist philosophy, loneliness is regarded as an opportunity to escape inauthentic existence in the anonymous mass, and of finding one's own self in solitary decision. Even if to some extent this is based on the cultural criticism of a now discredited mass psychology, the philosophical theme of man's self-realization remains a valid one, for man has to experience his social nature in self-awareness as well as in that of others. This requirement is taken over by a theological anthropology in its view of man. By the transcendence which characterizes him, and the profoundly mysterious character of his life, he stands before God, ultimately alone, yet at the same time bound always to practise this relationship with God as a member of the whole of mankind which is called by God, in other words, the *society*. Solitude is therefore not a value in itself, but a function of the God–man relationship, which cannot be founded on pathological feelings of loneliness, but only on the richly human self. Solitude is therefore a necessity for the existential discovery of meaning, not a-social but

rather constructive, affirmative polarity of the social.

4. *Ethical significance*. Christian ethics has not to regard loneliness as a pathological phenomenon which admits of no moral conduct one way or the other (see *Love*). It provides norms by which solitude can be used as an opportunity for personal, social and religious self-realization.

Man is perpetually and in all phases of his development faced with the task of reducing old contrasts, coping with losses due to circumstance (see *Aging*) and striving to make new contacts (adaptation appropriate to the stage reached). He is failing in an essential duty to himself and others if he does not realize this, and if, for instance, he seeks refuge in the feeling of melancholy (inhibiting action) and despair (tristitia) or the mood of boredom, which in its sensation-seeking consumer attitude denies man any activity of interpretation (see *Indifference*). On the other hand, the way to full individuation and socialization leads through painful endurance and bearing of loneliness. Man has the capacity to block interpersonal interactions (by egocentrism etc.) and thereby to bring himself and others into interior and external isolation. Against this stands the moral obligation to cultivate sensitivity (see *Love*) to the concerns of other people. A high degree of sensibility and imagination is required to perceive how individual and collective prejudiced behaviour (see *Prejudice*) and its results in isolation and loneliness can be eliminated.

'Other-directed man' (Riesman) predominates in our modern world. This refers to the behaviour which undermines the personal autonomy and identity required for mental health, and which creates for itself security and a source of decision in the collective ego (see *Education*). The human being of this kind loses himself in busy activity and trivial contacts, which relieve him of the need for confrontation with his own anxiety-ridden, because insecure, ego. Old monastic traditions called this attitude 'acedia'; it consists in despair of one's own ego and its capacity for transcendence. Where the individual is no longer prepared for loneliness as a return to himself (see *Spirituality*), all social relationships lose depth and seriousness, and the hidden God (*deus absconditus*) becomes a symbol of a distressing experience of dereliction and emptiness (see

Faith).

F. J. Illhardt

Loyalty. See *Reliability*.

LOVE

Love is an activity involving the whole of man's being. Unlike a pure impulse, drive or instinct, it is not something that simply seeks to satisfy its own needs. It also affirms what is different from the person expressing it—it affirms the other person. The fact that the concept 'love' has so many different meanings points to the many different levels present in the phenomenon itself, a reality that cannot be confined either to purely physical or corporeal aspects or to purely spiritual elements. Love, then, is orientated towards the whole person of the other, body and spirit. In the same way, it is also rooted in the whole person of the one who loves.

1. The self and love. Man's ability to love grows from his experience of being loved. From the very beginning of its life, the child needs its mother's love. It experiences that love in receiving nourishment, in its close physical contact with its mother and in fulfilling other natural needs. To begin with, the baby experiences a complete unity with its mother. As it grows and develops, the child continues to experience this unity in its attempts to imitate its parents in order to remain close to them. The mother also experiences it in her feeling any threat to her child as a threat to herself. Finally, it is experienced in those forms of affection in which the well-being of one person gives satisfaction to another. This disposition to spontaneous affection has its parallel in mature men and women in a permanent need for acceptance, recognition and social assertion. People whose emotional life is undeveloped or unhealthy, perhaps because they have experienced rejection in childhood, are less capable of sustaining a loving relationship and of maintaining a satisfactory social attitude. Love of oneself and love of another person are not mutually exclusive, but mutually determinative. It is possible to love others only if one accepts oneself. Whenever one's own interests are in conflict with those of another person, it is essential

156

therefore not to seek a solution by simply satisfying one's own desires. If the dictates of love are followed, what will probably be sought is, as far as possible, the equal good of both persons involved. On a higher plane of love, it may even be necessary to sacrifice one's own interest entirely for the sake of the other person's.

2. *Love of one's neighbour.* The person who loves his neighbour above all tries to meet the other's need in all its various forms. (see *Mercy*). If this love of neighbour is truly moral, it will not be expressed in attempts to satisfy purely bodily needs or to create purely utilitarian values. It will above all work towards the unfolding of the other's moral personality. It is, after all, only in this way that the other will find fulfilment of his deepest hopes and deep, lasting happiness. On the other hand, however, the other person can only do justice to the claims of morality by loving in his turn and this means that the aim of all moral love must be to make the other a loving person. This cannot be achieved by allowing the other to misuse his own readiness to serve or to undervalue his own personal dignity. True love of one's neighbour has therefore to include an expectation of a response and a claim that one's own person and rights will be respected. If it did not include these demands, the other's selfishness would perhaps be confirmed and he might even remain close to the claims of morality. It is, of course, true that this claim that one will be respected by the other person cannot simply be expressed by coercing the other or subjecting him to certain conditions. On the contrary, it usually becomes clear in each situation whenever an injustice is borne without complaining or whether forgiveness is granted; it also emerges what is understood by a moral attitude and therefore what can be expected from the other person.

Love of one's neighbour has, then, to be expressed in serving the other persons needs, which are often natural and corporeal. It is therefore important to take into account the external, natural circumstances in which the other is placed. Love has therefore to be objective. It should not assume forms which seem to the other or to the person expressing love to be momentarily advantageous, but which may, in the long run, have predominantly negative effects. This reveals an aspect of love that is essential to our understanding of the human person and personal love. Love must, in other words, not simply be concerned with the other person's present appearance—it must above all accept him as a historical reality. Man exists consciously in history. For this reason, he must be affirmed in his future and in his future needs. In loving one's neighbour, one must always be conscious of his future. Love therefore always includes a promise (q.v.) of faithfulness. If this were not so or if this promise of faithfulness were given in advance and only for a limited period, this would amount to a failure to acknowledge the other as a historical person. It would be 'loving' him simply because of the utility or other limited value that can be offered to him.

Love has similarly to be concerned with the other's past. Every man is determined by his past and can only be known insofar as his past is known. In the same way, he can only be loved insofar as his past is affirmed as an essential aspect of his being. This always includes a concern for the guilt (q.v.) incurred by the other person and must therefore take the form of forgiveness and understanding.

3. *The transcendental structure of love.* Love transcends the present and points to a future without limits. It even transcends the limits which the other imposes on his worthiness to be loved by his guilt, rejection and failure. Love cannot therefore be understood simply as a reaction to what the other person is at a given moment or to the way in which he behaves at that moment. If it were merely based on the person or the personality of the other, this transcendental aspect of love would be incomprehensible and meaningless. It points, however, to the fact that love itself is unconditionally meaningful in its essential structure and that this does not depend on whether it is reciprocal or whether it encounters rejection and hostility. This unconditionally meaningful structure can only be understood if it is seen as a relationship with the absolute and transcendent reality of God. If he is to find happiness, man needs a Thou to whom he can give himself completely. Perfect happiness is therefore only possible when that Thou transcends the limits of finiteness, transience and guilt, in other words, when the Thou is God. God cannot, of course, be seen

158

simply as the condition that makes it possible for man to achieve the fulfilment of perfect happiness. The latter can only be reached when man loves God as such. It cannot be found so long as man is simply looking for himself in God.

The love of God and of one's neighbour are not independent of each other. God's claims to love are expressed in the many different obligations that man experiences with regard to his fellow men. Similarly, all the many different ways in which man expresses his love of his neighbour point to the absolute Thou of God. Love of one's neighbour is not an alternative to the love of God—it is the symbol of that love and the way in which it is communicated.

4. The moral consequences of love. The commandment to love is absolute. It can and should give way to nothing. This means that man does not exist as a person simply for his own sake. He finds himself and is fulfilled only by being present for others and for the sake of others (see Mt 10. 39 par). This law of the dialogue of love means that the moral subject of love cannot be autonomous. Living and acting for the sake of the other person implies a concern for the other's will. It is only possible to give full consent to his will and treat him as a free person if his free decisions are taken fully into account. For this reason, it is not possible to deduce the concrete content of a demand made by love purely on the basis of one's own understanding—it can only be known in dialogue with the other person. This also applies, of course, in an extended sense to our relationship with society as a whole. The will of God is communicated to us in the lawful demands made on us by society.

At the same time, there is also an eschatological reservation with regard to the meaningfulness of love of one's neighbour. The experience of such love is not necessarily one of the ultimate meaning of human life. The successful expression of such love is subject to certain natural preconditions which are beyond the control of free choice. In so far as the experience of this love is dependent on human attitudes, it is not a full and unequivocal expression of man's inner freedom to choose. Limits can, in this experience, be imposed on man's moral freedom that can only be overcome by God, who is 'greater than our hearts'

(1 Jn 3. 20).

Freedom, as the fundamental structure of interpersonal love, is the direct consequence of the fact that interpersonal love points to the ultimate fulfilment of human hope, although it is not that fulfilment itself. Love makes the other person free. It is not simply a reaction to the other's benevolence and does not presuppose a corresponding counter-reaction. It is a free gift to the other person, with the result that love cannot be demanded from the other as a right, although it can be accepted gratefully as a free gift if it is received. Love therefore always implies an obligation and makes a claim on the other person, namely that he will accept the gift of love. This claim will always of necessity be, however, an appeal to the other's freedom. For this reason, it must always respect the other's freedom of decision.

There is a close connexion between love of God and love of one's neighbour. This connexion is above all apparent in the way in which God's love is communicated to men and the claim that is linked with it is conveyed through men. According to the New Testament, then, the ultimate basis and reason for the commandment to love is not to be found in human nature, which is common to all men, or in an immanent human dignity (*q.v.*), which is again common to all men, but rather in the fact that God loves men. We read in the fourth gospel: 'A new commandment I give you, that you love one another; even as I have loved you, that you also love one another' (Jn 13.34) and in Paul's letter to the Ephesians: 'Husbands, love your wives, as Christ loved the church and gave himself up for her' (Eph 5. 25). In the same way, men ought also to forgive each other, so that God will forgive them or because he has forgiven them (see Mt 18. 23–35; 6. 12–15). A demand for love that is based exclusively in one's fellow men can never explain an absolute claim or the radical commandment to love one's enemies. Such a moral claim cannot also be based on purely natural structures. If it is true to say that morality finds its highest and most all-embracing expression in the commandment to love, then it can only be based on the freely given love of God. A theologically based morality, then, does not take its point of departure in the purely natural laws of interpersonal behaviour or in a purely philosophical concept of the human person. It is, on the contrary, firmly rooted in the place where God's free love of man appeared, that is, in the history of salvation in general and in Jesus Christ in particular.

The connexion between love of God and love of one's neighbour is especially important in the question of the overcoming of guilt through forgiveness. If morality were really to be found simply at the level of fellow-humanity, then moral guilt (*q.v.*) could also only be found at that level. If that were the case, however, a complete overcoming of human guilt would not be possible. It is not enough, when a man has failed with regard to his fellow man, for him to try simply to cleanse himself of his guilt—he has to be reconciled through the word of forgiveness. Purely human forgiveness, however, is not sufficiently radical in its effects and is always limited. It can also be refused. Complete forgiveness is only possible if it can be hoped for as an action of God's grace. This divine forgiveness is not dependent on forgiveness by one's fellow-man or on the extent of the forgiveness or mercy felt or shown by one's fellow man. It is, however, connected with the extent to which the guilty person is converted and therefore with his will to be reconciled with his fellow man (See *Mercy, Forgiveness*). See *Ethics*.

Bibliography: **Cardenal, E.**: Love. London, 1974. **Dominian, J.**: Proposals for a New Sexual Ethic. London, 1977. **Kosnick, A. et al.**: Human Sexuality: New Directions in (American) Catholic Thought. New York & London, 1977.

H. Rotter

Loyalty. See *Promise; Truth*.

M

Man. See *Anthropology*.

MANIPULATION

1. *Analysis of the phenomenon.* Manipulation (the word comes from Latin *manus*, hand and *pleo*, a handful; to grasp with the hand, handle) is found in every kind of expression of individual and social life whether in relation to self or to other people. Even if many things have to be 'manipulated', i.e. handled, dealt with, in a good sense (correct diet, medical treatment for health; political, scientific and technical measures to promote the common welfare), at the present time the threatening because hidden and secretly operative aspect of manipulation is focussing attention. Individuals and groups see themselves exposed to this kind of influence. As 'social manipulation' (H. Rombach) it happens consciously and of set purpose. It aims at 'handling' people in the domain of social interaction. Modes of behaviour are to be produced and firmly directed to goals established but not disclosed by particular interested persons. For example, fashion seeks to induce a lot of people to dress fashionably on the motto of 'That is what is being worn now'. The economic interests that lie behind this are not disclosed. Valuable as sound information about products and their qualities undoubtedly is, the whole domain of advertising is also the field of the 'hidden persuaders' (V. Packard). Manipulation by every form of mass communications, by ideologies, which often claim to be indispensable political, economic and technolog-

162

ical solutions but in reality conceal techno-bureaucratic rule by officialdom, is thrusting forward as a public force in so-called free societies. For many people this process is mysterious and confusing. They feel themselves at the mercy of that sort of manipulation. Restriction of information in the form of indoctrination by a political party, as practised in totalitarian systems, is also felt as a kind of manipulation. Particular types of manipulation of the human organism e.g. of genes, are felt by many to represent defenceless surrender to 'man-makers' (R. Kaufman). 'The manipulated soul' appears as an 'uncanny possibility' (Th. Löbsack). Also the whole realm of pharmaceutical preparations has links with manipulation, for seriously questionable effects are evident here in the shape of doping, present-day use and abuse of drugs, particularly in narco-analysis and brain-washing (see *Addiction*).

What is dangerous about manipulation in this pejorative sense is the idea that everything, including man, is constructive and can be fabricated, so that manipulation ultimately proves to be an instrument of power and domination of men over men (see *Liberation*), though, of course, by seemingly innocent methods, while the harsh purposes are hidden. As many people nowadays, because of the specialization of their rôles, lack a critical eye for things as a whole, there are many opportunities for manipulation to seize and its effect is literally undermining. The 'administered world' (Horkheimer) of manipulated man can present things in such a way that people think they are living in a civilized society whereas in reality it is a society of semblance and illusion because it has no guiding values; human beings are manipulated by what is drummed into them.

2.   *Moral counter-action.* Despite this universally perceptible social manipulation, counter forces are at work. A well-developed, critical personality does not succumb to any and every manipulation, but is able to see through it and ward it off or eliminate it. Because manipulation seeks to persuade, it cannot convince anyone capable of judging, even when it resorts to social coercion and resistance brings personal disadvantages. Of course, when manipulation contrives to make use of democratic majority decisions,

with consequences for legislation and social institutions, it can bring hurt to the perceptive and discord to society.

Ethical consciousness recognizes that manipulation as we have described it derives from a superficial idea of man and a frivolous attitude to human beings. A view of man that really does justice to reality, demands respect for the fundamentally equal value of each human life (see *Human dignity*). It is a basic moral principle that men should be treated honestly and sincerely and not manipulated for disguised purposes. Manipulation insinuates itself precisely where human beings are no longer being treated as persons in the full sense, but handled like manufactured products determined simply from outside. Here the realm of fundamental personal rights and justice is violated. A proper sense of personal dignity contributes to the prevention and defeat of manipulation, which is a calculus of what is technically feasible.

3. Responsibility of believers. Christian faith sees man as God's image (Gen 1.26), to whom God the Lord has offered a partnership relation of alliance and friendship, especially in Jesus Christ (Jn 15.14 f). He calls every man to salvation and therefore to conversion from oppressive manipulation.

An ethos of true freedom stands at the service of liberation from anything inimical to man. Social life should promote the growth to maturity of personalities determined by values and able to distinguish between necessary manipulation at the service of man (e.g. education in values or medical operations undertaken for personal welfare on the principle of sacrifice of the part for the whole, with the patient's own consent) and the manipulation which is an inhuman indignity because it treats human beings as things to be processed.

Bibliography: Brown, J. A. C.: Techniques of Persuasion. Harmondsworth, 1963. **Clinard, M. B.**: Sociology of Deviant Behaviour. New York, ³1968. **Häring, B.**: Manipulation. London, 1975. **Huxley, J.**: Brave New World. London, 1932. **Marcuse, H.**: One-Dimensional Man. Boston & London, 1964. **Orwell, G.**: Nineteen Eighty-Four. London, 1949. **Packard, V.**: The Hidden Persuaders. New York & London, 1957. **Rahner, K.**: Meditations on Freedom and the Spirit. London & New York, 1977. **Wolstenholme, G. (Ed.)**: Man and his Future. London, 1963. **Zamiatin, E.**: We. (trans. G. Zilboorg). New York, ²1959.

F. Beutter

Man-without-God. See *Godlessness*.

MARRIAGE. I

1. Biblical point of departure. The relationship between man and woman is emphasized in the fundamental statements of the biblical account of creation. Woman is man's companion. The 'community of one flesh' existing between man and woman in marriage is accompanied by God's blessing of fertility (Gen 1. 28). In the Old Testament tradition, marriage is given a prominent position as the institution for the preservation of the man's lineage. In marriage, children are seen as God's gift and blessing and to be unmarried is regarded as shameful. Old Testament man hopes for a share in the messianic salvation through his offspring. All this gives great prominence to the idea of fertility. Even certain forms of polygamy are accepted in the interests of the continuation of the clan or tribe and for economic reasons. As the head of the family, the man has more rights than the woman. A partnership with equal rights for the husband and the wife does not exist in the Old Testament.

In the New Testament, Jesus goes back to the basic statements contained in the account of creation and at the same time takes the Old Testament teaching about marriage to a deeper level by rejecting the practice of divorce and affirming the deepest meaning of marriage as God's way of achieving unity between man and woman in love and faithfulness (Mk 10. 1–12). Jesus' teaching contains another change of emphasis. Whereas the Old Testament over-emphasized the importance of marriage as the only way to salvation and the only means of perpetuating the race, Jesus relativizes the institution in both senses. His teaching stresses that marriage is a secular reality which will pass away with life in this world (Mk 12. 25). With Jesus'

165

coming, the kingdom of God has already commenced on earth and with it a special call to remain unmarried 'for the sake of the kingdom of heaven', which is parallel to the vocation of marriage. This unmarried way of life is meaningful, even though 'not all men can receive this precept' (Mt 19. 12). The historically conditioned superiority of the man over the woman is preserved in Paul's teaching, although the foundation is laid for an equal partnership between husband and wife. The differences between the sexes are unimportant in the light of faith. Marriage is seen as a model of the loving relationship between Christ and his Church (Eph 5. 21–33). The basic point of comparison is the unreserved and total giving of both partners to each other and their mutual love and faithfulness.

2. *The anthropological and theological understanding of marriage.* The Christian understanding of marriage and sexuality (*q.v.*) has been deeply influenced by external factors throughout the history of the Church. In the past, Christian marriage was above all seen in the light of its value as a means of procreation and of satisfying sexual needs. The predominantly patriarchal structure of western society that prevailed until late in the nineteenth century also led to the Pauline teaching in Eph 5 being interpreted as a theological justification for male superiority over women. Nowadays, however, it is personal rather than purely biological factors which form the basis of partnership and sexuality in marriage. These factors are also the prerequisite for any really human expression of total self-giving and for any morally justifiable creation of new life.

3. *Marriage as a sacrament.* According to the Catholic understanding of marriage, the love and faithfulness of two Christian partners for each other are not only a sign of the Lord's love for his Church, but also the realization of that love (Eph 5. 29, 31–32). The Church is actively present within the community in the expression of marital love and self-giving. This idea of marital love receded in the course of history and was insufficiently emphasized in the Church's sacramental understanding of marriage, but was revived in the sixteenth century Roman catechism. The renewed teaching stressed, in addition to the procreative

aspect of marriage, the intense bond of love between the Lord and his Church. This bond was seen as a model for the relationship between man and wife and pointed not only to the human need for procreation, but also to the community of love which the partners had to strive to achieve as the real basis of their marriage.

The papal encyclical on marriage, *Casti connubii* (Pius XI, 1930), emphasized the special value of marital love, although this was still expressed in Augustinian terms of marital faithfulness, the sacramental aspect and offspring as the primary purpose of marriage. The personal factors in the Christian understanding of marriage were later stressed in the Pastoral Constitution on the church in the Modern World (*Gaudium et spes*, 47–52) of Vatican II: 'As God of old made himself present to his people through a covenant of love and fidelity, so now the Saviour of men and the Spouse of the Church comes into the lives of married Christians through the sacrament of matrimony . . . Authentic married love is caught up into divine love. . . Thus the Christian family (*q.v.*), which springs from marriage as a reflection of the loving covenant uniting Christ with his Church and as a participation in that covenant, will manifest to all men the Saviour's living presence in the world and the genuine nature of the Church. This the family will do by the mutual love of the spouses, by their generous fruitfulness, their solidarity and faithfulness and by the loving way in which all members of the family work together' (48).

The Second Vatican Council, then, clearly rejected a purely biological and reproductive evaluation of marriage. Marital love and faithfulness were stressed as the foundation of the sacrament. A sacramental marriage in this sense can only come about if the unity and the indissolubility of the marriage are freely accepted by both partners and this united, indissoluble bond is extended, if that is possible, by free consent of both partners, to the foundation of a family. This will then form and continue to be the basis for partnership in marriage and a responsible creation of new life. An essential aspect of such a responsible marriage is also a conscientious regard for birth control (*q.v.*).

Because it is nowadays so difficult to experience marriage

167

in a really personal way, there is a need for certain aids and supports to marriage. These ought not simply to be applied just when the marriage is on the point of finally breaking down. It is clear that some form of initiation ('asceticism', *q.v.*) in the relationship between the partners and communication (*q.v.*) between them are necessary not only during the period of preparation preceding marriage, but also throughout married life.

Whether it is freely chosen or enforced by circumstances, the unmarried state may be a meaningful and subjectively satisfactory way of life, especially when the unmarried person is fully integrated into the environment in which he is working and is not living in isolation. It is, however, not possible to justify the tendency to give unmarried people the right to full sexual relationships so long as this does not cause harm to anyone and a full partnership is guaranteed. This is because the statements about sexuality (*q.v.*) in marriage show that the preconditions for such an extra-marital sexual relationship do not exist. In a full sexual relationship, both partners, after all, only come to accept full responsibility for each other when they have decided to share their lives fully together. Without this total commitment, total self-giving in love can easily become either a lie or a meaningless sacrifice. The will to marry is therefore the essential prerequisite for full sexual relationships.

4. The marriage contract. Marriage should not be regarded simply as an arrangement concerning only the two partners. In most societies, marriage is celebrated as a socially significant event. Since the Christian is, after all, a living member of his community, that community has a right to be involved in his marriage and his foundation of a family. This is especially important in the sacramental understanding of Christian marriage. The Christian's promise, made in public, of his will to marry and to be indissolubly united in faithfulness to his partner provides that partner with a certain protection against a possible denial or withdrawal of that promise later. The legal form and consequences of this public contract of marriage have, of course, changed a great deal in the course of history, but such a public contract has always been made, since serious reservations have always been felt towards a 'marriage without any sign of marriage'. As long, however, as there is no real will to marry, any insistence that a marriage contract should be undertaken, even when the couple are cohabiting, has seemed irresponsible. The need for a personal understanding of the meaning of Christian marriage makes a fundamental preparation for marriage essential. The marriage contract can only be valid so long as at least some understanding of the unity and indissolubility of the personal relationship is present and accepted by both partners.

5. *Mixed marriages.* It is precisely because there is also a religious dimension to this necessary understanding of the nature of Christian marriage that the unity of the partners may be disturbed by their not belonging to the same community of faith. This problem cannot be solved simply by suppressing the religious aspect of married and family life. Mixed marriage between two members of different Church communities—now subject to increasing care on the part of the Church—can be dangerous, but it also provides an opportunity. It may lead to authentic toleration (*q.v.*) and religious openness. In the case of a Christian and a non-Christian partner in marriage, the intensive religious life of the former may lead to the 'consecration' of the latter (1 Cor 7. 14); on the other hand, the result may be religious indifference on the part of the Christian partner and a loss of faith on the part of the whole family. The Church has made it much easier to contract a mixed marriage, but requires the Catholic partner to promise to do everything within his power to guarantee a Catholic education for his children. The marriage contract can be celebrated ecumenically.

6. *Breakdown of marriage.* Since the Lord has forbidden his followers to divorce, the Christian clearly cannot ask when divorce is 'permitted'. It is quite a different matter, however, to state that married love and faithfulness have broken down irreversibly. We live, after all, in a world that is not yet saved. There is evidence in Scripture of practical concern for broken marriages. The Church has tried to find a helpful compromise solution by forbidding remarriage rather than divorce and by the erection of impediments to

169

marriage. Partners whose marriage has broken down are not excluded from pastoral care. It is, of course, still not possible for divorced Roman Catholics who have remarried to receive the sacraments, but it remains to be seen whether, despite the Church's present ruling, it is justifiable for 'exceptional' cases of such Catholics to receive the sacraments under certain conditions.

Since there is at present no satisfactory anthropological basis for a bond of love in faithfulness and indissolubility as a precondition for the sacrament of marriage, we are bound to include within our pastoral care those 'marriages' or unions resembling marriage which are either not able or not yet able to be sacramental.

Bibliography: Dominian, J.: Marital Breakdown. Harmondsworth, 1968. Id.: Proposals for a New Sexual Ethic. London, 1977. Häring, B.: Marriage in the Modern World. London, 1965. Kosnik, A. et al.: Human Sexuality: New Directions in (American) Catholic Thought. New York & London, 1977. Schillebeeckx, E.: Marriage: Human Reality and Saving Mystery. London, 1966.

J. Gründel

MARRIAGE. II

Marriage is the exclusive and permanent personal union between a baptized man and a woman, commonly but not essentially for the procreation and education of children.

Marriage and the family form the basic social union in the community within which life—the life, that is, of the spouses and their children—is nurtured. Marriage has a history which precedes Christianity; the development of marriage in the Christian tradition reflects first the taking over of established customs in different parts of the world and the gradual Christianization of those social norms.

From the very beginning—that is, in the Old and New Testament—marriage had a special place as a symbol of the relationship first between Yahweh and his people and later between Christ and his Church. This basic insight prepared the way for the mediaeval view of marriage to be regarded as a sacrament and it was defined as such by the Council of

170

Trent. But after that definition, the question remained of what the essential characteristics of this sacrament might be.

In due course it became clear that the ministers of the sacrament were the man and the woman who in the presence of a priest and two witnesses expressed their assent to the mutual bestowal and acceptance of one another for life. The irrevocable consent which initiates the marital relationship is transformed into an indissoluble, permanent union through the first act of sexual intercourse. But what is the purpose of marriage? The goods or ends of marriage have been described as the permanence of the relationship, mutual faithfulness, and the procreation and rearing of children.

The accumulated results of dogma and practice have inevitably focussed on the wedding day as the main event of marriage. Recently, and in particular after the second Vatican Council, thinking on marriage has moved from the strictly legalistic approach which surrounded the sacrament in the post-Tridentine period to its more personal terms; this move has been described as from law to love. The family—that is, the relationship of the spouses and that between parents and children—has been described by Vatican II as a 'community of love'.

This community, while retaining the traditional characteristics of permanence and exclusiveness, is now seen increasingly in terms of the capacity of persons to initiate, sustain and maintain a relationship of love which expresses more than the social characteristics of a couple living together under the same roof, and sharing one bed and one table. The personal relationship of love permeated by grace is considered to have the capacity to sustain, heal, and facilitate the growth of the couple.

Expectations of personal fulfilment from marriage far exceed the requisite preparation for the support of the sacrament, and currently all societies but particularly Western ones are experiencing a wave of marital breakdown and divorce which indicates the gap between rising expectations and changing social conditions and effective means of coping with them. Divorce in particular has presented a challenge to Christianity for, unlike other sexual moral issues, the indissolubility of marriage is one of

171

the most clearly proclaimed teachings of Christ about life in the kingdom of God. Recently there has been a renewed interest in this sacrament as, gradually, it has been realized that after baptism and the eucharist it is the most important sacrament in the life of the Christian community.

Bibliography: Baab, O. J.: 'Marriage', 'Sex' in Interpreter's Dictionary of the Bible. New York, 1962. **Bailey, D. S.**: Common Sense about Sexual Ethics. New York, 1962; The Man-Woman Relation in Christian Thought. London, 1959; **Bowlby, J.**: Attachment and Loss. London, 1969; **Cole, W. G.**: Sex and Love in the Bible. New York, 1959; Declaration on Certain Questions Concerning Sexual Ethics. Rome, 1976; **Delhaye, P.**: 'The Development of the Medieval Church's Teaching on Marriage' in Concilium 55. London, 1970. **Dominian, J.**: Authority. London, 1976; The Church and the Sexual Revolution. London, 1971; Proposals for a New Sexual Ethic. London, 1977; 'Birth Control and Married Love' in The Month. London, March 1973. **Dubarle, A. M.**: Love and Fruitfulness in the Bible. De pere, Wisconsin, 1968. **Erikson, E. H.**: Identity. London, 1968. **Häring, B.**: Medical Ethics. Notre Dame, 1972. **Harrington, W.**: The Bible on Marriage. Dublin, 1963. **Horner, T.**: Sex in the Bible. Rutland, Vermont, 1974. **de Jong, B.**: 'Christian Anthropology: the Biblical View of Man' in Sex, Family, and Society in Theological Focus, ed. by J. C. Wynn. New York, 1966. **Kosnik, A., et al**: Human Sexuality. New York, 1977. **de Kruijf, T. C.**: The Bible on Sexuality. De Pere, Wisconsin, 1966. **Piper, O.**: 'Sex in Biblical Perspective' in Sexual Ethics and Christian Responsibility, ed. by J. C. Wynn. New York, 1970. **de Riencourt, A.**: Sex and Power in History. New York, 1974. **Schillebeeckx, E.**: Marriage. London, 1976. **Soane, B.**: 'Rethinking Medical Ethics' in The Clergy Review, July 1976. **Stoller, R. J.**: Sex and Gender. London, 1968. **Vatican II Documents 1967**: The Church Today. Fostering the Nobility of Marriage and the Family. **Winnicott, D. W.**: The Maturational Processes and the Facilitating Environment. London, 1965.

J. Dominian

MARXISM

Marxism is not usually viewed as contributing much to ethical theory, even when it is taken seriously in other respects. Marx's contribution in fact lies deeper than the solution of particular problems; his work offers a new way forward from behind the mistaken views that have dominated ethics since the Renaissance.

Before then classical ethics, derived from the Greeks, was expressed by a theory of natural law. Ethics is the way of deciding whether the needs we desire to satisfy by our actions are true or false: it provides a criterion of judgment. Natural law saw this as conformity to the discernable fixed character of the action. This still remains the official ethical thinking of the Catholic Church; contraception is morally wrong, runs the familiar argument, because it contradicts the (biological) character of the sex act. Most people are unconvinced by this but counter it at a quite different level: morality depends on whether or not the intention is correct, whether we act lovingly or not.

Such a move is natural to us because of the dissociation of 'the world' into 'objective' and 'subjective' that also took place at the Renaissance (stemming from the rise of capitalism, Marxists would say). As this division was given shape by the empiricist philosophers, there was a 'real world', independent of our subjective judgment, and thus of values, 'out there': it could be described, understood, controlled by natural science. Opposed to it was the personal 'world in our head', private to each of us, the place of aesthetic and moral judgment. The connexion between the two was tenuous. As Hume put it, the moral 'ought' cannot (as classical ethics held) be derived from the 'is' of a factual world. With German subtlety Kant fixed the division for all time; not merely for philosophy, but for common sense as well, moral thinking today is largely 'subjective', whatever the Church may say.

Now Marx called himself a 'materialist' because he did not accept this dissociation (the term as he uses it has nothing to do with reduction of all explanations to those of physics). There was a single human world, he insisted, though it could be analysed at many different levels. The basic one was economic, to be sure; but correct analysis

173

here was not independent of the other levels (the crude idea that a separate 'superstructure' is entirely explicable in terms of the economic 'base' is foreign to him). There is constant feed-back from one level to another—the relationship between them is 'dialectical'.

At the centre of this approach lay the insight that it was centrally the way in which a society *produced* goods (not, as had been supposed, its consumption of them) that determined the relationships between its members and thus its cultural patterns—remembering the dialectical nature of this 'determination'. At the present era of western history—not before or, hopefully, after—the mode of production is 'capitalist'. This requires for its continuance the accumulation of capital (rather than its consumption in extravagance, say), in other words requires growth. A necessary consequence is that the workers who produce never receive back the real value of the labour they sell to the capitalist owner. Marx showed in great detail the effect of this exploitative relationship on every aspect of society, and his method is equally effective for analysis of the developed capitalism of today.

The effect of such analysis is to expose a gap between appearance and reality. People's real needs are masked by the nature of the capitalist system, being substituted by a set of false ('ideological') ones. This is not by deliberate conspiracy to deceive on anyone's part: the reality is hidden from the class that benefits as much as from the class that is exploited. Marx believed, however, that as more people become aware of the reality they would act to change the situation (mode of production) so as to bring into being a more rational set of relationships and a new social formation (socialist society). This was by no means automatic—he was not a determinist—but neither was it a matter of 'applying' an abstract theory to the situation. Theory and practice were intimately bound together in dialectical relationship; as people grew conscious of their situation they acted to change it, and thereby deepened their awareness.

Marx's achievement was therefore to restore the classical ethics of 'natural law' in a more satisfactory and dynamic way, behind the subjective approach that makes morality, in the end, a matter of opinion and mere feeling. He discovered how, in the present era of capitalism, people's real needs could be distinguished from their ideological ones, so that in acting to satisfy them they were acting 'rightly' in the ethical sense.

Of course there is an immense literature on the analysis of different sectors of society in these terms, exposing the gap between appearance and reality; because of the direction ethics has taken in the post-classical world, such analysis is not usually seen by its authors in moral terms. A few random examples must suffice for illustration.

The family lies at the centre of much ethical thinking. Christians in particular hold it in high regard, and condemn any moves which might relax permanent monogamous relationship through increased sexual permissiveness, or change its male-dominated character through questioning of roles within it. Yet analysis shows how this particular form of nuclear family grew with industrial capitalism, and now has the prime function of maintaining the work force as it is. Women stay at home to bear and socialize the future workers, thereby providing cheap unpaid labour. The unit itself is necessary to maintain levels of consumption (necessary if capitalist production growth is not to run into the sands of recession) since rivalry between nuclear units is far more wasteful than collective policies would be.

A second and connected area concerns education. Behind the arguments for the right of all to literacy lay the need for a work-force that could operate the more complex type of modern machine; behind the division into grammar and 'modern' education lay the need to produce management and its auxiliaries on the one hand, manual workers on the other; behind the arguments for 'comprehensive' schooling lies the certainty that 'streaming' will continue, in masked form, to maintain the divisions between classes that are the necessary product of capitalism.

Even more obvious is the propaganda that disguises modern war as patriotic 'defence', rather than the means of defeating capitalist rivals for the world's markets or maintaining these areas of exploitation against the indigenous population.

Clearly these examples represent the briefest indications of what has received far more extended and subtle

175

MASTURBATION

treatment from Marxist analysts. The main point to be made is that such considerations are in fact ethical, once ethics has been freed from its self-indulgent concern with 'loving behaviour'. Marxism thus offers to Christians the possibility of being 'doers of the word, not hearers only'.

Bibliography: Avineri, S.: Social and Political Thought of Karl Marx. London, 1968. **Baran, P. & Sweezy, P.:** Monopoly Capital. London, 1966. **Turner, D.:** 'Morality is Marxism', New Blackfriars (February/March 1973). **Dupré, L. K.:** Philosophical Foundations of Marxism. London, 1966.

L. Bright

MASTURBATION

Masturbation is a self-induced means through which men and women at any age but particularly post-pubertally obtain sexual pleasure with or without achieving an orgasm.

Modern studies have shown that masturbation is practised by young children but that the peak for masturbatory activity is post-pubertal and pre-marital. Some men and women continue to use masturbation as an alternative or supplementary form of sexual stimulation other than coitus.

Masturbation is surrounded by secular and religious taboos and anxieties. At various times it has been held responsible for all kinds of disordered behaviour including mental illness. There is no iota of evidence to support these fears and it is likely that they reflect a much deeper anxiety about sexual behaviour in general.

Traditional Christian teaching which related sexual activity intimately to procreation has found masturbation trebly difficult. Since sexual pleasure was obtained in isolation, in the absence of sexual intercourse and without procreation potential, it was condemned on all these grounds. Recently a much more lenient view has been taken of the seriousness of the offence on the mitigating grounds of restriction of freedom and lack of maturation of the young people involved. A further ethical development which considers masturbation as an essential and transitional part of
176

adolescent behaviour has been put forward. Such a view however remains condemned in the official teaching of the Catholic Church: in, that is, its treatise on the subject, *Declaration on Certain Questions Concerning Sexual Ethics* (1975).

Bibliography: 'The Declaration on Certain Questions Concerning Sexual Ethics' in The Clergy Review. London, June 1976; **Dominian, J.**: Proposals for a New Sexual Ethic. London, 1977; **Greeley, A.**: Love and Play. Chicago, 1975; Sexual Intimacy. Chicago, 1973; **Hare, E. H.**: 'Masturbation Insanity, The History of an Idea' in Journal of Mental Science 108. London, 1962; **Kosnik, A., et al**: Human Sexuality. New York, 1977; Maier, H. W.: Three Theories of Child Development. New York, 1969; **Spitz, R. A.**: 'Authority and Masturbation' in Psychoanalytic Quarterly 21. London, 1952; **Sullivan, P. R.**: 'What is the Role of Fantasy in Sex?' in Medical Aspects of Human Sexuality 3. London, 1969.

J. Dominian

Maturity. See *Asceticism; Authority; Epiekeia; Family; Freedom; Identity.*

Meaning. See *Action; Body; Ethics; Faith; Love; Norm; Human dignity.*

Measure. See *Abstinence.*

Meditation. See *Spirituality.*

MERCY

Within the scope of purely rational or philosophical ethics it is not at all easy to discover the meaning of mercy as a moral requirement. In this field results are largely negative. Thus Stoicism places mercy (*eleos*) among man's downright vicious attitudes. It does not seem compatible with the idea of apathy or freedom from passion. Nietzsche discredited mercy in the light of other considerations. Since it is devoted to the life of the weak and suffering, it is opposed to the justice which only a strong and healthy existence can claim. And it can be exercised only by someone who is ineffective in his own life and is therefore not in a position to give to a weak life the only appropriate response, which is that of contempt.

1 *Theological interpretation*: There is scarcely any moral theme in which the peculiarly theonomous character of Christian ethics becomes more evident than in that of mercy. In the New Testament this term more than any other signals the entry of divine mercy into the reality of human misery, as it is expressed in the action of Jesus. Compared with the contemporary evaluation of mercy outside Christianity, as an emotion unworthy of man, the presentation of God himself as 'Father of mercies' (2 Cor 1.3;cf. also the parable of the prodigal son, Lk 15.11ff) and Jesus' admission of his compassion for the people must have seemed like extreme provocation. Nor is it by chance that the cry 'Lord, have mercy on me' acquires the meaning of a confession of faith in Jesus' divine authority. It is thus obvious that the reason for mercy between human beings is to be seen in the mercy of God and not in human considerations: according to the parable of the wicked servant (Mt 18.23–35), the requirement of mercy for a fellow-debtor is justified by the master's previous unlimited mercy. It is the same with the beatitudes with the promises of God's mercy. It is only logical therefore that Paul should exhort the faithful to pass on the divine mercy they have experienced (2 Cor 4.1; Rom 12.1) with cheerfulness (Rom 12.8), so that mercy in particular becomes a distinguishing mark of the disciple and unmercifulness is to be understood as an utter perversion of the knowledge of God.

In the light of this interpretation of mercy by God himself new standards emerge: because mercy is given wholly to the person dependent on our mercy, with all the personal, material and social aids at our disposal, it is a grateful response. At the same time no questions are asked about the recipient's worthiness nor about any gratitude to be expected from him. Finally, mercy which is passed on will be the criterion of the last judgment on man.

2. *Human perspectives*: Compassion is a precondition and—so to speak—the factor which releases mercy as a gesture of human devotion. Both as emotion and as anticipatory readiness it is directed not only to perceive the suffering and distress of the other person, but to be drawn by it, touched by it, to identify with it: that is, to make it as much our own concern as if we ourselves were in the same state. We should not fail to notice that it has become very difficult today to mobilize compassion: confronted often involuntarily by indescribable distress in the whole world, many are no longer stirred to compassion but have become insensitive, so that the power to react appropriately even to the human predicament as seen at close quarters has been impaired.

The act of mercy itself is shown in the will to remove the distress of the person whose whole situation, whether brought on by his own fault or not, has become known to us; and, if it cannot be entirely removed, at least to alleviate it. According to biblical teaching, mercy is especially called for when someone has obligations to us which he cannot fulfil. In this sense mercy means a release from existing liabilities. For the rest, mercy is the uttermost and final opportunity 'of saving man in his naked existence when he is faced with the immediate negation of that existence' (W. Schulz). It should be obvious that the exercise of mercy does not permit us to stress or to parade our own superiority, nor must it be obtrusive; the sufferer's sense of honour and of his own value must not be hurt. And mercy must not be allowed to cripple the needy person's own initiative. This is particularly important in the provision of *Development aid* (*q.v.*). See *Forgiveness*.

B. *Stoeckle*

Might. See *Liberation*.

MILITARY SERVICE

1. The present position. Most modern societies (though not the United Kingdom) on the one hand require their citizens to perform compulsory military service and on the other allow exemptions, for example to women, clerics and objectors with various conscientious grounds. This situation embodies both the state's fundamental claim on its citizens to participate in its self-preservation, if necessary with violent means, and the fact that this claim cannot be enforced absolutely, and not at the expense of *conscience* (*q.v.*). Normally it is not so much military service itself which may provoke a crisis of conscience as the unavoidable possibility it entails of being summoned to active service itself which may provoke a crisis of conscience as the unavoidable possibility it entails of being summoned to active service in the event of war, with weapons which may violate the moral relation between means and ends. Conscientious objections may be of various kinds: to active service with specific weapons (atomic, chemical and biological), to any active service as a possible consequence of military service, to any military service as training in the use of weapons which kill and injure, and finally to peaceful alternative service as participation in the secular state (Jehovah's Witnesses) (*Life*, q.v.).

2. Conscientious objection. All these varieties of motivation are summed up in the term 'conscientious objection'. It is sometimes believed, erroneously, that the question of conscience exists only for objectors, but in fact entry into military service is, or at least ought to be, also a question of conscience. However, it is principally conscientious objection which creates legal dilemmas. On the one hand, positive law is not capable of distinguishing between very different conscientious grounds, and in any case testing the force of a conscientious decision by legal means is a dubious procedure. The only long-term solution seems to be the abandonment of investigatory tribunals, the creation of more possibilities for alternative service (social service, peace service) and the punishment of complete refusal by administrative sanctions. The rational basis of conscientious decisions is hard to examine, and in any case it is not the intellectual suppleness of the objector which is the object of the investigation. From another point of view, of course, if the right of the state to self-defence is recognized, compulsory military service can be seen as an equally important obligation in sconscience.

3. *Ethical assessment.* The question of conscience is part of the dilemma of violence and non-violence. On the one hand, as Vatican II says, (*Gaudium et Spes*, 79), the legitimate right of defence cannot be denied provided no other possibilities exist. On the other hand some means of defence are morally unacceptable, as 'far exceeding the bounds of legitimate defense' (*op. cit.*, 80). Within these limits military service is a moral obligation arising out of the common good, though this obligation must be within a context of efforts to secure peace and security by other means. It could be maintained that military service could only be a moral obligation within the framework of a defence system which was accepted as objectively rational. Whether this framework only exists in peacetime or can continue to exist in war is a question which the individual can only answer with difficulty and he must therefore answer it by giving the benefit of the doubt to his state. Even within this framework the ability to defend oneself has only the priority of a provisional necessity, even though there may be no sign of any end to the necessity. This temporal priority is transcended by the supra-temporal eschatological priority of the ethics of non-resistance, and this is perhaps implicitly recognized. It is therefore impossible to formulate a single *norm (q.v.)* for all. A norm is a guide for independent moral decisions, but does not replace them. Consequently, from the moral point of view, the individual is free to choose either what for him is the absolute preference for symbolic non-resistance or the relative, realistic and objectively rational preference for military preparedness (cf. *Gaudium et Spes*, 78, 79). Both choices can be regarded as contributions to peace in the sense that peace, in the present world, marked as it is by sin, is always caught in the dilemma between absolute and relative peaceability, non-violence and the security of peace and *justice (q.v.).*

D. Mieth

181

Mind. See *Body; Humanity.*

MODEL

1. The concept. The term covers behavioural models in the widest sense. Normally it implies a subject-object relationship and designates an object of imitation distinct from the subject, but the subject's own behaviour in a particular situation can also be a model for him. Unlike other branches of learning theory, learning from models or learning by imitation offers the possibility of acquiring not just individual types of behaviour, but more or less whole behavioural patterns. In the socialization process behavioural models take on the fundamental function of patterns of orientation, which can initiate changes in behaviour both immediately and in the future.

2. Model and imitation. The intensity of imitation depends on particular characteristics of the model. A model which satisfies the need of the learner will be imitated more vigorously. Models of high social status are more likely to be imitated because they promise successful attainment of advantageous goals. Friendly and attractive people inspire more spontaneous imitative behaviour than people who lack these qualities. According to empirical studies, the effect of models 'in the flesh' seems to be more lasting, though the influence of film models should not be underestimated.

On the effect of emotional relationships between models and learners the data are conflicting.

3. The effects of models. The behaviour of the model has two main effects. Models draw attention to behavioural alternatives, they give prominence to a particular type of behaviour and so propagate social norms. They also provide information about what is appropriate behaviour in particular situations by setting an example and helping to create an obligatory pattern and by contributing to the definition of the situation. For moral behaviour, White was able to show that examples of behaviour produce more effective change in behaviour than moral admonitions.

182

Wyss says that the living moral pattern (the virtuous man, *virtue*, q.v.) is clearly superior for the humanization of human existence than mere law or any imperative code. The imitator adopts the system of norms and values of the model. This may also produce a rational awareness of the necessity and logic of these values and norms, but this is not a strict requirement. Morally good behaviour is the result of processes of socialization in which models have played an important part as patterns of morally good action.

4. Models in Christianity. Since every group lays down specific norms as rules of behaviour, the Christian community functions as a model in the transmission of norms and values. One of its chief tasks is to provide models which can be imitated as patterns of Christian life. All these models derive from 'the model of our action', Jesus Christ. In terms of learning from models, the veneration of the saints is also of fundamental importance, although if it is to produce more vigorous imitation it requires considerable revision.

A. Schulz points out that the idea of the 'imitation of Christ' has only a very minor place in the gospels, though it cannot be denied that the gospels also show signs of a later primitive Christian 'model ethics' (e.g. Mk 10.45). Following (*akolouthein*) and imitating (*mimeisthai*) are not identical concepts in the New Testament. The concept of following is totally a religious idea. 'Referring to a caree, 'following' denotes primarily the collaborators in the Messianic work of the historical Jesus. . . . On the other hand the group of words based on 'imitate' . . . and the idea of the example of Jesus Christ belong, throughout the New Testament, to the sphere of model ethics. They have a definite place in its ethical message' (Schulz). Imitation of Christ the model includes the different forms of his divine and human existence, as distinct from following, which is restricted to companionship with the historical Jesus.

These data from the theory of socialization and biblical theology show how Christian life as lived in practice is able to transpose the behaviour learned from its models into different real social situations. The transmission process required for this is made easier the more relevant models of

Christian behaviour are available (*Education*, q.v.).

A. Biesinger & W. Tzscheetzsch

MODERATION

1. Concept and scope. The virtue of moderation (*temperantia, sophrosyne*) is one of the four cardinal virtues. It concerns the control and regulation of man's egocentric impulses. It is concerned specifically with man's need for food (temperance) and drink (sobriety), his sexual drive (chastity) (q.v.), ambition (humility), aggressiveness (gentleness), his need for retribution (meekness), his tendency towards arrogance (modesty) and his curiosity (restraint in the pursuit of knowledge). The aim of this virtue is the true "mean", which avoids Manichean devaluation as well as the unbridled indulgence of human desires (instinct).

2. Moral relevance. Moderation is the last of the four cardinal virtues, because it is concerned solely with man as an individual, whereas prudence (q.v.), justice (q.v.) and fortitude are more immediately relevant to man in society. This attitude is evident even in the chief knightly virtues of medieval times (faith, moderation, loyalty). Strictly speaking, however, the practice of moderation does not in itself constitute a moral act or attitude but is merely a pre-condition of its fulfilment since the concept of moderation implies directly only a certain order and control of human desires, unless its relevance to an ultimate purpose (and this constitutes an essential aspect of morality) is made explicit. For a moral evaluation it would be necessary to consider from what motives moderation is practised, whether from natural disposition, utilitarian considerations, narrow-mindedness or perhaps vanity or whether in obedience to a genuinely moral imperative. Only the examination of this motive reveals the dynamic and 'immoderation' inherent in love of God and one's neighbour, which is fostered rather than excluded by the control of natural impuses.

3. Moderation in practice. Like every virtue moderation demands constant practice (askese = practice). The purpose

184

of this learning process is to ensure that the correct moderate frame of mind is acquired, so that it becomes the response even in situations where freedom of choice is reduced. It is equally a question of achieving an inner distance from the limited values of human life, as the christian hope in salvation demands (hope) (q.v.). Consequently a conscious fast or renunciation of food is meaningful. It in no way implies a fundamentally negative evaluation of human needs or of the fruits of human labour, but presumes an exercise of the freedom which makes it possible for Christian hope to be the ultimate goal in contrast to the "penultimate goods" (Bonhoeffer). Traditionally "mortifying the flesh" was regarded as being a preparation for dying and relinquishing, an interpretation which runs the risk of presenting a dualistic devaluation of worldly goods.

H. Rotter

MORAL EDUCATION

Traditionally moral education has been seen as the handing on of a body of accepted values principles and rules. It has also sought to cultivate through exhortation, example or exercise, recognized virtues and strength of will. The increasing and more evident pluralism of the contemporary world has called this approach in question. There has also grown up a much more sophisticated psychology of moral development and a systematic application of moral philosophy in the educational field. These factors combined have led in recent years to a different style of moral education.

This began with an attempt to lay the foundation of a 'value-free' programme of moral education. If you think of morality in terms of a set of abilities or skills—for instance that of foreseeing the probable consequences of one's acts or that of applying a principle to concrete cases—then it might be possible to filter these out leaving behind the substantial (and controversial) value-questions. These abilities could then form the basis of an educational programme acceptable to any value system. Although this approach has come under heavy criticism, most recent material for moral education is quite deeply marked by it.

One criticism of it has been that in morality, ability and substance cannot be rigorously separated. Another is that the 'abilities' selected do not constitute the timeless essence of morality but are those which are highly valued in the liberal West. Yet another is that to promote free-wheeling abilities in children is as likely to lead to cynicism as to real moral autonomy. It is also argued that effective education requires the engagement of a teacher with all his won moral values and beliefs. To see him as a neutral chairman prodding children towards autonomy is to cast him in a thin, bloodless teaching rôle.

Among recent writers on the subject, there has been a certain renewal of interest in questions of substance; or at least an acknowledgment that moral education cannot be reduced to one single, simple process. There are several kinds, each of which has some claim to be taken seriously. In the United States especially, some progress has been made in developing a positive education in values, through the process known as 'value-classification'.

Bibliography: Hirst, P.: Moral Education in a Secular Society. London, 1974; Kohlberg, L.: Stages of Moral Development as a Basis for Moral Education in Beck, Crittenden & Sullivan (Eds.): Moral Education. London, 1962; Lord, E. & Bailey, C. (Eds.): A reader in Religious and Moral Education, London, 1973. Macy, & Blackham, (Eds.): Let's Teach Them Right. London, 1967. McPhail, P. et al: Moral Education in the Secondary School. London, 1972; Peters, R. S.: Reason and Compassion. London, 1973; Piaget, J.: The Moral Development of Children and Adolescents. London, 1965; Wilson, J.: An Introduction to Moral Education. London, 1966; Wright, D.: The Psychology of Behaviour. London, 1971.

K. Nicholls

Morality. See *Ethics; Ethos.*

MORALS

In general, the principles of ethics (*q.v.*) which govern

action or consideration of action: values, responsibility, legality, social concern. If held to be inherent in the nature of man, they may be said to be 'propositions about the nature of man translated into obligatory norms' (Rahner). In situation ethics, morals may be said to arise from a specific social or individual situation, or complex of situations. See *Norm; Ethics*.

Moral theology. See *Ethics; Ethos*.

Mourning. See *Indifference; Joy*.

N

Neighbour, Love of one's. See *Aging; Biblical ethics; Ethics; Ethos; Freedom; Love; Marxism; Socialism.*

New Testament ethics. See *Biblical ethics.*

NORM

1. State of the question. Neo-scholastic theology understands by (moral) norm a 'rule which influences the will as "what ought to be" and morally binds it while leaving it psychologically free' (Mausbach-Ermecke). In this view human actions in their entirety in all situations have to be guided by an ontologically normative and hierarchically structured order of values having its absolute origin and ground of validity in God, prior to any historical and social determinations. −Rigid adherence to this conception of the position of man within a divinely created and redeemed reality which is developed into the doctrine (deriving from the Salmanticenses) of the natural moral law, has prompted severe criticism from modern thought (see *Ethics*). It also inevitably resulted in a far-reaching failure of Christian morality to reflect on fundamental problems of modern living. In view of the straits to which moral theology was thus reduced, and which in the end were impossible to deny, it became increasingly clear, especially after the controversy on situation *ethics* (*q.v.*), that a specifically theological definition of the initial conditions of human action will require a re-interpretation of moral imperatives within the framework of a different kind of epistemological model; that it will have to be recognized from the start that the substrata of *action* (*q.v.*) are socially constituted and vary with the history of culture, and that this does not entail the disappearance of the absolute character of moral obligation.

2. The norm of the natural moral law. The natural moral law thesis, often simply termed 'natural law', is presented in three substantially different forms. In Aquinas the term law (S.Th. 1a 2ae, 90–108) denotes the ontological structural principle which belongs analogically to Creator and creature. The lex aeterna as all-embracing teleological determination of all that is, binds human action, however, only mediately through its modes of existence as lex naturae i.e. as natural moral law, and as lex divina in the sense of God's positive self-revelation in history ('law' of the Old and New Testaments). –Since Aquinas, in contrast to Aristotle, equates the concept of nature with that of essence (S.Th. 1a q29 a1 ad4), the natural moral law signifies exclusively that formal powers which distinguishes man's essential nature, his rationality: the power in analogy of God's creative power, of being a law-giver oneself in the realm of action ('propidentiae particeps, sibi ipsi et aliis providens', S.Th. 1a 2ae q91 a2). Concrete action—understood as 'syllogismus in operabilibus'—is guided by propositions which on the presupposition of the one general 'principium per se notum quoad nos': to do good and avoid evil, are *not* necessarily self-evident to all human beings. Their contents, ascertained with the help of the doctrine of the 'natural inclinations', are not regarded by Aquinas as belonging to natural moral law, but to the *ius gentium*. What he is therefore ultimately concerned with is a 'metaphysics of action, which does not establish and judge norms, but exhibits their metaphysical foundations' (Oeing-Hanhof).

A new conception of the natural moral law is found in later scholasticism in Spain. The primary theoretical purpose now is to overcome the voluntarism of the Nominalists by a new grasp of the concept of order. Vásquez, who like the other theologians of Salamanca appeals to Aquinas, discerns the natural moral law in the rational character of human nature. In this he is still largely in accord with

Aquinas' intentions; what is new, on the other hand, is his specifically epistemological concern which is to establish the possibility of conceiving an essential nature of man independently of God. His critic Suárez, on the other hand, attempts to prove that the natural moral law does not contain simply the notification of a norm, a knowledge of good and evil, but actual precepts and prohibitions; that is to say it represents an 'emanation of the eternal Wisdom ordering and ruling the world' (K. Werner). With this idea, Suárez links a detailed casuistry of the metaphysical nature of the actus hominis and thus founds the modern tradition of an objectively given morality of separate acts. Subsequently the theory of natural moral law disappeared completely from the manuals; its place was taken by ever more extensive catalogues of its alleged contents.

Neo-scholasticism on the whole repeats the Suarezian postulates. It is claimed that the moral demands of the natural moral law possess ontological quality, direct 'natural' self-evidence, immutability and universal validity, a directly legal character, and finally are authentically interpreted by the Church's magisterium; their contents extend for instance from indissoluble monogamy to the biological, physiological integrity of each act of sexual congress. –In fact this kind of concept of norms amounts to 'the establishment of legal positivism' (G. Otte) in moral theology. The 'situational' approaches (cf. 3) directed against this, however, are in general unable to make the 'connection of ground' (Korff) between the creative and saving action of God and the individual moral action of the human subject. Only the recourse to the original systematic function of the natural moral law in Aquinas appears theologically to justify the 'Christian anthropocentrism' (Metz) which it assumes, the relation of entailment between 'autonomous morality and Christian faith' (Auer) or between the 'autonomy' and the 'theonomy' of the moral sphere' (Böckle). On this basis it then becomes possible to form a conception of norms as prescriptive statements which will have some 'chance of affecting the reality of human existence and of becoming convictions actually lived' on the way towards 'an ethos open to amendment' (Korff).

3. *Norms of action and situation.* The older situation ethics condemned by the Church's magisterium (DS 3918-3921) and the contextualist 'new morality' (Fletcher, Robinson) resemble one another to the extent that they either equate the concept of norm with *conscience (q.v.)*, or understand it in the sense of a subjective imperative or as the substratum of Jesus' commandment of love. The resulting reduction of morality to the purely inward sphere of intentions, does as little justice to the positively active character of conduct as to its intersubjective structure. The proposal to replace the 'statics' of the New Testament by 'dynamics', and to introduce the 'ethical directives' of the New Testament as 'models' or as 'prescribing goals' of binding interpretations of a situation, eventually leads to the same result. –Much the same applies to B. Schüller's view that love should be regarded as 'attitude of mind and deed' in an 'ordo bonorum'; this culminates in a doctrine of value-preference, unelucidated in status, for it plainly presupposes a successful 'rehabilitation re-trial . . . for the doctrine of the natural moral law'. It remains an open question how for instance in practice the postulated principle of subjective freedom of conscience in the sense of freedom from repression, is to be combined with the claim to validity of normative expectations. Korff's epistemologically and methodologically explicit demand that we should reject 'any flight into a meta-rational sphere of authentic reason beyond the positive, as the essence of the normative', makes it possible for Böckle to introduce the following general concept of norms; it can be extended by substantial empirical scientific considerations on the structure of moral norms: Norms are . . . 'general rules of human behaviour (customs, habits, moral and legal prescriptions and laws) (1) which are current in a particular social group (2) and have some chance of meeting with agreement and obedience (3).'

4. *Phenomenology of norms.* A human being attains his subjectively and objectively structured reality by way of complex processes of socialization. The world of the real and the possible is opened out to him through cultural symbol systems (language in particular), in which social norms have the function of limiting the individual sphere of

experience and ensuring the predictability of the behaviour of actors in a given situation. Norms must therefore on principle be regarded as artificial products of human culture, which guarantee the permanence (extremely flexible though it may be) of human experience and action, by means of 'mutual establishment of identity' (Popitz). Their validity does not rest on an abstract cognitively standardizable 'law' above or behind the reality accessible to experience, but primarily on the ability and readiness of those interacting to react with sanctions against aberrant behaviour. –A priori the individual experiences his own action under a presupposed subjectively meaningful integration of the habitual expectations of other people. These expectations, as rôle-norms, not only decide the structure of the status hierarchy in a society, but also predispose to certain types of behaviour in certain situations. The 'resistance to disappointment' (Luhmann) of particular norms, which may be prohibitions, or norms of action, verbal norms or opinion norms, depends essentially on the extent to which they correspond to the institutionalized rôle-structure. Their development from the static social order of the Middle Ages, based on custom and usage, down to modern stratified society based on law and bureaucratic administration, has been described by M. Weber as a process of rationalization and depersonalization. The individual is free from the burden of comprehensive (external) control by *one* group; on the other hand he experiences frequent conflicts between the contradictory rôle-norms to which he is subjected. This is the historical source of the individuating of the subject; the location of specifically moral action in contemporary conditions of human life proves to lie in the subjectively conscious zone 'beside' (G. Simmel) rôle relationships.

The assumption of an analytical connexion between norms and *values* (*q.v.*), has proved to be correct only as regards small groups. Only here can norms be understood primarily as aids to orientation in difficult situations—elsewhere they have more the character of conflict solutions—and their acceptance by all members of the group be taken for granted. On the other hand, with small groups nowadays it is not a matter of self-sufficient social structures, but largely of very unstable not strictly functional formations, mostly associative in character, and which presuppose the existence of general legal norms guaranteed by state authority. From this point of view it seems extremely questionable to refuse to attribute to the concept of moral norms the character of objective claims to performance or abstention, for if reality is harmonized and transfigured in this kind of way, the sheer force of brute fact—described in a trivializing way as 'the secular world'—is withdrawn from any possibility of criticism. This is the explanation, too, of the patent dysfunctionality of natural law ideas in modern industrial socities. –The thesis of group pluralism in the neutral state, the political adaptation of the formula of social differentiation of modern societies, can no longer at the present time hide the 'crisis of legitimation' (Habermas) in the domain of public, compulsorily normative authoritative action. What applies to politics in particular applies to morality in general (cf. the concepts of 'praxis' in Aristotle) (see *Action*); norms derive their legitimacy *not* primarily through the construction of cognitive schemata on the part of particular headquarters and institutions, but as a result of far more complex social processes. The formulation of verbal norms in the shape of standards of evaluation, can be regarded in the domain of morality only as an aid to communication for those actually engaged in action. And here the application of such potential sanctions as are still available to the ecclesiastical 'norm-giver' must not be guided by the innocuousness of the particular intervention, but by objectively communicable necessities. It is precisely from the point of view of the empirically uninterrupted mutual interaction between the provision of grounds of legitimacy for norms and the factual currency of norms because of subjective value consensus combined with renunciation of forcible sanction mechanisms, that it would ultimately be possible to give a more intelligible account of the specific character of Christian morality than can be produced by purely logical extrapolations of a completely abstract indicative statement of the redemption or of the commandment of love.

5. *Norms of Christian morality.* Moral norms are a matter of generalized standards relating to particular *values* (*q.v.*) or value models drawn from an *ethos* (*q.v.*). Arrived at by

193

active appropriation of historically and socially changing reality, they serve to interpret and justify human behaviour. The translation of such prescriptively formulated imperatives into norms of action (i.e. actually observable and subjectively meaningful regular types of behaviour) takes place by means of various social mechanisms (customs, manners, convention, law, fashion); their acceptance, on the other hand, is necessarily based on subjective, free consent interpreted in terms of value (conscientious decision). The distinctive features of Christian normativity consists in its being grounded in the historical context of revealed faith in the Old and New Testaments and its documentary sources. These, as the concrete practice of the Church's faith interpreted on the basis of Jesus Christ's redemptive action, enter as sources of moral and ethical reflection into present-day Christian morality. A central problem of Christian normative action at the present time is the need to organize integration of divergent situation definitions within the Church and of heterogeneous explanatory models in such a way that on the one hand the exclusively subsidiary functions which pastoral care, theology and the Church's magisterium have to exercise in the field of moral communication about problems arising for believing agents are re-defined, while on the other hand the historical identity of Christian morality is also retained institutionally in theory and practice or is re-established in regard to the totality of human reality. On these assumptions the conventional private morality concerned with single actions can no longer be defended. It must be replaced by a greater ability of people to act despite the shock and uncertainty about their subjective competence to act which has naturally resulted from the rapidity of social change, so that they will actively co-operate in solving problems for their own and other people's action. In view of the obvious dysfunctionality of neo-scholastic moral casuistry, including its 'dynamic' manifestations, it is for the moment primarily a matter of scientifically based grasp of some precarious areas of action, their analysis and public and explicit discussion, and finally the presentation of alternative ideas for their solution, the adoption of which is not to be imposed by legal sanctions. Any kind of norm-giving action must take its own potential consequences and by-products as a subject for prior reflection and as a point of view from which to judge its own value. See *Ethics*.

H. Oberhem

O

Oath. See *Promise*.

Obedience. See *Authority; Norm; Resistance*.

Old age. See *Aging*.

Old Testament ethics. See *Biblical ethics*.

P

Pacifism. See *Military service.*

Pardon. See *Forgiveness; Mercy.*

PLEASURE

Three attitudes stand in the way of an objective treatment of the phenomenon of pleasure. The first is the fashionable interpretation of pleasure entirely in terms of libido. The second is the negative connotation pleasure has received in the theological tradition, which has led to the frequently expressed generalization that 'the Church is hostile to pleasure'. Finally, there is the contemporary view that the experience of vital sensual pleasure is the highest form of human fulfilment.

1. *Pre-Christian attitudes.* The concept of pleasure had an inherent ambiguity from its first use in Greek philosophy. In the period of Plato and Aristotle pleasure was understood as the enjoyment of the good, the beautiful and the true, and true pleasure and rational activity were regarded as practically identical. It was not long, however, before the question was asked, 'Is pleasure a "good" or an "evil"?' Different answers were given. Some schools, notably the Cyrenaics and the Epicureans, continued to regard pleasure as good, but the Stoics and Cynics, who were the main influence on later popular philosophy, denounced pleasure derived from the experience of sensual satisfaction. The

197

increasing pessimism of late antiquity was another cause of this rejection of pleasure. The fundamental assertions of the Old Testament (for example, that man is made in the image and likeness of God) give no support to a negative view of pleasure, and in the Proverbs and the wisdom literature (especially the Song of Songs) there are clear signs of a favourable attitude to it. Nevertheless, under the influence of late Jewish apocalyptic a more cautious attitude towards pleasure became unmistakable.

2. *The New Testament Revelation and the Theological Tradition.* In the New Testament writings, especially in Paul, the negative side of pleasure is clearly prominent. As pleasure of the flesh or pleasure of the eyes, it is one of the characteristics of a strongly egocentric attitude to life which is opposed to the altruistic ideals of Christianity. In the subsequent period, however, it was the influences of dualism on Christianity which were mainly responsible for the hostile view of pleasure. In contrast to the previous tradition, Thomas Aquinas tried to reach a broader and more balanced judgment, but in the Church's practice the influence of the Augustianian view remained predominant. It is this view which was embodied in the missionary work of the Irish and Scottish monks, and in the rules of the medieval penitentials. Some responsibility for the negative view of pleasure should also be attributed to the influence of social groups such as the nineteenth century bourgeoisie.

3. *The modern rethinking.* A new opportunity for a positive evaluation of the phenomenon of pleasure had to wait for the discoveries of psychoanlysis. The existence of experiences of pleasure in early childhood (the oral, anal and phallic stages) made Freud regard the pressure principle as a fundamental principle of psychoanalysis. The principle says that the human *psyche* has a tendency to seek pleasure and avoid pain. The main instinctual energy (*drive*) which impels human beings to seek increased pleasure is libido. In early childhood the pleasure principle urgently demands the immediate satisfaction of instinctual demands. Later, however, the tyranny of the instincts is balanced by the so-called reality principle, the realisation that the immediate satisfaction of instincts would

198

make people incapable of normal life. Freud regarded the ability to defer instinctual satisfaction as highly important. In his view it helps to strengthen ego consciousness and through the sublimation of energies is responsible for the growth of culture.

The widespread modern tendency to make pleasure an absolute, (which is even supported by uncritical appeals to Freud), brings with it a number of extremely dangerous consequences. The danger that pleasure may be used in manipulation and even to produce addiction, has been impressively illustrated in animal experiments by United States neurological researchers. Rats were induced to press a bar which released electric impulses which were then led by means of a probe directly to the pleasure centre of the brain. As time passed the rats gave themselves more and more stimuli (as many as 10,000 a day), began to neglect food and sleep, and finally died from total exhaustion. It may be deduced from this that pleasure which is not co-ordinated with the overall structure of drives and sensations may become a danger to life. The pressure to repeat it may lead to *addiction* (q.v.), with the consequence of complete isolation and a refusal of any form of social life or *communication* (q.v.).

Another important consideration is that an unrestrained striving for pleasure often builds up very harmful aggressive impulses, since any demands or obstacles which stand in its way are immediately swept aside. Another consequence of a fixation on pleasure is a shortening of *time* (q.v.) perspectives: all that counts is the present moment, which becomes an absolute criterion. All calls to forgo immediate pleasure for the sake of future happiness then become unacceptable. Finally, the fact that actions which involve no pleasure, such as sacrifice, effort and abstinence, make up an essential element of human life is totally forgotten.

4. *Pleasure in moral theology.* While a theological evaluation is impossible without the data of the human sciences, there are other aspects which point to the need to situate pleasure theologically. Theology's most important contribution is to draw attention to the provisional and incomplete nature of our human existence, and so to reject

199

the reduction of *happiness* (q.v.) exclusively to immanent possibilities. This means that the believer will take care not to make this-wordly things, such as pleasure, into absolutes in the knowledge that they are all only 'penultimates'. At the same time he will make an effort to integrate pleasure into the total structure of his personality in the knowledge that by a right use of this-wordly things he can attain his ultimate salvation. This critical distance makes it possible to put the experience of pleasure in a larger context, along with personal maturity, inter-personal relations, and also love, forgiveness and the need for salvation.

Bibliography: **Dominian, J.**: Proposals for a New Sexual Ethic. London, 1977. **Freud, S.**: Beyond the Pleasure Principle. London, 1959. **Marcuse, G.**: Eros and Civilization. New York & London, 1962.

W. Hesse

Pluralism. See *Social ethics; Value.*

Political theology. See *Freedom; Politics; Liberation; Socialism.*

POLITICS

1. The range of the concept. The *concept* of politics is today given very varied interpretations. In a narrow view, politics is seen as the ability of the specialist in assuming responsibility and taking decisions in society which enables him to be successful in terms of winning power, creating a consensus and resolving conflicts. As a result of 'democratization' (not just of democracy itself), this predominantly technical view of politics has been steadily extended to include the idea of universal participation in power and responsibility in society (*Codetermination*, q.v.). In the former case, political activity is the activity of the (professional) politician; in the second it covers every form of self-determination and co-determination in the community, so that ultimately every sort of socially relevant activity, even in a restricted circle, can be labelled 'political'.

The movement from the narrower to the wider concept of politics is connected with the change from an approach based on the concept of the state to one based on that of *society*. To the extent that a citizen's actions are actively 'relevant' to society, they are political. Indeed, according to the most radical concept of politics, a person's every act or omission, even if emphatically apolitical, must be called political since it cannot evade relevance to society. It is necessary to keep a balance between a too narrow concept of politics which regards politics as essentially constitutional expertise and its exercise by office-holders and too broad a concept in which the outlines of the political melt away completely before the social. The awareness that even an unpolitical attitude to life can be of prime political significance should not be allowed to overshadow the sphere of private action. In other words: part of the definition of political action must be active participation involving a rational consideration of power, goals and real possibilities of success.

   2. The tasks of political science. The contribution of political science here is direct or indirect according to its presuppositions. Since breaking out of the restrictive framework of the normative sciences—in which political theory belonged to law and political ethics to moral philosophy—it has found greater affinity with social studies and has become political sociology. As such it is more closely concerned with the empirical and analytical study of the factors influencing politically relevant behaviour. Here too there is a danger that the move away from a narrow framework will lead to politics being totally dissolved into sociology. In such a situation, political science becomes concerned ultimately only with those rule systems governing human behaviour (power, *conflict*, q.v., consensus) which it would be culpable ignorance on the part of any politically active person not to be familiar with. Normative concepts of the common good increasingly disappear as political science loses its interest in natural law. This can lead to a situation in which the state and law appear only as functional components of a system, and the laws by which they function are of more interest than their moral status (systems theory, functionalism). Here again, a balance has to be held between the legal positivism of political authorities, ontopraxological moral concepts (whether derived from Marxism or natural law), and systems theory analyses of hypothetical situations.

3. *Principles of political action.* To the extent that politics functions primarily within the confines of given possibilities, and can even be partly defined as the art of the possible, we are constantly driven back to the relationship between reality and possibility. This is the starting-point of political action, and includes ideas such as basic human rights and the common good, *justice (q.v.)* and law, as well as constitutions and the power of the state. The real possibilities of politics are not the product of any fixed and immovable order (the ideology of law and order) but of real differences within the order itself. Such differences can exist between the intentions of a constitution and the extent to which it is implemented, between the intention to be just and existing law, and between a democratic outlook and the actual distribution of power. The object of politics is therefore not exclusively the maintenance of the political system—as sometimes implied in functionalist models of system survival—but its development through the reconstitution of its humane intentions. An example will illustrate the connexion between the common good—the possibility of everyone enjoying the good life—justice and the basis of the state in constitutional democracies. As the basic idea of (hierarchical and indirect) participation by all is increasingly stifled by restrictive power structures (the 'pressures of the system'), the need for the reconstitution of those structures (the 'democratization of society') becomes stronger and stronger. This does, however, involve the danger that this legitimate need may go beyond the bounds of the real possibilities contained, though sometimes suppressed, in reality and so take on a utopian or revolutionary character. Such a need is no longer political in the strict sense of the community (in antiquity the polis) defines the limits of politics differently. Only when the framework of given possibilities is accepted—as it is in democracy—can politics fulfil its proper function. In this sense politics is impossible until agents accept the basic intentions of the social framework within which they act. The basic intention

of the modern social framework derives from the variants of
the idea of democracy. These reduce ultimately to two
(Even non-democratic societies today proclaim democracy
to be their underlying value). The first view of democracy is
based on a defence of a pluralistic freedom which itself can
only be maintained by the parliamentary constitutional
state. The other rests on the postulate of a uniform general
will (*'volonté générale'*, 'popular' needs, the will of the
working class). Historical experience shows that the two
forms cannot be practised simultaneously; the politics of
one basic form exclude those of the other.

4. An ethics of politics. The choice between different
fundamental political directions and the choice of a specific
alternative in political action are the object of political ethics
seen as the science of human *action* (q.v.) in and for society.
In ancient onteopraxology the whole of politics was
absorbed into, political ethics, and there was no real
distinction in area between politics and *ethics* (q.v.). The
same is true, matatis mutandis, of models of the political
ethics of change based on a dialectical view of history, but a
distinction has to be made today between political science
as an investigation of state of affairs within the framework
of the social sciences on the one hand, and political ethics
as a normative theory of practical activity on the other. If
the factual investigation is absorbed by the normative
theory the price is a loss of empirical rationality. If, on the
other hand, the normative approach is replaced by the
competition and conjunction of desirable interests, the price
is paid in a loss of rational responsibility for choices. In both
cases politics evades all-round rational testing. Political
ethics is therefore ultimately better defined as the *ethics of
politics*. This enables connexions to be made between
normative, empirico-analytical and critical theories of politics. The political sciences' exemption from value judgements would then be not a prerogative but an opportunity
for a political ethics reconstituted on the basis of moral
philosophy. It would be the task of the ethics of politics
critically to elucidate the humane potential of political
power through an analysis of political reality, though in its
approach it would be no different from the general theory
by which norms are established in social ethics. The term

'political ethics' can also, of course, be used to imply that
ethics should free itself from its concentration on individual
problems and no longer be primarily a guide for private
action.

5. *Political theology*. This topic can be included under the
heading 'theology and politics' since it was one of the
issues that led to the development of 'political theology'.
From having been more or less notoriously identified
during the Middle Ages, theology and politics were driven
by the modern rise of the autonomous secular state into a
complex opposition. On the theological side this was often
'resolved' by an insistence on the separateness of religion
and politics while in practice the influence of ethical views
was kept alive by the institutional presence of the
Churches. To this extent the privatizing tendency of
theology, through the influence of the Churches, was able
to retain considerable political significance, often to the
benefit of the status quo. For example, the unpolitical
nature of theology allowed curial diplomats in the Nazi
period to see their main task as the defence of the Church's
interests, a course which, though not totally crushing
humanitarian commitment, left it much weakened. A
radical disengagement of theology from politics on the
ground of a fundamental dichotomy between the *world*
(q.v.) and *salvation* risks producing an uncritical political presence. Political theology argues from this that
the power of the existing institutional presence of the
Church should not promote its partisan interests but its
eschatological message. This path of synthesis is narrow,
and is defended by the proponents of political theology by
a refusal to allow their political critique to go into the detail
of political programmes—a reserve they justify by invoking
eschatology. Nevertheless, the analogy by which theological anthropology should be applied in social criticism
remains disputed. Also disputed are the implications of the
idea of the Church as 'an institution of socially critical
freedom', since dissent about criticism of society should
presumably continue to exist even among Christians.
'Political theology' is more defensible as a corrective of
theology than of society. The broad interpretation of the
concept of politics in political theology enables it to coincide

with theology's connexion with practical activity and society, though if the concept is more narrowly defined 'political theology' comes into conflict with its self-imposed restrictions. It nevertheless remains an open question in what way the Christian faith can testify to its power outside its call to individuals in the sphere of political action. If the rule of God proclaimed by Jesus is not limited to the relationship of the God who speaks and the man who listens, that is if the autonomy of politics is placed by faith within the context of a divine order, theology and the Church retain a critical function within an ethics of politics. Their critique should take account of the empirical data provided by the political sciences, but test their value judgements. It should investigate the ability of political theory and practice to improve the conditions of human existence in society, and lastly it should bring the historical experience of the actualization of *salvation*, including the mistakes, into the dialogue with the various forms of political humanism. See *Marxism; Socialism*.

Bibliography: **Adorno, T. W. et al.**: The Authoritarian Personality. New York, 1950. **Allardt, E. & Rokkan, S.**: Mass Politics. Studies in Political Sociology. New York, 1970. **Assmann, H.**: A Practical Theology of Liberation. London & New York, 1975. **Christie, R. & Jahoda, M. (Eds)**: Studies in the Scope and Method of 'The Authoritarian Personality'. Glencoe, Ill., 1954. **Coleman, J. S. (Ed.)**: Education and Political Development. Princetown, 1965. **Cunningham, A. & Eagleton, T. (Eds)**: The Slant Manifesto. London, 1966. **Eagleton, T.**: The New Left Church. London, 1967. **Eysenck, H. J.**: The Psychology of Politics. London, 1954. **Fromm, E.**: Escape from Freedom. New York, 1941. **Gutierrez, G.**: A Theology of Liberation. New York & London, 1973. **Homans, G.**: The Human Group. New York, 1950. **Rokeach, M.**: The Open and Closed Mind. New York, 1960. **Wicker, B. & Clements, S. (Eds)**: The Committed Church. London, 1966.

D. Mieth

Possessions. See *Liberation; Love; Marxism; Socialism*.

Power. See *Authority; Communication; Conflict; Manipulation; Politics.*

Prayer. See *Faith; Leisure; Spirituality.*

PREJUDICE

1. According to general linguistic usage, prejudice is an opinion influencing knowledge and viewpoint (to be distinguished from presuppositions which are, from the outset, intended and applied as provisional guidance only), which is adopted, formed or retained without any serious attempt to get at the facts oneself or examine them critically. In order to bring knowledge, life and freedom into a meaningful context, man depends on judgments and perspectives derived from tradition and environment. There can be no objection to adopting other people's opinions without prior, serious consideration, when there are substantial grounds for accepting a convincing *authority (q.v.);* when past experience has proved them satisfactory and presumably will continue to do so; when a judicious trust is placed in human surroundings, providing that one is always willing to revise this should reason be given. In view of the predominantly irrational nature of such motives, there is a real threat involved in the dependence on emotional factors.

The main reasons for a deficient growth and consequent effect of prejudices lie in child development, when unconscious experiences make a particularly strong impression (educational influences on development and fixation: instruction, *model (q.v.),* the emotional transference of personal views, reaction to and self-assertion in the face of authority, and so on); in a life-style dictated for the most part by personal interests (overcompensation in self-assertion, slow and obstinate self-determination, suggestibility); in all kinds of environmental influences which are generally hard to identify (expected behaviour and rôle distribution, manipulation of public opinion, status symbols in sales promotion).

Of particular importance are the so-called social prejudices. These group-bound, traditional and controlled prejudices function as established, emotionally charged schemata, which make it easy to come to an agreement because of their communal and stereotype nature. As such they constitute an important means of orientation and distribution within society, create consensus between the members of a group and turn their expectations of co-existence into set rules, although the marked emotional content frequently reveals a totalitarian tendency. Prejudices have long served to strengthen the position of those with power and wealth. They can easily bring about a preconceived, socially and emotionally highly negative judgement of other groups, minorities or foreign peoples and races (e.g. Negroes, Jews). A strong emotive force combined with mass suggestion provokes aggressive attitudes (*behaviourism, q.v.*).

2. *Ethical and religious aspects.* Since the Enlightenment, the geneaology and phenomenology of prejudices find their place in the growing philosophical self-reflexion, in the criticism of *ideology*, and also in the sociology of science (with its formal ideas of social structure). Modern rationalism and scientism are, however, themselves biased when they suppress and reject the irrational. Depth psychology sheds light on the extremely complicated area of psychic and mass psychological conditions, correlations and regulations. On the other hand, the increasing difficulty of understanding modern living conditions, the widespread incompetence to come to terms with the irrational, the systemization and materialization of human and social relations and behaviour, the almost endless possibilities of manipulating public opinion, meet with a greater degree of readiness to activate and spread prejudices. For this reason it is imperative that every attempt should be made to free personal psychology and social causes from distortion and, furthermore, to discuss generally but thoroughly the human basis of existence, being careful to give a factual representation of the irrational aspects and tendencies.

Christ's decisive *criticism* of contemporary religious prejudices and partialities must provide the Church with an indispensable guide-line for critical examination in all fields of religious life. A look at the latest and most anti-religious criticism of prejudices, although itself biased, is revealing. It is absolutely essential to clarify constantly and thoroughly, intellectually, historically, socially and psychologically all manifestations of Church and faith within a religious and moral framework, all possible links between a Christian consciousness and sociocultural, political and social conditions; all signs of self-assertion and domination through the mixing of ecclesiastical life with religious questions and all cases where others are condemned for the sake of self-justitification. Such as critical attitude is also then required when contact with prejudice puts faith in jeopardy. However, the belief in the divine relevation considerably deepens both insight and the sense of security because of its transcendental dimensions, Man's orientation towards God and salvation and because of its claim to a natural inwardness.

Bibliography: **Adorno, T. W. et al.**: The Authoritarian Personality. New York, 1950. **Allport, G. W.**: The Nature of Prejudice. Cambridge, Mass., 1954. **Banton, M.**: Race Relations. London, 1967. **Berkowitz, L.**: Aggression: A Social Psycological Analysis. New York, 1962. **Christie, R. & Jahoda, M. (Eds)**: Studies in the Scope and Method of the 'Authoritarian Personality'. Glencoe, Ill., 1954. **Dollard, G. et all.**: Frustration and Aggression. New Haven, 1939. **Rokeach, M.**: The Open and Closed Mind. New York, 1960. **Sherif, M.**: In Common Predicament: Social Psychology of Intergroup Conflict and Cooperation. Boston, 1966.

R. Hofmann

PROMISE

1. Basic meaning. A promise is the most fundamental way of committing oneself or entering into obligations towards a person or a number of people with their knowledge. The moral significance of promises derives from the fact that without promises and fidelity to promises human society is impossible. There are simple promises and can also be unspoken promises, by which the person who makes them is bound when the other party accepts them. There are also contractual promises of unilateral or bilateral action. A special form of commitment is created by a sworn promise. In addition, specific types of obligation are created by a promise according to its degree of publicity and the person to whom it is made: for example, particular publicity is given in the Church to a Catholic priest's promise of celibacy, and religious vows are addressed to God. According to their type, promises can be understood from philosophical, social, legal and moral points of view.

2. Morally relevant aspects. For a promise to be valid it is always necessary for the promised action to be something morally, socially or legally acceptable, and for the person making the promise to be both in a position to carry it out and willing to do so. The promise must be 'true'. It must also be made with 'knowledge and intent', i.e., with the appropriate degree of freedom.

In a promise a person creates a model of the future. He gives a certain shape to himself, his social and possibly his religious relationships for the *time* (q.v.) ahead. The moral foundation of promises is the human capacity for loyalty. The obligation of fidelity which derives from a promise has various dimensions, fidelity to oneself, to another person, to the group of which one is a member, and religious fidelity.

In philosophical terms, to be capable of making a promise or pledge of fidelity a person must be capable of trust and love, and able to commit himself in relative *freedom* (q.v.). He or she must possess a firmly based fundamental confidence in themselves, an active capacity for unselfish and responsible *love* (q.v.), and their capacities for realistic perception value judgements and decisions must have been developed.

Promissory obligations do not come into being if the above-mentioned external or personal conditions are not fulfilled when the verbal promise is made. When a person who mistakenly makes a promise becomes aware of this situation, which creates a nullity, he is no longer directly bound, though he may face social or legal consequences.

Obligations in fidelity or justice arising out of a promise lapse when one of the essential conditions for a promise is

209

missing.

3. Particular issues. Various points should be remembered with respect to difficult cases. Oaths as religious reinforcements of promises are only justified when all magical elements are eliminated. With regard to vows, the reifying tradition which sees them primarily as promises to God to perform specified material acts should be rejected; vows are an expression of personal dedication. With regard to the clerical promise of celibacy, it is important, on moral and legal grounds, to note that the greatest possible freedom is allowed in making the promise and that in the case of withdrawals from the undertaking for whatever reason and social and legal community rules out unjustified sanctions.

H. Kramer

PRUDENCE

1. General. Prudence has been regarded as a basic virtue in the Graeco-Christian ethic since Socrates, together with justices (q.v.), fortitude and moderation. As a basic and personal stance, prudence implies an openness of mind, attitudes and dispositions which enable, prepare and train a man to recognise truth and to do what is morally right. It implies not only an intellectual ability and awareness, but also a willingness and capacity for volition and action in concrete situations. So in the context of man's moral life prudence fulfils a clarifying and diagnostic function and also provides an inspirational stimulus for action.

2. Doctrinal tradition. The definition of prudence given by Thomas Aquinas, according to the medieval image of man, is illuminating anthropologically. Prudence may be divided into different stages: 1) reflection and interior consideration 2) assessment of the situation 3) initial decision and subsequent effective action. Therefore attributes of prudence are judgment, deeper insight, a willingness to learn and memory, accuracy of aim, foresight, circumspection and discretion.

Prudence enables a man to judge an ethical situation

210

correctly and to form his conscience (q.v.) accordingly. It is conscience acting in a concrete situation.

3. *Anthropological level.* Modern anthropological research indicates that prudence is more precisely defined as the moulding of emotion and conscience (q.v.), the dual authority in the control centre of the person, the "heart" in biblical terminology; from this source a just and realistic appraisal of real life can be made, the moral values of the actual concrete situation weighed up, then the decision taken and finally the impulse for action given. The description is laboured, but the process in reality is a rapid, smooth and even happy one.

A humane culture which touches the deepest levels of the human personality and the concentration of all human talents are thus preconditions of the virtue of prudence. But this is not to be judged as a merely human achievement; it is rather man's prudent readiness to see the way open for the Spirit of God (Jn 6. 25) with his gifts of wisdom and counsel.

4. *Christian prudence.* There is a false prudence which is a 'wisdom of the world' (1 Cor 1. 20) and is 'to set the mind on the flesh' (Rom 8. 6); in contrast, true prudence is 'to set the mind on the spirit' (ibid.). Through this true prudence the Christian finds wisdom in the cross of Christ, where those who do not believe find only folly (1 Cor 1. 18–25). From this passage it is incontrovertibly clear that even if Christians are exhorted to be 'wise as serpents' (Matt 10. 16), the virtue of prudence is far removed from cunning, slickness, mere cleverness, or slyness.

A proper Christian respect for prudence and a pedagogic emphasis on the human attitudes which provide the natural preconditions for it, should mean that the virtue of prudence will lead to the independence and competence in all life's situations, put forward as the ideal of the mature Christian in the Second Vatican Council's Pastoral Constitution on the Church in the Modern World.

Bibliography: **J. Pieper:** *Prudence.* New York, 1959.

H. Kramer

R

RACISM

1. Summary. Racism in its pre-fascist and fascist forms has now been conclusively refuted. This form of racism maintained that both individual characteristics of aptitude, mentality or character and social and cultural characteristics of whole groups were racial characteristics, causally determined and hereditary. Its postulate of the absolute superiority of one race (e.g. the white or Nordic) and the inferiority of others (e.g. the black race or the Jews) received world-wide condemnation in the proclamation of the Rights of Man (UN Charter of 1945). Nevertheless, the phenomenon of 'racism' continues to exist in a variety of forms in almost all societies. Ineradicable prejudices in large sections of the population, together with the existential or religious positions of individual groups or nations, or their interests in power, the economy or employment, constantly bring about new polarizations, between white and black (South Africa, Rhodesia, Namibia, USA, rich and poor (the industrialised nations and the countries of the Third World, indigenous populations and foreign workers—and also, in a sort of counter-racism, between black and white (the 'Black is beautiful' and Black Power movements) or poor and rich (the oil-producing countries and consumers).

2. Forms. One form of racism is discrimination against the (minority) group, which is wholly or partly excluded from economic, social and cultural benefits and from the legitimate exercise of political power. The minority may also be economically exploited and politically repressed. Other

212

forms of racism are efforts to assimilate the minority which require it to sacrifice totally its characteristics and autonomy (monist integration), to segregate it by forcing it into a ghetto and so isolating it (pluralistic integration), or finally, in extreme cases, to eliminate it, sometimes by physical extermination (cf. the 'final solution' of the 'Jewish problem' under the Third Reich).

3. Moral assessment. Racism is not only an attack on *human dignity* (q.v.), but also a threat to internal and international peace. Its eradication requires the use of all conceivable measures both on an individual level and in social policy. Among individuals, prejudices must be broken down by information and education towards a self-critical and tolerant attitude. A readiness must be aroused for contact and reconciliation, for identification with and commitment to the victims of discrimination. On the political level a diagnosis of the causes and forms of racism is required: unjust social conditions, laws and structures must be brought to light. An attempt must be made to create a society which guarantees the dignity and freedom of all individuals and peoples, and racist systems should be the object of political and economic boycott.

The problem of foreign workers is a particularly difficult one to solve, for two main reasons. Firstly, the foreign workers themselves form an extremely heterogeneous alien group because they have different origins and very different languages, religions and cultures. Secondly, the problem affects the common good not only of their country of residence, but also that of their countries of origin and of the wider international community. For this reason it is not enough to remove all forms of discrimination and create more human living conditions (accommodation, opportunities for informal and cultural contact, legally backed guarantees of equality); international agreements are also needed, such as the right of free movement within the EEC and the right of emigration and immigration.

Since racism is a direct affront to the Christian message of a love which transcends all distinctions (col 3. 11; Eph 2. 13), it offers a challenge to the commitment of all Christians and their Churches (see *Toleration, Prejudice.*)

A. Elsässer

RELIABILITY & LOYALTY

1. *Human and theological aspect*: The structure of personal existence is essentially that of a dialogue. Speaking and hearing represent primitive situations in which human truth is evidenced, in a free open and receptive encounter. Factual communication follows upon free personal communication, which demands unconditional spontaneous solidarity on the part of the listener. The spoken word and freedom in life are complementary and one interprets the other. The saving encounter with Jesus Christ is the point at which God's free communication of himself reaches a climax in an immediate tangible historical form. The believer is the hearer and at the same time the willing companion. In this unity he finally integrates his unjustifiable history.

The claim of this original encounter extends in the physical and spiritual descent of God's incarnation to embrace the reality of human encounter. In the act of incarnation the unity of the human race is finally proven beyond all doubt, so that all moral acts performed by the Christian rest on its continuing realization. Complete openness towards God makes man open towards his neighbour. This is one of the basic anthropolitical implications of the decision of faith (*q.v.*): all human contact is part of the incarnate presence of God. The basis for all further proof of God's nearness lies in the attentive listening approach to man's neighbour. Man's basic need for self-communication is then validated. The fact of acceptance creates a loving community.

2. *Reliability in the context of truth and the love of one's neighbour*: Thus reliability is revealed as the original manifestation of Christian neighbourliness. In communicating in words, the neighbour is accepted for himself and acknowledged in his unique personal dignity. In the receptiveness of the listener the first step towards a loving approach is made (see *Love*); at the same time every sort of active love of our neighbour is already projected in advance. This presupposes a high degree of strength of character, which does not project itself, its own wishes or prejudices onto the other person, because it cannot

214

tolerate that person's difference. It rather exposes itself in sober truthfulness to the full claim and so to the burden of his truth. Reliability is thus the first proof of Christian love of truth (q.v.). The man who is a true believer has the strength to be put to the test by his neighbour, because he has already previously been put to the test by God (see Love). He does not relapse into exaggerated justification of himself, which is merely a symptom and an unconfessed weakness. On the other hand reliability is by no means the revelation of a cynical scepticism, which has already surreptitiously given up hope of recognition as well as the pursuit of truth. It presupposes rather a keen readiness to recognize the limited nature of its own insight without illusions. It bears eloquent witness to its own search for a truth, which it understands how to accept. Seen from this viewpoint, it proves itself as the school of tolerance, which never breaks off the dialogue in resignation. To the extent that listening is the preliminary plan for action, reliability develops into that unconditional readiness for reconciliation, which has its source in Christian brotherhood. Only then does it succeed in creating that relationship of confidence, which is a basic condition of the experience, of all true speech. Last but not least, truth arises from listening. Rooted in freedom, truth is bound up with the experience of solidarity with others: it is revealed as the result of indisputably achieved faithfulness.

3. *Requirements*: Reliability demands great self-discipline, informed by sympathetic love. It is a reminder of the manifold demands of conversion, demands involved in religious decision. It is the intermediary through which religious and personal maturity are integrated.

K. Demmer

Reconciliation. See *Forgiveness; Conflict; Love.*

Regression. See *Addiction; Guilt; Identity; Loneliness.*

Renunciation. See *Abstinence*

Repression. See *Abstinence; Prejudice.*

Resentment. See *Jealousy.*

RESISTANCE

1. The state of the problem. The problem of resistance appears at every level of the exercise of human power. The rules of almost every association and society devote attention to the limits of obedience and loyalty. Given the premiss that obedience (*authority*, q.v.) and loyalty are not unilateral rules of behaviour, applicable to the subordinates in any relationship, but always presuppose a just interaction, there can be no subordination at the cost of the justice of the relationship. Obedience and loyalty cannot be regarded as formal virtues in either asceticism or politics. Ascetical misunderstandings in the Catholic tradition and subservience to authority in the Protestant tradition (derived from Rom 13 and Mt 5.39) have at times obscured this connection. A correct understanding of power and *authority* (q.v.) must include their relation to *justice* (q.v.).

2. Resistance as a Right and Duty. In a just social order specific forms of resistance become forms of proper participation; the legal tradition of the past included examples of this, for example the Germanic view of law. In modern states resistance clauses, with their liability to misuse, have been replaced by rights invested in the legislative and judicial power to control the executive. The division of powers makes just resistance legal. As a result the individual's right of resistance becomes less prominent, but in an emergency, if the state controls are not effective, have ceased to function or do not function fast enough, it has the full support of the constitution. There is a general right of resistance in primary justice to unjust acts by the state when the common good is endangered and when the power of the state is used to make illegal attacks on the basic rights of citizens (cf. resistance against the Nazis). In some circumstances resistance can become not merely a right but a duty.

3. Forms of resistance. Among the early Christians the New Testament example of non-violence was invoked to sanction only passive resistance in support of the faith (martyrdom). The development of the theory of natural law in scholasticism broadened the field of ethics and extended sanction to active resistance for the benefit of the common good. The main case considered in this view, however, was the special one of the murder of tyrants, which was justified in the case of an incomplete usurpation. Nowadays this special case—last discussed in connexion with the 1944 attempt on Hitler—is seen as no more than a consequence of a right of active resistance which can use any political or legal means and even force. Violent resistance can be justified only by analogy with self-defence (see *Liberation*). To avoid the dangers of a purely subjective assertion of the necessity of resistance, which could lead to its indiscriminate use, it must be possible to point to objective criteria for a situation calling for social self-defence. These might include unconstitutional action by the executive, the destruction of the community itself or the infringement of human rights. Practical resistance must be recognizable as counter-force and justifiable by the proportionality of its means and the prospect of success.

4. Revolution and resistance. There remains a distinction between resistance and revolution even when resistance uses force. The aim of resistance is the restoration of perverted legality, while revolution has the transformation of the social order as its primary aim, and derives its justification and motive from this. Nevertheless, as human rights and social justice become more widely accepted as obligations binding on all states, it seems more likely that resistance in totalitarian states should be thought of in revolutionary terms. This would mean that it no longer limited itself to restoration, but actively linked its success with ideas of social change. A distinction would then be necessary between revolution as a primary aim and revolution which developed and drew its justification from just resistance, but was forced, almost in a secondary development, to go beyond resistance if success was to lead to real change.

5. *The ecclesiological aspect.* To the extent that resistance is an integral part of the relationship of authority itself, it also has applications within the Church (cf. Gal 2. 11). Resistance as the rejection of unjust orders is not even nullified by what is known as 'religious' obedience—the subordination of knowledge and will—as the rules of many orders show. The Church needs the productive resistance which comes from a rightly directed obedience of faith insofar as authority in the Church too is connected with its brotherly responsibility in the community.

D. Mieth

RETRIBUTION—RESTITUTION

1. *Essentials.* Action in society is based essentially on an exchange of services. Forms of behaviour which meet the needs of others are recognized and rewarded, while others are rejected and punished. If someone injures another, he is required, so far as possible, to make restitution. People learn very early to take this social aspect of their actions into account. The development of *conscience* (q.v.) and the effectiveness of social norms would be inconceivable without sanctions, which give individuals an effective motive for being concerned not just about their own welfare but also about the common good.

2. *Responsible retribution.* In the measure that a person attains the use of reason and freedom, it is necessary to get away from a rigid correlation of norm-governed behaviour and corresponding sanction. A person has to learn to understand *norms* (q.v.) in terms of their aims and, when necessary, to override them (see *Epieikeia, Freedom*). Society, on the other hand, must allow individuals a certain degree of freedom. Human action cannot be guided entirely by general norms of behaviour. Sometimes it is necessary to take liberties which other people at the time neither understand nor reward. Human behaviour is mainly influenced by a sense of the likely consequences of actions and by acceptance of an ultimate, transcendent goal of life.

Correspondingly, retribution of a wrong ought not to be the mere reaction of an injured sense of right (revenge), but must have regard to bringing back the wrongdoer to social behaviour. The dignity of the individual person also requires that sanctions should not exclusively benefit the community, but should also take account of the welfare of the individual. Retribution should not destroy the individual but arouse and develop his moral sense (Resocialization).

3. *The Word of God and retribution.* Corresponding to the change in understanding of basic theological truths, the Bible shows a change in its attitude to retribution. In the Old Testament, there was no idea at first of anything other than this-worldly retribution of human action. In this view, God rewarded morally good acts and punished morally bad ones in this world. As a result, good or bad fortune was interpreted as a blessing or curse of Yahweh. Moreover, as a result of the idea of the covenant between God and his people, retribution in the earlier periods was thought of predominantly in collective terms. Only gradually did a more personal attitude develop. These ideas produced a corresponding view of justice between men. Like was to be repaid with like. Human revenge was the direct working out of God's punishment.

The difficulties created by the belief in historical retribution (see Job) only began to be overcome as belief in a judgement after death and hope of eternal life at length gained a foothold. The New Testament combines the ideas of punishment in time and at the end of time. The Kingdom of God is 'already' present, but at the same time 'not yet' present. Reward and punishment no longer consist in earthly prosperity or earthly deprivations, but in a person's positive or negative relationship o God. This relationship ultimately constitutes a person's definitive *salvation* or damnation.

When someone voluntarily accepts the punishment or other consequences of guilt in order to restore the disturbed order and demonstrate his repentance, we speak of expiation. To the extent that human *guilt* (q.v.) is also guilt with regard to God, expiation is only conceivable through God's initiative in the incarnation of Christ and his redemptive

219

death. Christians are nevertheless called upon to accept unavoidable suffering in faith in the mercy of God and to see in it the redemptive action of God in the present.

H. Rotter

Reverence. See *Ethos; Human dignity; Life; Virtue.*

Revolution. See *Liberation; Marxism; Resistance.*

Riches. See *Capitalism; Marxism; Socialism.*

Robbery. See *Theft.*

S

SCANDAL

1. Fundamentals: The concept as such is directly biblical in origin and its literal sense embraces both the prising open and snapping shut of a trap (*skandalon*) or the stumbling over an obstacle lying in the way (*proskomma*). From the ethical aspect what is described as scandal is usually understood as 'causing scandal' or 'being scandalized' (adj. offensive, scandalous). Seen from this point of view, scandal refers to actions or ways of behaviour, which are calculated in themselves, or as a deliberate result of the conduct, or through circumstances, to disconcert another person or group of persons, to cause uncertainty, to bring about a state of outrage, to lead others into unworthy reactions. Sociologically, it is a certain type of deviation from set roles, an affront to the accepted attitudes sanctioned by the community. It must be taken into account too that in many cases something ranks as 'offensive' which relates to the sphere not of morality but of 'good manners' or convention. From this general basic definition there has arisen a tendency to qualify scandal in every case as something which is not as it ought to be and therefore to be rejected. Yet a careful clarification seems necessary. It is common knowledge how often actions which are in themselves good and justifiable can unintentionally cause scandal, just as conversely actions which are definitely bad are not felt to give rise to scandal. Whether something is felt to be scandalous or not, clearly depends to a very large extent on subjective sensitivity: on age, degree of personal excitability, inner emotional stability, to what extent a

221

person is educated and informed, just as much as on its connection with morals and customs. Apart from this, by no means everything that provokes, shocks and challenges can be regarded as giving scandal. If it were a moral precept to remove every human source of scandal and to avoid anyone ever taking offence, this would lead ·to a stifling of life, to a dictatorship of the staus quo. If the relationship between human beings is to take a fruitful form, if peace is to be maintained and progress made possible, 'giving offence' is necessary especially in the sphere of mere convention and so scandal cannot be altogether avoided.

2. Biblical-human guidelines: necessary scandal. The N.T. bears witness that Jesus himself was often a source of scandal for his contemporaries, in fact he himself represents the greatest scandal. He is that stone which is the corner-stone of the community, but which can also cause some to fall, he is the stumbling block of scandal. It is his unexpected messianic conduct which gives cause for scandal, his ready acceptance of the Passion, but in particular his liberal way of dealing with the law and with sinners, his critical attitude towards human precepts, his radical re-interpretation of the concept of purity. Finally Jesus gives scandal through the cross, as the radical contradiction of man's self-glorification. If Jesus becomes a source of scandal in this way, it is because of the reluctance to believe (see *Faith*) of those who find themselves face to face with the gospel. It follows that the Christian too must reckon with his faith provoking scandal, if it is expressed unadulterated and undistorted: for faith forces people to consider subjects which, because they are difficult to face, are often pushed to one side (sin, guilt, the need for salvation, egoism, impossibility of self-redemption). So the Christian should not let himself be misled into softening or 'embellishing' the faith of which he should be the witness, so that his mission of being a 'sign of contradiction' goes by default or is sacrificed to a superficial humanistic conformism.

3. The question of avoidable scandal. Next to the scandal of the gospel which may not be pushed to one side, there is also human scandal which can be avoided. So Paul gives strict injunctions that inside the community the strong are not to give offence to the weak nor hurt their conscience (Rom. 14: 13-21; 1 Cor. 8 : 9). He is referring to actions which are in themselves good and blameless, and so lay claim to justifiable freedom, but in an actual real-life situation yet run the risk of hurting certain of their fellow-men. Where that happens an offence is committed against love of our neighbour and an obstacle placed in the way of the gospel (1 Cor. 9: 12–19). For this reason even morally unexceptionable actions are only justifiable, insofar as the offence arising from them can be accepted as helpful by those who are offended. Moreover, the believer is bound to keep his distance from deeds and forms of conduct which because of their worthlessness and their tendency towards evil are liable to infect his fellow-man and lead him to what is bad. It is true that scandal of this sort is part of the susceptibility of the age (Mt. 18: 7; Luke 17. 1), but woe to the man through whom such scandal comes. This applies in particular to the scandal given to the little ones, not yet of age, still uncertain of their moral convictions (Mt. 18, 6 cp. also Col. 3, 21:) 'Fathers, do not provoke your children lest they become discouraged'. Finally each and every one of us should beware that he does not bring about his own downfall through evil looks or deeds (Mt. 5, 29f). Notwithstanding these admonitions it is sometimes necessary to give rise to scandal in human relationships as part of a moral therapy: in order to bring a man out of his state of blindnessl self-satisfaction and dogmatism, it can be quite in order to have recourse to words and actions which the person in question mat at first find highly 'offensive'. But in such cases great care and even certainty are essential. In themselves even therapeutic scandals usually have a destructive effect, if the value which they can only make effective in a provocative way is not put forward clearly and persuasively enough and so the attitude of resistance is stiffened rather than reduced. The actual stress which the other person can stand must always be kept in mind. Moreover, many causes of scandal may be spared if justifiable actions which might cause offence are properly expressed and presented.

B. Stoeckle

Scriptural ethics. See *Biblical ethics.*

Self. See *Body; Identity; Masturbation; Sex.*

Self-love. See *Love; Masturbation; Toleration.*

SEX & SEXUALITY

1. Meaning. Sexuality determines the whole of human existence as man and woman. Sexual differences are not simply confined to individual sexual characteristics—they affect man in the whole of his being and behaviour. They point to the fact that man is created as man and woman and continues to be dependent on this polarity at all times. The different aspects of sexuality are determined by man's whole understanding of life. Insofar as interpersonal relationships are communicated through the body (*q.v.*), sexuality makes it possible, in a very special way, for personal affection and love to be expressed and experienced in a particularly pleasurable way and for one partner to give himself to and be accepted by the other. Sexuality is always directed towards the begetting and bringing up of a family and in this way provides the experience of fatherhood and motherhood (see *Marriage*). Man may experience, in the course of his life, various aspects of sexuality, but it is also possible to abstain from sexual activity without harming himself physically or spiritually. This abstinence (*q.v.*) may be the result of circumstances or it may be the result of a free choice made with the highest motives. (see *Promise*). The pattern and form of man's sexual behaviour is determined by the different aspects of his sexuality (see *Chastity*). In all this, of course, the legitimate desires and interests of the partner must be taken fully into account.

In the past, the Christian morality of marriage and sexuality was determined to a great extent by a short-sighted view of human sexuality. This view was based on non-Christian hostility towards the body, a one-sided biological interpetation of the phenomenon and a negative attitude towards pleasure (*q.v.*). In addition to these factors,

224

the earlier Christian view of sexuality was also determined by Old Testament cultic influences. Christianity is now in search of a new understanding of the whole phenomenon.

2. *The biblical basis*. Sexuality is part of God's creation. According to the plan of creation, man exists in two sexes and this form of existence is meaningful because the partners are mutually complementary and together have the task of procreation. Neither a hostility towards the body and a resulting repression of sexuality on the one hand nor a frenzied exploitation of sexuality on the other can do justice to its true meaning. Apart from the proclamation of the indissolubility of marriage, the New Testament contains no direct pronouncements by the Lord on sexual behaviour. The relevant texts in the epistles cannot be applied directly to present-day situations, since they are historically conditioned. What is clear from the New Testament, however, is that Jesus made human behaviour in general subject to the norm of a radical love (*q.v.*) and faithfulness, which form the best Christian expression of personal responsibility for one's partner in marriage. The teaching attributed to Jesus (Mk 10. 5–9), which goes back to the Old Testament, is not a law that is imposed from outside, but the expression of mutual responsibility and equal partnership.

3. *Personal evaluation*. Human sexual behaviour has to be evaluated in personal terms, since it is intimately connected with love. Without love, sexuality becomes atrophied and defrauded of its real personal content. It is the aim of chastity (*q.v.*) to encourage the growth of the sexually determined capacity for personal love and to integrate sexuality into love. Christians who are concerned nowadays with the question of sexual morality have to examine critically such as happiness (*q.v.*), love (*q.v.*), satisfaction and fulfilment and clarify them in the light of the Christian understanding. Man is characterized by drives, which he has to express or abstain from. According to Christian teaching, sexuality and sexual love, together with their inherent satisfaction and pleasure, are good. They form a constitutive part of man's existence as a person and express a mutual fulfilment within the framework of consummated

225

personal love. In this context, the Christian understanding of love is essentially orientated towards such biblical statements as that concerning the love of the Lord for his Church, which constitutes a norm governing all human love that can never be, in the Christian view, superseded (Rom 5. 8; 1 Jn 3. 16).

4. *The inductive approach.* The experience (*q.v.*) and behaviour of young people must be taken into account in the formation of human behaviour generally. Within the individual phases of human development, the growth and maturity of sexual behaviour constitute a moral task. A completely neutral view of man's behaviour in connection with his sexual urges does not do justice to the total personal meaning of sexuality. In an expression of sexuality resulting in total mutual surrender, a kind of knowledge is experienced by the two partners, who recognize in this unique and non-interchangeable experience that they belong to each other and cannot separate again from each other just as though nothing had happened. They remain orientated towards each other and interrelated in a way which might later be an obstacle to marriage with a different partner.

It may well be, of course, that many people have no such knowledge in their sexual relationship with another person of this unique and non-interchangeable kind and therefore do not have any experience of belonging to each other. This may be because they are not yet sufficiently open and mature. Their self-seeking prevents them possibly from being alert to the other's desire to belong for ever to this one partner. This means that it is not really possible to achieve a total sexual surrender unless responsibility is accepted for the other person. It is clear from the Christian understanding of man's personality and his unique nature that the partner can never be reduced to the level of a pure object and that the relationship can similarly never be treated simply as a means to an end.

To return to the question of young people, their concrete sexual behaviour is often a clumsy expression of tenderness or of a desire for security. It often reflects immaturity. Even if two young people agree that their relationship should be uncommitted and without obligation, taking the form, for example, or premarital sexual intercourse, their attention should still be drawn to the existence (in their unconscious minds) of certain expectations and obligations. This is, after all, in contradiction with the ultimate meaning of this act. A 'trying out' of a sexual relationship cannot be justified if what is intended as marriage (*q.v.*) cannot be experienced without the desire for mutual giving and accepting—quite apart from the fact that personal relationships and love cannot simply be 'tried out' on an experimental basis, because of the special value of the human person.

The psychological and personal relationships are more important than sexual techniques for the success and durability of marriage. A distinction has to be made in pastoral care between the demand made by the norm and, without prejudice to its validity, the pastoral action to be taken in each case. It is of great importance that the young person should be made aware of the reasons for accepting and forming his sexuality. Abstinence from sexual urges easily becomes repression if his motives are insufficiently understood.

5. *Premarital sex.* An encounter between two people of different sex with the aim of finding the most suitable partner in life is, of course, a form of preparation for marriage. What is required in such encounters is a readiness on both sides to test out and correct or reject a choice of partner when this is recognized to be faulty. To this extent, the relationships between the partners will correspond to the non-definitive character of the encounter itself. The partners' sexual harmony and mutual compatibility and the ultimate stage of their belonging to each other cannot be finally and definitively reached before marriage. In the period preceding marriage, there is a wide spectrum of erotic and sexually tinted relationships of various intensities and expressing themselves in different ways, amounting ultimately to a whole scale of degrees and forms of tenderness. The sexual act should be an expression of a profound physical and psychical unity existing between the partners. As the sign of reciprocal personal love and faithfulness, it tends to perpetuate and deepen the relationship between the partners. Marriage, then, is the place where complete sexual relationships acquire their deepest

227

meaning and therefore their legitimate expression. It is not possible to give oneself without reserve before marriage or outside it. Premature sexual relationships before marriage make it difficult freely to choose a partner or to correct a choice.

6. *The problem of homosexuality.* Everyone is subject to the law of bisexuality. Both man and woman are bisexual insofar as they both possess female and male hormones, but the distribution of these hormones is different and correspondingly dominant. This bisexuality is also present in each sex at the level of depth psychology. Man and woman are therefore not totally different from each other. Their sexuality is also influenced by society. All the same, the physical and psychic differences and the corresponding sexual distinctions between man and woman have persisted throughout the ages. The relationship between the two sexes and their involvement with each other is based on these differences. The difference between the sexual organs also points to the bisexual (or heterosexual) disposition of man and woman.

All this indicates that homosexual encounters are 'abnormal'. They are, moreover, only practised by a minority, which is pressing for recognition in society. The aim of human sexuality is fundamentally bisexual love and possible procreation or sharing in creation. Homosexuality is therefore a restriction of man's possibilities to live and grow. In cases of permanent homosexual propensity, however, it is more correct to speak of a wrong inclination than of sin· or guilt (*q.v.*). If therapy produces no results, homosexual men and women should be encouraged to accept themselves as such and to make their propensity part of their life's task (see *Celibacy*).

Bibliography: Beach, F. A. (Ed.): Sex and Behaviour. New York, 1968. **Broadhurst, A.:** Abnormal Sexual Behaviour Female. In: **Eysenck, H. J. (Ed.):** Handbook of Abnormal Psychology. London, ²1971. **Dominian, J.:** Proposals for a New Sexual Ethic. London, 1977. **Ellis, H. & Abarbanel, A. (Eds): The Encyclopedia of Sexual Behaviour. 2 tols., New York, 1961. Feldman, M. P.:** Abnormal Sexual Behaviour Male. In: **Eysenck, H. J. (Ed.):** Handbook of Abnormal

Psychology. London, ²1971. **Id. & MacCulloch, M. J.**: Homosexual Behaviour: Therapy and Assessment. Oxford, 1970. **Kinsey, A. C. et al.**: Sexual Behaviour in the Human Male. Philadelphia, 1948. **Id.**: Sexual Behaviour in the Human Female. Philadelphia, 1953. **Kosnik, A. et al.**: Human Sexuality: New Directions in (American) Catholic Thought. New York & London 1978. **Maccoby, E. E. (Ed.)**: The Development of Sex Differences. London, 1967. **Masters, W. H. & Johnson, V. E.**: Human Sexual Response. Boston, 1966. **Winokur, G. (Ed.)**: Determinants of Human Sexual Behaviour. Springfield, Ill., 1963.

J. Gründel

Shame. See *Body; Celibacy; Guilt; Sex.*

SIN

The subjective, i.e. conscious, violation of God's revealed, i.e. clear will. 'Sin as an act is the free decision of the whole personality against the will of God as manifested in the orders of nature and grace and in verbal revelation; it presupposes clear knowledge, free consent and grave matter. By mortal sin a creature rejects the Creator's will for the basic structures of his creation and his covenant (as in the Old Testament conception of sin) and God's will to communicate himself to his creature in grace, and thus contradicts his own nature and the purpose of his freedom, which is to love the highest value of all, the personal God' (Rahner & Vorgrimler). See *Biblical ethics.*

SINS, SEVEN DEADLY

In traditional, pre-psychological, understanding these are: pride, covetousness, envy, lust, gluttony, anger, sloth.

SOCIAL ETHICS

1. Definition: In contrast to individual ethics, social ethics is

229

'concerned with right conduct between human persons and groups within and by means of the social institutions existing in the historical world. So it covers not only individual and group conduct, but also the structures of the institutions in and with which this conduct takes place.' (Rich).

Any changes in the traditional division of power and property; in the danger zones for group conflict; in judgment on society's failings, or any alteration in the harmony or disharmony between an economic system and economic thinking—these and other new elements of social change delineate and influence social man's responsibility for proper organisation. And from this angle they are the subject of socio-ethical reflection.

We may similarly understand the reference in *Gaudium et spes* to the 'sacred obligation to count social necessities among the primary duties of modern, man and to pay heed to them.' (GS 30).

2. *Social virtues.* The Pastoral Constitution on the Church goes on to deal with the social virtues which should be encouraged and brought to bear on society (GS 30).

Realization of the Good in moral acts points to the reality of the world, to the truth of that reality which contains the Good, by charging this reality with the task of realizing the Good. This raises the decisive question of 'what proves its worth in the world as meaningful and good.' (J. L. Döderlein).

An appeal to 'social' virtues implies that every attempt to organize human social life needs to fix aims and means reliably, if it is to have any permanent success.

It is for this 'virtue for tomorrow' that the caritas politica (GS 75)—aided by the insights, information and communication of as many people as possible—is striving.

Social virtues (including constant readiness to learn, sympathetic feeling for other ways of thinking and behaving as an aid to overcome fear of the risks of self-reliance) make clear that the Good does not come about simply as the result of isolated decisions.

It is part of man's joint task to ask questions and act in the face of any conduct towards people and things which concerns him.

230

This is taken into account by the Council's declaration that 'created things and societies themselves enjoy their own laws and values which must be gradually deciphered, put to use and regulated by men.' (GS 36).

3. Basic assumption of social ethics. For the 'right ordering' (GS 3) of society therefore, the humane political and economic possibilities of society must be discussed. In this way the question of what is socially important and just, which—as an appeal to responsible behaviour—'precedes' the social state of affairs, is given over to reflective experience (q.v.).

This question is posed already in the dialogue, or discussion, on the 'basic assumption' of all social ethics (however these are based) that the human is 'right' and inhuman 'wrong.'

As experience shoes, the concept of 'humanity' as a central ideal of social ethics can quickly fall into the grasp of Ideologies (q.v.) and special interests, if ethical thinkers suppress critical thought in their own sphere and give up the notion of free assent.

Among the symptoms of this, ideas have developed according to which pluralism should be given an integrating authority. This authority would be determined, where possible, by a permanent conflict of force and counterforce, carried out according to agreed rules. (Conflict, q.v.). Nowhere is the recognition of common values seriously discussed.

A reference made by the German Catholic Bishops Conference reveals a different approach. They say that by common values is meant 'not values of faith in the narrower sense, but general human rights. On the basis of these the Church seeks that which is ethically binding within modern pluralism.' (Document on The Church in the pluralist society and in the Modern Democratic State. Trier 1969. Art. 25).

Something very useful but not entirely new is being said here as is proved by glancing at social ethics in the more recent social teaching of the Church.

By presenting 'values which are seen as the collective task given by God to the world,' (A. F. Utz) the underlying theological concern has never been denied, although the matter is not pursued along purely theological paths (for if it is philosophical and empirical it is at the same time not beyond the scope of theology).

4. *Relation to the idea of humanity (q.v.)* Such 'natural law' thinking makes headway as soon as it reflects—with F. Böckle, W. Korff and others—on the non-arbitrary nature of moral judgment (social order) and the irreversibility of historical processes of understanding and cultural development.

The outcome is that if we are to take the non-arbitrary element as a 'structural timetable', as a basis for setting moral norms, then man will always appear to his fellow man simultaneously as a being in need, as an aggressor and as a provider.

In determining right conduct, social ethics therefore remains bound up with the totality of mutual penetrating conduct (a sort of 'flow balance'), which is at the same time practical-need oriented, competitive and selflessly concerned for others.

The possibility of a certain plurality of ethical systems (but not of an open-ended systematic pluralism) rests in turn on the possibility of giving preference to this or that element in an ethic based on justice or love, where a Christian social ethic—because of the truth of God's love revealed in faith—is able to see the unifying factor in the element of selfless concern (love, q.v.).

At any rate, the belief that all points of view (elements) must somehow be brought to bear belongs to those 'insights beyond which man cannot return if he is to determine his life in a rational, humane way.' 'Take the Declaration of Human Rights. Here the discontinuity of ethical norms, determined by historical change, is borne along by a continuing and irreversible process of understanding' (Böckle).

This is supported not least by the fact that an understanding of science, in which the question of the meaning of man and the world is not scientifically answerable, does not take away from man the challenge of determining his existence in a meaningful way, i.e. with the help of constructive principles (ethics, q.v.).

'Metaphysics is not essential for this. But one does need,

at least in the modern world, a good deal of perception and a positive attitude to one's fellow man—one needs humaneness.' (H. Mohr).

This question of what man needs recurs in economics and the economic community as an 'anthropological turning point,' and in the social sciences generally as a debate on how far assembling points of view on man's social existence can remain 'open-ended' if statements are being made about a society fit to live in.

It is therefore with some hope that Gaudium et spes records the 'birth of a new humanism' in which 'man is defined first of all by his responsibility towards his brothers and toward history.' (GS 55).

5. *Function of faith.* It is no doubt true that the eye of faith is needed to have the 'certainty' (evidence, q.v.) 'that the way of love lies open to all men and that the effort to establish a universal brotherhood is not a hopeless one.' (GS 38).

But we cannot expect that insights of faith should directly regulate conduct that is structurally and institutionally conditioned and must therefore be approached in these terms.

At the same time, that is not to say that such insights do not have significance for social ethics, nor to play down the question of the socially significant content of revelation.

The New Testament, in the Christ-event, points to the tension of for example the statements in Rom 13 (political power as a handmaid of God) and Apoc 13 (the 'State' in the service of satanic power).

We are faced with the task of thinking out these statements systematically if a Christian social ethic is to aid attempts to give meaning to political activity with didactic principles (e.g. as Church social teaching) and is to take a stand with more than 'impotent declarations.'

The Church too remains always in need of such reflections, as confirmed by the historical experience of almost unlimited changeability in the relationship between Church and State.

There is a long and twisting path from the casual criticism by Jesus of the state power which concretely opposed him (Lk 22.25) to the interpretation of the same words in the

233

Bull of Boniface VIII (1302) Unam Sanctam, which understands Jesus's reference to the 'two swords' (Lk 22.38) as justification for anticipating through the Church the final revelation of God's dominion.

If we contrast this view with the natural-law based approach of a political ethic which emerges strongly with the late scholastic period in Spain (Ethics q.v.), a very varied picture will result of the way in which the State–Church relationship is theologically and historically determined—and the present-day value of this picture for determining rational, humane principles is not apparent.

An attempt is therefore being made—in a system of social ethics based primarily (but not solely) on Protestant theology—to 'recast' socially meaningful principles of biblical faith into 'central axioms', i.e. terms which are not a 'foreign currency' for modern society and its organization. Nobody wants the foreign currency, and it can be cashed neither against real problems nor against attempts to solve them.

Terms (programmes) such as 'critical solidarity and openness' and 'responsible participation' have in consequence always only hypothetical character (in contrast to the biblical reference). They must be 'verified' in systems and situations in such a way that they can be shown to work or not to work.

6. *Human responsibilities.* Social organization is legitimate in proportion to its effectiveness in forwarding the common good 'dynamically understood' (GS 74).

That does not mean reflections and judgments as to why men prefer one form of 'co-operation'—legal, economic, ethical etc.—to another would be adequately answered by a consensus of those involved.

For any plan or model of conduct must take adequately into account the non-arbitrary nature of social organization (already noted) and the irreversibility of historical processes of understanding.

If we think of the social inequality entrenched in the world, it is clear that alongside or beneath those involved in certain societies is the mass of people adversely affected by inequality. Their absolute poverty corrupts the humanity of mankind as an inseperable whole.

The 'existential discord' expressed here—which lets man love himself more than God and his fellow man and consequently rules out love as a condition for a vision of justice—is a problem which must be overcome both at the personal and institutional level.

Anyone who includes 'solidarity' in his ethical code must be convinced of this—and must persuade others that he (and every other person) has ethical reference only when and where all have such reference.

So it is properly a matter of regret that the concept of 'interests' is generally not dynamic enough. It is used only in the sense of 'legitimate egoism'—but every interest is alway 'full of contradictions' (D.V. Oppen). For it always involves both a direct individual interest and an indirect general interest—which makes every protection of interest a political act.

Fundamental interests (needs) of individuals and social groups are satisfied in society by (basic) institutions. The interaction of these—e.g. in the marriage relationship (family, q.v.); in educational institutions; in the existing organisation of property, finance and business; in communities of faith and denomination; and in national and international centres of state authority and power—determine to a great extent the structure of societies (social structure).

In view of this, social ethics has the (co-)responsibility for giving advice on how to balance the progressive splitting up of social functions with 'stabilizing' forces, and also the duty to critically examine institutions and see if and how far they make possible a joint approach to given aims.

Conflict research and planning for peace intermesh here. But any leaning towards peace as a 'basic socio-ethical norm' (F. Beutter) should not blind one to the fact that the development and testing of legal relationships is at stake, and not only (nor primarily) the fostering of sentiment.

From the humane point of view, the way in which certain things must be done is always open to question.

Dignity, stability and peace (GS 48) will be characteristics of an institution's interactions to the extent that these are 'humanly perfected' ?(GS 49).

This is most easily seen where solidarity is experienced as

235

directly as in the family (*q.v.*), as in communities of the faithful which show brotherly understanding, or in action groups aiming at direct help.

This sense of solidarity will be found rather less in the notion that specialist areas of culture (such as the economy) have autonomy. Here determinism often acts only as camouflage for not wanting to do what is possible.

If economics is understood as 'a special technique without value in itself' which helps to attain goals solely 'beyond the economic sphere' (A. Lowe), then the justification and practicality of economic ethics—which can never be more than a part of social ethics—would be in question.

It may be said of the so-called economic principle (rational principle) which underlies every economic system that it rests fundamentally on the aim of winning the greatest possible success (output) with given means, or of winning a given success with the smallest possible input.

Insofar as this approach is 'not accompanied by any social norms—such as fairness, justice or social value,' it has 'given rise to many negative effects' (F. Maltz).

So there will have to be agreement that production involving 'efficiency' and 'profitable' input has economic-ethical significance and needs interpretation, since it sets norms for man's relation to man and to the economy.

The more that business is judged on whether it furthers the common good (social justice), the more clearly must social and political aims be brought into play. And this will raise the 'not exclusive' question of standards beyond the economic sphere.

The considerable attention paid—of considerable importance too to the business world—to codetermination, development aid, protection of the environment and of health demonstrates the fact that industry and commerce are a service.

The call to 'be businesslike' is a demand of the business ethic which involves keeping the internal laws of economics. But it takes on full meaning only when seen in the full context of social life.

Bibliography: Barth, K.: The Humanity of God. London & Richmond, 1963. **Cox, H.**: The Secular City. London & New

York, 1966. **Gutierrez, G.**: A Theology of Liberation. Maryknoll, N.Y. & London, 1973. **Sleeper, C. F.**: Black Power and Christian Responsibility. Nashville, 1968. **Wilder, A. N.**: Kerygma, Eschatology and Social Ethics. Philadelphia, 1966. **Welty, E.**: A Handbook of Christian Social Ethics. 2 vols. London & Edinburgh, 1960. **Yoder, J. H.**: The Politics of Jesus. Grand Rapids, 1972.

R. Henning

SOCIAL GOSPEL

A liberal Protestant notion which sees sin as inherent in evil social systems, and the kingdom of God and a truly human this-worldly social goal not only as compatible but often as one and the same thing.

SOCIALISM

1. Different uses of the term. 'Socialism' is equally at home in the mouths of protesters and in academic social analyses. It is used by social reformers and political parties in East and West in as many different senses as there are groups, and it may also be reduced (as in Hitler's 'National Socialism') to the level of slogan or camouflage. Nevertheless no study of modern social history can ignore it. This does not mean that its content can be clearly defined. For Karl Marx socialism was the social form of the 'transition' from capitalist to communist society (*capitalism*, q.v.). Because of this the word—which occurs for the first time among the English workingmen's associations in 1827—retains in the eyes of many 'socialists' a definite aura of the provisional, strongly influenced by the advantages and disadvantages of capitalist attitudes and approaches. It is largely the presence of these 'remnants' and varying attitudes to them that have created a variety of 'roads to socialism', such that socialism today can normally only be thought of, by its adherents as well as by outsiders, in association with explanatory adjectives such as 'Marxist', 'African', 'Democratic' or 'Christian'. If one nevertheless wishes to talk of socialism as such, both accuracy and an examination of social movements and theories will single out as its essence a belief in the need for a total liberation of man from inhuman dependencies and pressures which are largely socially (structurally) determined. It follows from this that for socialists of all shades arguments about the 'true' meaning of socialism, or the 'correct road', are an essential part of this process of liberation. Rudi Dutschke's 'attempt to bring Lenin down to earth' was not the first of such attempts at correction, nor will it be the last.

2. *The aim of socialism.* Not all, but most, socialist movements derive from an idealistic impulse which must be regarded as significant for socialism's intellectual history and as having had powerful effect on its practical politics. This impulse is the attempt to replace 'belief in blind development', or to weaken it, in socialism by the claim that socialism is 'the temporal form of an eternal drive towards a moral social order' (H. de Man). In socialism as a regulative moral idea, an 'actual utopia', in which the law of the future at last comes true, one is reminded of the 'Christian Socialism' of thinkers like J. H. Wichern (1808–81). This 'Christian Socialism' set out to be on the one hand the 'true form' of the ('scientific') socialism which had been constructed on an atheistic basis by Marx and Engels, and on the other a salutary reminder of the beginnings of Christianity, which in its early stages tried seriously to go from ideal fraternity to real solidarity. It is no coincidence that in many German working-class homes at the beginning of this century the picture of Bebel was still accompanied by the motto 'Jesus Christ was the first Socialist'. Marxist socialism, given its premises, methods and aims, naturally has no time even for this emotional attachment of Christianity and socialism—or rather it regards it as dangerous. It seeks a 'liberation' in the world and in history of a totally different kind from what it regards as the ideological (and therefore ineffectual) illusion offered by religion and Christianity. 'The call to give up illusions about a state of affairs is the call to give up a state of affairs which requires illusions' (Marx, 'Towards a Criticism of Hegel's Philosophy of Right').

3. *Transformations in the idea of socialism.* The usual vague

238

reference to 'transformations of socialism' derive essentially from the continuing discussion within socialism about paths towards and the form of a socialist society, which remains 'the constant aim of socialism'. To support revolutionary violence and oppose the status quo (reforms), or the reverse? Issues such as the 'contradiction' between social production and private appropriation can no longer be raised in socialism today without an attempt to define the relationship between historical necessity and human freedom, and a solution to this dilemma has to take account of the inescapable features (or imperatives) of human nature (*humanity*, q.v.). A 'developed socialism' of this sort—cf the Dubcek period in Czechoslovakia—challenges the assumption of Lenin's concept of democracy (of which no discussion is allowed) that the interests of the political leadership and the socialist society are identical. It is also a challenge to the claim by a 'new' class (the bureaucracy) that the role of a socialist party as the universal administrator of the common good is automatically immune from any criticism. The 'Basic Programme' of the West German Social Democratic Party (1959), which claims that democratic socialism in Europe is 'rooted in Christian ethics, in humanism and in classical philosophy', also emphasizes, in spite of a good many reformulations, 'the priority of theory over practice, for the sake of human freedom' (A. Schwan and G. Schwan). The practice of a democratic socialism of this sort, insofar as it is guided by principles such as the free development of every individual (*human dignity*, q.v.), and values social and cultural plurality, certainly does not deserve the neo-Marxist accusation that it is a form of pragmatism without theory or insight. On the other hand, neither do the intellectual foundations of such (or any) socialist programme make the 'case for socialism' unanswerable—as the SPD's Basic Programme seeks to maintain with its assertion that democracy is 'completed in socialism' (W. Mommsen).

4. *Assessment of socialism's fundamental aims.* All forms of socialism are characterized by a view of society which gives priority to common over private ownership of the means of production, and this is the origin of the preference in socialist programmes for the system of the controlled or

planned economy. Whether purely economic arguments are sufficient to recommend or rule out this system is disputed. According to Pius XII, a Christian morality cannot 'simply accept' such a social order 'as just'. On the other hand, socialist economic and constitutional policies cannot be regarded as unjust in themselves as long as they can be questioned by the people who live with them, and in this sense remain experimental. This applies both to the demand in the 'classical' socialist programme for the replacement of hierarchical industrial structures by the so-called council system and to the model developed in the Prague reform period of a 'socialist market' subject to guidance. What is acceptable in any system must be measured by the needs of the common good at any particular time.

5. *The Church's view.* The Church's 'official' criticism of socialism is also not directed at the legal or organizational constraints to which economic activity in socialist societies is subjected. It is concerned with the Marxist socialist doctrinal structure in which religion and Christianity are regarded as transitory because they are an expression of alienation—and certainly not a means of transcending it. A form of socialism which accepts this view is, in the judgment of Pius XI, 'always irreconcilable with the teaching of the Catholic Church' (Encyclical *Quadragesimo Anno*, 117). This judgment also condemns any form of socialism which sees itself as a movement covering every aspect of life and thereby disregards or obstructs the demands made by the complex nature of man and the world. A Christian cannot 'subscribe to Marxist ideology, its atheistic materialism, its dialectic or the way in which it absorbs personal freedom into the collectivity and so denies human beings, in their historical existence as individuals and communities, any aspect of transcendence' (Paul VI, *Octogesima Adveniens*, 26). Also to be regarded as irreconcilable with the teaching of the Church are attempts within religious socialism to interpret socialist movements deriving from Karl Marx or elsewhere as religious phenomena. These views, in different ways (E. Fuchs, E. Heimann, P. Tillich), prophetically attribute to the socialist movement a divine mission which the movement itself firmly rejects.

240

Committed religious socialists of this type 'refuse to acknowledge the limitations of historical social movements, which remain conditioned by their original ideology' (*Octogesima Adveniens*, 31). Papal statements have maintained that neither socialism nor revolution can belong to the heart of Christian theology, or be among its deepest springs. In other words, socialism is and remains 'a thing of this world' (W. Dirks). See *Marxism*.

R. Henning

Solidarity. See *Capitalism; Indifference; Justice; Liberation; Marxism; Social ethics; Socialism*.

Solitariness. See *Identity; Loneliness*.

Standard. See *Norm*.

SPIRITUALITY

1. Definition. This subject was dealt with in earlier times under the headings asceticism and mysticism, striving for perfection, piety, and so on.

By 'spirituality' is meant either (subjectively) the concrete spiritual life or (objectively) the theology of the spiritual life (spiritual theology).

'Spiritual life' refers to life 'in the Spirit' or 'of the Spirit' (in the New Testament sense). 'Spirit' has here the full richness of meaning that the word possesses in the languages of the Bible.

From its meaning of 'wind' or 'breath' the word can—already in the Old Testament—refer to the life force, the seat of the emotions and of spiritual fulfilment, the soul, the spirit of man. 'Spirit' is also a word used of God, and it can then mean a force emanating from God, but also God's own being: his spirituality, his imperishability, and his powerful presence among His people.

Finally, in the New Testament, the divine person of the Holy Spirit emerges clearly. God's spirit, the Holy Spirit, is given to man and becomes the centre of the human spirit.

241

'Spirit' can now refer to man's nature elevated by God, the divine sphere (in contrast to the Pauline 'flesh' and the Johannine 'world').

The spirit is the basis and dynamic centre of Christian existence. The Christian is 'in the spirit' (Rom 8.9), he 'walks by the spirit' (Gal 5.16), he brings 'fruit of the spirit' (Gal 5.22). Paul can refer to Christians simply as 'you who are spiritual' (Gal 6.1) (See *Biblical ethics*).

In this way 'spiritual' has become a technical expression for Christian existence. If 'spirit' was afterwards understood in contrast to body (*q.v.*), to material, this was due to later contractions of meaning.

If we speak of 'spiritualities' (in the plural) or of schools of spirituality, we refer to the variety of concrete historical forms which the one Christian spirituality has adopted. These derive less from differing theological principles than from various types of spiritual experience (Franciscan, Carmelite, Ignatian spirituality) or from the various ways of life and different tasks within the Church (religious, lay and priestly spirituality).

2. *Sources and place in theology.* The main source of spirituality is the word of God in Scripture, which acts as the 'norm and critic of all spirituality in the Church' (von Balthasar).

Of great importance too is tradition—the piety of the past, lived through and reflected on. We encounter this above all in the liturgy, which proclaims the mystery of faith through the word of God and effects through the sacrament living contact with him.

The saints have a special importance for spirituality (see *Model*), for they constantly let the inexhaustible riches of the mystery of Christ shine forth in a new and exemplary way in different historical circumstances.

The Church's magisterium has rarely commented on matters of spirituality, and then mostly to ward off false views and practices. The Church presupposes the positive aspects from the devoutness lived through and handed on by the faithful.

Much has been said on the place of spirituality in theology. Many authors approach it from an empirical standpoint, for example in the phenomenology of grace from prayer (Poulain). But spirituality is dealt with mainly in moral theology.

The listing of moral commands and spiritual counsels—where these are put forward as the science of Christian perfection (Tanquerey, Noldin, Jone)—is rarely undertaken today because of the exegetical and theological problems.

Often the entire ethical conduct of the Christian is assigned to the moral sphere, while to spirituality are assigned the paths, steps and aids for the more intensive realisation and perfection of the Christian life (Vermeersch, de Guibert, Truhlar). Alternatively, spirituality is characterised as only those activities which relate expressly and directly to God (Bouyer, Vanderbroucke).

Other authors range spirituality under dogmatic theology (Garrigou-Legrange, Gardeil, Stolz). H. Urs von Balthasar calls spirituality 'the subjective aspect of dogmatic theology', the 'mystery-dimension of objective dogmatic theology'.

It is dealt with systematically mostly in connexion with the doctrine of grace and the theological virtues. All these attempts to compartmentalize spirituality but raise their own problems and have their fuzzy edges. Spirituality is inseparably bound up with dogmatic theology, exegesis, moral theology and history of devotion and is dependent on the knowledge contained in these subjects. It consequently shares in their present-day uncertainties.

Because it is so close to experience, spirituality cannot ignore the findings of psychology, sociology and educational theory. Because it is interwoven with other disciplines, spirituality has been called a 'cross-section science'. But perhaps this expression raises expectations which spirituality, as a science, cannot meet.

3. *Spirituality in practice.* The practice of the spiritual life is very varied and covers the whole breadth of Christian existence: the theological virtues, prayer, the stages of spiritual development, spiritual experience, mysticism, worship and liturgy, asceticism and response to suffering, work and service to mankind and the world, charismatic gifts and special vocations. We shall refer more closely here to only a few basic forms of the spiritual life.

Theological virtues and gifts of the Holy Spirit. Spiritual life develops mainly through the dynamic force of the theological virtues Faith (q.v.), Hope (q.v.) and Love (q.v.), which mark the special character of Christian existence and were already seen in the New Testament as a unity (1 Thess 1.3; 1 Corr 13.13; Rom 5. 1–5).

The virtues are the active, dynamic extension of the grace which makes man's innermost being Godlike in its capacities.

Through these virtues the Christian's whole personal, spiritual activity is directed towards God (hence they are called theological or divine virtues). Since God makes possible the performance of these virtues, they are also called supernatural or infused virtues (cf. Rom 5.5). But they need further development by man and are perfected in all moral acts, even if they are not expressly evoked (see *Virtue*).

Growth, development and perfection of the spiritual life are traditionally ascribed to the seven gifts of the Holy Spirit, where the figure seven is no doubt meant to express fulness. They represent the more passive side of the life of grace and bestow a particular lightness on the Christian life in faith, conferring receptivity and a willingness to learn in the face of the Holy Spirit's prompting.

Prayer. Prayer arises from the grace of justification and from the theological virtues as the central act of adoration and of the childlike attitude induced by the Holy Spirit.

Prayer takes place between two poles, indicated by the traditional definitions of the 'ascent of the spirit to God' and 'talking with God'.

Since many people today find difficulty in addressing God as in a personal way, prayer could begin as an ascent to God, in the form of meditation. Meditation can start with reflection on one's own situation, which is illuminated by listening to God's word. Christian meditation is therefore ultimately directed outwards—to Scripture, to Christ, to mankind.

But the types of eastern meditation often practised today (Zen, Yoga) are valuable particularly because they allow people to find inner peace and recollection amid the rush of modern life.

But it is important to go beyond them into the Christian

sphere, to the personal relationship with God (see *Love*). 'Talking with God' is the goal of prayer. That we can and should address God in prayer (as the response of faith to God's word, as 'talking faith') is proved by the example and teaching of Jesus and by the unanimous tradition of the Church. The Christian's prayer to the Father is ultimately based on the mediatorship of Jesus (praying 'in the name of Jesus': Jn 15.16).

The main forms of prayer are praise, thanksgiving and supplication. The elements of praise and thanksgiving show that prayer is more than a merely internal affair. The highpoint of prayer is 'purpose-free' standing before God. This is achieved primarily in liturgical prayer, the 'official' prayer of the Church, which has celebration of the Eucharist as its climax. In the presence of the Lord in the word and the sacrament, meditation and explicit prayer find their source—which never runs dry. Personal prayer should constantly take its bearings from the objectivity of liturgical prayer.

Prayer of supplication raises special practical and theological problems. For it should not aim to change God's will in a magical way, but neither should it simply express adaptation to God's providence.

On the one hand, prayer of supplication should inculcate the right attitude on the part of the praying person, so he can receive God's gifts. On the other hand, God has eternally incorporated our daily prayer in his plans, since God's eternity and our time are not commensurable.

But behind every actual request is the greater plea for God's favour, which is constantly granted to us. Prayer demands regular practice, although the frequency will depend on the individual. As a general rule it may be said that time for prayer is needed in any stretch of time experienced as a unity.

Development of the spiritual life. The possibility of growth in the spiritual life is indicated by Holy Scripture (1 Cor 3. 1–3; Eph 4. 13–15). Tradition speaks of the stages of purification, enlightenment and union, or refers to beginners, the more advanced and the perfects. But these stages should not be misinterpreted as a rigid system: they can in fact recur at an ever higher level.

245

Progress in the spiritual life consists in the growing intensity and existential depth of the act (of faith, or love). Through a passive process of purification (the 'dark night' of the senses and spirit) prayer matures to ever greater simplicity.

But even in what is called 'mysticism', faith, the word and the mystery of God are not left behind. It is true that psychologically there seems to be an essential difference between mystical and ordinary ways of experiencing faith and prayer. But theologically no great difference between the two is assumed.

Rare associated phenomena—such as visions and ecstasies—should be treated with great reserve. The ultimate goal of the spiritual life is not unworldly contemplation but 'finding God in all things' (see *World*).

Charismatic gifts. The Spirit of God operates not only for the personal perfection of the individual, but bestows special gifts for the use of others. Paul lists several catalogues of these 'charismatic gifts' (1 Cor 12. 8–11; Rom 12. 6–8). The variety of gifts finds its unity in their source—the same Spirit—and in their purpose: the 'common good' (1 Cor 12.7), and 'building up the body of Christ' (Eph 4.12).

Charismatic gifts are not necessarily miraculous, going beyond the powers of nature. They may also be due to natural ability, awakened by the inspiration of faith and placed in the service of the Church. Charismatic gifts are a sign through the ages of the Spirit dwelling in the Church.

It is true that since the age of the New Testament there has been friction between the magisterium and the charismatics ('fanatics'). Hence charismatic gifts must be subject to criticism, to 'the ability to distinguish between spirits' (1 Cor 12.12; Thess 5.19-21).

Marks of the 'good spirit' are: joy, peace, consolation, sound teaching, membership of the visible Church, obedience, humility and love of the Cross.

Marks of the 'bad spirit' are: restlessness, confusion, disobedience, wilfulness, selfishness.

Training people to listen for personal guidance from the Holy Spirit and to 'discern' or 'distinguish between spirits' is an essential aim of all 'spiritual direction'.

Bibliography: **Bouyer, L.** (**Ed**). A History of Christian Spirituality, 3 vols. London & Baltimore, 1963-5. **Mühlen, H.**: A Charismatic Theology. London & New York, 1978. **Rahner, K.**: The Spirit in the Church. London & New York, 1979.

G. Switek

Sterilization. See *Birth control.*

Strike. See *Marxism; Socialism; Work.*

Suffering. See *Aging; Ethics; Ethos; Happiness; Hope; Humanity; Identity.*

Suspicion. See *Reliability.*

SUICIDE

Suicide refers to all acts which are deliberately intended to terminate one's life. It has been condemned in Christian tradition on the grounds that God is the author of the initiation and termination of life, and that man is not entitled to usurp this right. The severity of Christian censure—which at times excluded the possibility of burial in consecrated ground—has been gradually waning. The reasons for this relaxation have been the insights gained from the psychological sciences which have clarified the diminished freedom of those intending or committing suicide, and the increasing realization that suicidal behaviour is intimately linked with changes in mood. Hence suicide often occurs against a background of severe depression, which may arise from depressive illness itself; and from the life situation: in particular the individual's isolation in an unstructured and rapidly changing social environment.

The despair regarding the future which is an essential background of those who kill themselves is thus no longer considered as an expression of selfishness or cowardice but as a result of depressive changes triggered off by illness or personal or community factors.

247

Those who commit suicide have to be distinguished from attempted suicides. The latter are often men and women who do not desire death but have reached a point of desperation in their own life. The attempted suicide, usually an action far short of what is necessary for death, is then a cry for help, calling the attention of relatives, friends, and others to the need for support in order to negotiate a particularly difficult life situation.

Recognition of the needs of those in despair has led to the evolution of organizations to meet them, such as the Samaritans in the United Kingdom, and similar organizations in other parts of the world. Hence suicidal behaviour is emerging from the traditional condition of moral disapproval. It is currently recognized as being, in the overwhelming majority of cases, a manifestation or expression of despair arising from a depressive response to a life situation or depressive illness.

Bibliography: The Myth of Sisyphus. London & New York, 1955. **Durkheim, E.**: Suicide. London & New York, 1952. **Häring, B.**: Medical Ethics. London, 1972. **Melinsky, M. A. H.**: Religion and Medicine, 2 vols. London 1970–3. **Stengel, E.**: Suicide and Attempted Suicide. Harmondsworth, 1964. **Towell, H.**: The Unfinished Debate on Euthanasia. London, 1973. **Williams, G.**: The Sanctity of Human Life and the Criminal Law. London, 1955.

J. Dominian

Sympathy. See *Love; Marxism; Socialism; Mercy; Virtue.*

T

Teaching office. See *Birth control; Ethics; Ethos; Faith; Godlessness; Sex.*

TECHNOLOGY

Man does not take the world as he finds it but opposes the powers of nature and the forms of evil he encounters and tries to adapt himself to things but only as far as his purposes seem to demand. Technology in a basic sense might be thought of as everything artificial or manmade as opposed to that which is natural. The possibilities and scope of technology and its goals are decided by the laws of nature, the conditions of human social life and an ideal, ideological and moral framework determined by historical experience, understanding of the world and religion. Man can work for a better world but he can also try to escape from it or even oppose it. Since the future is hidden from us, what is materially better is always perceived as the next best thing to be worked for piecemeal.

Industrial technology is characteristic of the modern era. It includes scientific progress, research, economy in the sense of the production and distribution of material goods and services, and all rationally manipulable phenomena (including man himself). This process has led to the liberation from need of great numbers of people, to a rapid increase in population, and finally to a firm dependence of the technologically underdeveloped nations on the rich countries of the world. On the other hand there has been an increase in the (uneasy) awareness of the value of the individual and of the community of all mankind (the United Nations).

Technical progress has made everything seem possible in theory. But development has seemed also to escape human control and even to threaten man and his values. Man has become more dependent on the laws of nature, as his plans have become the more complex and inclusive. In several instances the natural equilibrium of evolution has been disturbed. The dangers and side-effects of misuse grow with the technical possibilities. Technical activity is never free from value-judgments but morally relevant goals and norms have constantly to be decided.

If things continue as they are catastrophe would seem to be assured. A great part of mankind close their eyes to the possibilities; others despair. The solution of technological problems requires increased commitment and rational engagement. It is not a question of abandoning industrial technology but of working through it and beyond it. It is important to gauge as precisely as possible the complex results of present practice (systems analysis, futurology and conflict research). But the results of such research need worldwide peaceful co-operation if they are to bear fruit. General agreement among nations and renunciation of all dreams of world domination are essential. Control mechanisms have to be established to counteract the misuse of power, and it is essential to bring about universal well-being and the assurance of the real interests of all mankind.

Christians have no pat answers to the problems of technology, just as they cannot banish death or bring about an essential moral improvement in the world. But they see and show the alternatives more precisely. Christians are concerned to prepare the way of the Lord, and therefore to persuade the whole world to decide for or against Christ. In view of possible future technological developments, men are always subject to the temptation of deciding for a happiness that men themselves think they can bring about by means of a perfectly functioning society. That could make Christ and Christianity seem superfluous. Christians have to work with all men of good will without any illusions, and in a technically appopriate way, in order to remove political tensions, raise productivity and obtain a just distribution of the goods produced by the economy, to

250

stop the waste of natural resources, and bring about a spiritual community throughout the world. See *Environment; Liberation*.

H.-H. Schulte-Vieting

Ten commandments. See *Biblical ethics; Ethics; Ethos*.

Terrorism. See *Marxism; Conflict; Liberation; Resistance; Theft*.

Testimony. See *Evidence*.

THEFT AND HOSTAGES

1. General definition. Theft, exortion and blackmail, kidnap and the taking of hostages are generally considered as criminal offences, and as such are examined from a purely legal standpoint. But underlying the law's concern to preserve the smooth running of societal relations are questions about the moral significance of such offences at an inter-personal level.

Theft is the seizure of another's property and can involve the threat or employment of violence against life and limb. The particular immorality of this offence against property lies in the concomitant diminution of freedom, intimidation or threat or injury to bodily integrity. In this sense gang-robbery and looting are unethical, but so are extortion and profiteering.

2. The problem of kidnap. Kidnap, abduction and the taking of hostages pose special moral problems, the full ethical implications of which must be carefully weighed and considered. The hostage is held captive as security for another's conduct; against his will he is deprived of his freedom, threatened with reprisals, and under certain circumstances with death. It is similarly important to give due weight to ethical considerations when passing moral judgment on the holding of prisoners of war or the taking of hostages. What is at issue here is the question of reprisals: these constitute an offence against human dignity and freedom for an innocent person his held liable for the actions of another. Moral liability is not transferable and the killing of the innocent is unethical.

251

As a general principle therefore, the taking and killing of hostages must be morally condemned. Nevertheless, in this world, with all its acknowledged imperfections, moral judgments about the taking of prisoners of war must be critically weighed and examined, lest an absolute pacifism and absence of violence appear to be advocated. Present-day methods of warfare give rise to situations so complex that a policy of non-involvement may be morally the greater of two evils and an act of intervention need not be condemned as unethical (value judgment).

Here one could speak of guilt by implication or 'transferred moral liability', were guilt not to be understood in a purely personal sense. There should be a far greater public awareness of and adherence to the condemnation of the taking of hostages by the Geneva Convention in 1949. Observation of the prohibition would clarify the situation to the extent that an ethically neutral and uncommitted position with regard to the taking of hostages would be no longer tenable. See *Liberation; Resistance.*

H. Kramer

TIME

1. Time and temporality as fundamental features of human existence. Time for human beings is at once a fundamental constraint, a gift and a task. They have to dominate it without forgetting their dependence on it. Time contains the possibility and the claim to give life a meaningful form for oneself and the world as a whole in the same way as the Creator by using all its three dimensions. This remains true even in spite of the large measure of human impotence before him. Human beings are impotent before the flux of time as manifested in growth and decay, and before the unknown moment of its limit in death. The coincidence of impotence and aspiration leads to a tension which issues in the longing to break through finitude into infinity. This fundamental aspect of human nature is both a torture and an inspiration, and man's task is to endure it and make it fruitful.

2. The practical significance of time. A number of fun-

damental rules for action follow from this. One essential
decision is the decision to accept one's own temporality.
Only a person who accepts life—his own or another's—as it
is can see it as a value with a right to be preserved.
Acceptance of one's temporality in the sense of being
subject to growth and decay is also essential to acceptance
of one's creatureliness, and so to the fulfilment of one basic
moral demand. An acceptance of time and temporality has
to be ratified in individual actions, and an essential
principle here is the effort to use one's allotted time as well
as possible (Col 4.5). However, time can only be organized
successfully when its character is realised, and in particular
its three-dimensionality. Overemphasis or neglect of one
dimension prevents the fulfilment of important aspects of
human nature and is a danger to a person's identity. Taken
to an extreme, an imbalance of this sort must lead to
despair, since the loss of a sense of history involves the
destruction of all coherence of values or purposes. A person
who tries to live wholly in the past alienates himself from
reality, loses sight of the real tasks and possibilities of the
present and also becomes unable to see beyond the limits of
time. He is incapable of creativity or spontaneity and only
interested in the restoration of the past. He has no interest
in progress. Conversely, the person who tries to shut out
the past thereby denies an essential element of himself, the
legacy of tradition which is active in him, and also rejects
the positive springs of action and life which he did not
create but which have been passed on to him in the
tradition (see *Truth*). Concentration on the present alone
is equally irresponsible. It leads to unconnected individual
acts, because no thought is given to man's past or his
future. A stress on staying young prevents proper preparation, externally or intellectually and psychologically, for
old age. The destructive effects on mankind as a whole of a
lack of forethought, sacrificing the future for the sake of the
present, are now becoming clear in problems such as
energy conservation and the preservation of the *environment*
(*q.v.*). Human powers have reached a stage at which
developments which are positive now are not necessarily
still positive when seen in the long term. This raises a
question which will have unprecedented repercussions for
the ethics of politics, economics and science and will be

253

crucial to the survival of the human race. Nevertheless, attempts to envisage all the consequences of actions must not lead to an obsession with the future. When the past is regarded as over and done with, and the present has value only in virtue of the future, man can exist only as someone who he as yet is not, and this deprives him of the possibility of gratitude and the experience of happiness. Sacrificing the present to the future means sacrificing people to ideas of utopia. In any case, this attitude is just as delusive as the obsessions with the present and the past, because it is based on the belief that the future is totally in man's power. Nor can it lead to real improvement because in it the work of building the future is not guided by human needs. Each of these three distortions has its own religious form. There is the anxious clinging to tradition which, combined with false trust in God and a lack of hope, leads to inactivity. Blind activism despises—often unconsciously—the achievements of the past and God's promise to act and expects everything from its own efforts. The hope which sets its eyes on eternity alone reduces even love of neighbour to a means. All these attitudes are varieties of little faith and also presumption, in that they mean that man is making his plans and his arrangement of history into absolutes. That is not to say that a weighing of different claims is excluded from his sphere of responsibility. The greatest possible self-determination in relation to time is the task that has been given to man, and it contributes to his fulfilment. The degree of wear and tear to which the individual may or should expose himself depends on the importance of the particular enterprise to the body and mind of both himself and others. A general attitude that, say, a shorter life in which (apparently) more is achieved is worth more than a longer life with less action, by making achievement an absolute, contradicts the gratuitous character of time. However much *work* (*q.v.*) is an obligation of man, it can never be more than a subordinate good. When values are reversed by constant stress and a compulsion to make use of every minute, the result, both for individuals and for society, is slavery and inner poverty. A precondition of balanced relationship of obligation and freedom in regard to work, and the precondition of the responsible organization of a person's life, is the achivement of an economical relationship with time. This involves adaptation to the natural constants of life in time, which leads to a way of life appropriate to a person's age and so both prevents exhaustion in attempts at the impossible and also makes possible the best use of the forces of each age, while being also the best answer to their corresponding needs. One's own needs and wishes are intrinsically no less deserving of attention than those of others. Training in *abstinence* (*q.v.*) and the postponement of satisfactions is not the only thing time demands; what is even more important is a constant effort to find the right moment in time for satisfaction. It is also important to free oneself as far as possible from the negativity of time, that is from total dependence on both human and cosmic time pressures and limits. This means planning one's own life on the basis of what is possible. This sort of positive atemporality can only succeed if not all one's time is filled with activity. *Leisure* (*q.v.*) is just as important as work, not only for the sake of maintaining life and efficiency, but also for meeting oneself, others and God.

3. Consequences for Christian morality. A Christian ethics in particular derives its claim, form and content from its attitude to time. Time must be felt as time so that eternity can be experienced as eternity and motivate action. A Christian ethics must therefore take account of the way its hearers' capacities for action are conditioned by their temporality and offer them a guide for implementing the claims and possibilities of that temporality. One way of doing this leads from the inculcation of an awareness of temporality and its consequences to the portrayal of a fundamental attitude of gratitude and joy on the one hand and on the other of an attempt to give time a structure which is autonomous but also at every moment subject to God. The other way begins with individual actions and is negative to the extent that it works by criticizing even objectively small failures. It must be realized that neither idling nor frequently having no time and sacrificing sleep and leisure are trivial faults, but both represent a rejection of fundamental gifts of God to men and a refusal to share with others the gift of time, for this is what having time really means. It must also be realized that these habits prevent man's self-realization and in the long run make qualities such as gratitude, loyalty, forgiveness and patience, which are necessary to human society. These and various other virtues should be reinterpreted positively in this context as possibilities.

Bibliography: **Orme, J. E.**: Time, Experience and Behaviour. London, 1969. **Ornstein, R. E.**: On the Experience of Time. Harmondsworth & New York, 1969.

M. Meesters

TOLERATION AND TOLERANCE

1. Prevailing interpretation. Nothwithstanding the view of D. H. Lawrence that it was 'an insidious modern disease' (*The Plumed Serpent*), and in spite of a good many distortions of itself, toleration has become a generally recognized maxim of social and political life. It requires us to accept without reserve not only the right to exist but also the legitimate ambitions of those who think differently from us, in particular minorities and marginal groups and including ideological deviants. Tolerance is a sign of the growing sense of the solidarity of the whole human race and shows an awareness that the problems of pluralistic societies, especially the various current threats to the existence of society such as the escalation of apathy (*indifference, q.v.*), intolerant fanaticism and acts of violence can only be overcome if individual sub-groups (states, philosophies, religions) feel and show mutual respect.

2. Tolerance and personal morality. It is important to realize that although tolerance is a fundamental attitude for social policy, it cannot be legislated for and that, in fact, its only hope of success is acceptance as a 'deep structure' rule governing every sort of human relationship. In this sense it means simply that everyone is expected to be prepared to accept that other people are different (*love, q.v.*). On the other hand, since tolerance has nothing to do with the 'nihilism that lets simply anything go' (A. Gehlen), with indifference or listless passivity, to be *capable* of tolerance a person must have a strong identity, and a high degree of

256

self-possession, integration (liking for himself/herself!), and also considerable resilience. This reflects the observation that intolerant behaviour always points to an inadequate personality paralyzed by helplessness in the face of its own inadequacies and weaknesses. The human and ethical motivation of tolerance is a conviction of the inalienable dignity and freedom of the individual human existence (*human dignity*, *q.v.*) and a recognition that other people have the right to their own ideas and pecularities, and even to misuse their *freedom* (*q.v.*). The chief implication of tolerance is that we cease to set up our own views as absolutes and, as a corollary, abandon attempts to force others into positions they have not chosen. This in no sense means, as Nietzsche believed, the sacrifice of 'one's own ideal', but on the contrary presupposes that one has an ideal. The other side of such abstinence is a willingness to allow others their otherness and to protect it in the face of threats. This includes accepting all the limitations and the fallibility which are an inevitable part of historical human existence.

Tolerance receives a particular vindication whenever we are forced to face up to the *guilt* (*q.v.*) and moral failure of fellow men for whom we are responsible. The ancients knew that, alongside threats and open opposition, tolerance fulfilled a most important function as an instrument for the prevention of wrongdoing. Of course in this rôle tolerance is not limitless. It is quite familiar with the injunction 'So far and no further'. As soon as the other person seems likely by his behaviour to do serious damage to himself or the community, other demonstrations of common human concern such as fraternal correction, rebuke and protest become appropriate.

3. Obligations from faith. The Christian is left in no doubt that he is called to tolerance. Does not the God in whom he believes reveal himself as the Father in heaven who makes his sun rise on the just and the unjust? His God is merciful to the ungrateful and wicked (Lk 3. 36) and reluctant to give way immediately to intolerant impulses to root out evil and opposition (cf. Mt 13. 24–30; Lk 9. 51–56). With good reason does Paul urge his communities to consider God's 'forbearance' (Rom. 2. 4; 3. 26). Confronted in this way with

257

the personal model of tolerance, the believer is required to be tolerant too. 'Bear with one another' is for this reason one of the most frequent admonitions in the apostolic preaching (Col 3. 12–13; 1 Cor 4. 12; 2 Cor 11. 1).

Finally, perversions of tolerance. Particularly with regard to the situation of our own time, it should be pointed ut that impatient zeal directed against others is not the only form of intolerance. Closing our eyes to the people around us, 'just not wanting to be bothered' about others, also shows a refusal to bear (with) them (*patience*).

Bibliography: Kamen, H.: The Rise of Toleration. London, 1967. **Rahner, K. (Ed)**: Concise Encyclopedia of Theology: Article on Toleration. London & New York, 1976.

B. Stoeckle

TRADE UNION

A labour union, or organization of those working in the same trade, vocation, and so on, in order to protect their basic conditions of work, payment, and living conditions, against exploitation and abuse.

Transcendence. See *Conscience; Evidence; Faith; Guilt; Hope; Love; Spirituality.*

TRUTH

1. Introduction. Truth is the fundamental requirement of human life, which can correspond to its reality only when existence, meaning and value are recognized and accepted. It is a prerequisite of self-consciousness and self-development within the environment and further for every influence on interhuman relationships and encounters. It enables, enlarges and increases the personal freedom of choice by opening up reality and meaning and thereby overcoming errors and mistakes. An initially unreflected and general conception of truth sees it as being intellectual knowledge and volitional action corresponding with a given

258

reality and not limited to a theoretical or logical relationship. Because ontology and epistemology pose questions of considerable import in their concern with truth, philosophy has long ago assigned itself this subject to work on. The relevant discussions are important for an ethical appreciation in so far as they deal with the question of the openness and recognizability of existence and the individual, personal ego, of the possibilities, limits, requirements and historical relativity of human knowledge and its universal realization in free man. Truth does not consist simply in knowing how to reproduce things and physical realities correctly, but in accepting, perceiving, experiencing and expressing the real relation of human consciousness to its objects. Its ultimate purpose is to shed light on human existence. Therefore it is also necessarily historical. The significance of individual, objective truths and the immediate criteria for the ethos of truth are restricted and subject to change. The all-embracing obligation to truth itself is indispensable. For this reason the extreme positions of sceptical indifferentism and universalism must be avoided. Historicity and a pluralistic knowledge of truth do not necessarily connote relativism.

The biblical revelation offers the whole of mankind the deepest insight into truth. The Hebrew word 'ameth', which implies steadfastness and includes in that constancy and faithfulness, was already geared in a special way to the process of life. God in his holiness is the absolute truth and source of all truth, from which the universe is formed. His word and deed can be relied on completely and thus he fulfils his promise to his people. Man is then committed to this original interpretation of truth. He must live and act in accordance with truth. Deceitfulness is the beginning of every downfall. In the New Testament, and especially in the gospels of John and Paul, the truth of the relationship between God and Man appears in the revelation of Christ 'to bear witness to the truth' (Jn 18.37 et all.). The truth manifested by Christ should be emulated with the utmost zeal. The Christian's path to righteousness follows the truth of the Gospel, which is light, strength and salvation. Injustice and evil can be turned aside by loving (love, q.v.), obeying and believing (faith, q.v.) in truth. The gospel of John stresses that truth, as the comprehensive term for the process of revelation, is the opposite to lies in the broadest sense, which, when overcome, results in 'freedom', 'life' and 'an existence in truth'. This New Testament use of language is not restricted to disclosing secrets and their intellectual experience, it refers to the faithful acceptance of the person Christ and the remaining true to his word. 'Live according to truth' (Jn 3. 21; 1 Jn 1. 6) is the demand made by the commandments (1 Jn 2. 4) and the testimony of the 'fellow workers in the truth' (3 Jn 8) to the world. Truth shows how life can be fulfilled according to God's will. This truth, a quality man cannot dispose with freely, is revealed through the spirit of truth.

2. *The nature of truth.* The purpose and content of an ethos of truth, the central value of which is truthfulness, is to comply with the existential and religious understanding of truth within the whole sphere of human existence. Knowledge of truth must be sought everywhere and at all times. In recognition of the relationship between the subsequent dependence of God and environment, the inhibitions and limits present in the character and the mental and psychological constitution must be overcome and one must strive unceasingly to arrive at a deeper, broader and clearer understanding of the facts of existence, meaning and value in human and interpersonal relations. The whole range of possible ways in which to shape one's life is determined by truthfulness. With the utmost clarity and integrity this life-style must be discovered and realized time and again as an all-integrating 'act of truth'. It is so deeply rooted in the personality that it cannot be treated objectively by general norms. Thus a person's whole attitude and the way he lives bear witness to truth, not the least when he clearly sides with truth when making public statements and testifying. This encourages a definite adversity to inappropriate compromises, wrong consideration and to the more or less conscious dependence of public opinion on the anonymous mass. A resolution to be truthful in thought and action is required if a true conscience is to be at all feasible and reliable. Being tolerant (*toleration, q.v.*) is neither a denial nor an indifferent treatment of truth, but is a show of respect for other people's opinions. Only after repeated effort and careful

thought can truthfulness in one's dealings with fellow human beings become a proclamation of truth. The first step is to search together for a deeper, broader and reliable approach to the whole of perceptible reality with a view to agreement and reciprocity. Collaboration of this kind occurs in all forms of communication. Difficulties and complications must be taken into consideration, especially the varying amount of knowledge possessed by the individual, and the problem of written communication which inevitably leads to an abbreviated form with new perspectives. The communication of thought and experience is just as dependent on the medium of expression available and the readiness to communicate as on the individual ability to receive it. A systematic communication of knowledge is adapted to the prevailing conditions and situation: i.e., to the whole structure of co-existence as it stands. Accordingly, love is the highest norm. A personal expression is not true merely because it satisfies the formal criterion of the correlation of word and thought, but because it takes account of human encounters and communication.

When a truthful statement is likely to injure the other person in a conversation, a third party or a group, a different problem arises. The practice of being truthful is designed to maintain and guarantee the basic social attitudes of trust and faithfulness within the group, just as the New Testament intended with its prohibition of oath-taking. This is even more important as the prssent state of public opinion is far removed from the original and proper forms of human and group *communication* (*q.v.*) and runs the risk of being dictated by materialistic and ambitious interests. When it comes to being truthful, openness, candour, sincerity and retinence are kept under control with these interests in mind. In individual areas of social and political life, in the press and public information, certain professional and social obligations exist, but do not interfere in any way with the commitment to truth.

In ecclesiastical life, the full and central significance of truth as outlined in the New Testament corresponds to a deeper religious responsibility which extends to all cases of human truthfulness. The certainty of the faithful that they have a set place in God's promise and work takes its cue from the spirit of truth and concentrates on eliminating any superficial confusion and ambiguity in life and on making clear standpoints and statements in which yes is yes and no is no. The Church has always considered the very difficult task of maintaining and ensuring the truth of faith as a prerequisite and even as a substantial basis of its existence. Dogma, loyalty and obediance to faith guarantee to defend both faith and truth without resorting to an inappropriate unity and traditionalism. Thus the Church is awarded the task of distinguishing truth from error, of recognizing the spirit of truth and exposing false prophets and of leading the faithful out of the confusion of conflicting doctrines to inspiration and spiritual guidance. With this as a foundation, the Christian becomes increasingly bound to truth and to bearing public witness to truth.

3. *Lie.* The direct opposite to a truthful statement in the widest sense of the word is a lie, which is clearly and decisively condemned in the revelation as a sin. In the history of moral theology up to the present day, the understanding and evaluation of lies have been subject to changes and uncertainty, partly caused by a one-sided, formal interpretation of the term. A lie is a deliberately false statement or announcement in the full sense of inter-personal communication. The moral negative quality lies then not in the formally false statement or in the dis-crepancy between thought or conviction and speech and its misuse, nor in the merely factual deception of the inter-locutor. It is in each case a distortion of the rules of communication, in so far as it is a discrepancy in personal experience and, at the same time disrupts human relations in general. Communication takes place each time in a personal situation where the question or expectation and answer or statement correspond to the individual competence in expressing oneself and the partner's ability to receive information. There are occasions in life when the speech situation is prejudiced, distorted or completely removed (for instance, an interrogation which, if necessary, unfairly forces someone to divulge a strict secret by threatening to hurt him or others). This problem is particularly acute in the genuine cases of the so called 'white lie'. It must be considered that an attempt is made here to avoid damage, but also that mutual trust and the general trust in any

statement can be diminished or even destroyed as a result of making a false statement. In other words, the speech situation as a whole must be examined. Sometimes superior obligations force one to keep back, even to cover up the truth. In the last analysis, a responsible sense of justice and love determine the possible extent, nature and presentation of each statement as the need arises. If the tradition of moral theology has decided against a casuistic definition of cases when a white lie is permissible and has therefore trusted to the Christian's general moral attitude to truthfulness and personal conscience to tell the truth when in a dilemma, then the very necessary, ubiquitous obligation to truthfulness, regardless of person or situation, is here given expression. The casuistic and much documented use of obscure language (ambiguity, mental reservations) in a hopeless situation takes place with the immediate aim of justifiably withholding true information or deceiving the other. By formally avoiding a false statement it attempts to uphold the general truth of the message. But since technique and skill alone have no moral advantage over a false statement, ingenious and obscure speech in itself does little to promote truthfulness. If lies are deliberately employed to injure another person in his private life (personality, spiritual or material rights, *honour, q.v.*), they are particularly serious (calumny, slander and deception). As long as an ethical interpretation and teaching cannot dispense with a casuistic treatment of lies when they occur, it must be done as a sign of Christian respect of truth.

R. Hofmann

Truthfulness. See *Manipulation; Truth.*

V

VALUE

1. The concept of 'value' is extremely complex and therefore difficult to define, not only in its everyday use, but also in scientific language. In general, everything can be regarded as 'value' or valuable that is seen, in the individual or in social esteem, as good, worth striving for, enriching, useful or in any way furthering man's interests. A distinction has to be made between various groups of values—there are, for instance, aesthetic, religious, artistic, economic and other values. Man's attitude towards such values can be respectful, consenting or covetous. Whenever he recognizes something to be valuable, his interest is aroused, he has to take up an attitude towards it and he is motiviated to think and act. On the other hand, he regards as a 'non-value' anything that repels, threatens, restricts or harms him. His reaction to such 'non-values' is rejection, resistance, defence or attack. It should be clear from this very general outline of the concept of value that the basic aspects of man's existence are subject to his recognition of or self-protection against values.

This applies in particular to moral values. These are the values towards which man directs his moral behaviour (his disposition, conviction, attitude or action) and which apply to his own qualities and modes of behaviour (justice, truthfulness, faithfulness and so on). In addition to these directly moral values, there is also a wide spectrum of values with a special moral interest (bearing in mind, of course, that all moral values can possess this moral interest). These include, for example, life, freedom, human

264

fellowship, friendship, the spirit of partnership and so on. The special moral significance of these values is to be found in the radical way in which they are impressed on the personal and intersubjective sphere of man's life and the enhanced readiness for responsibility that they require if they are to be given a concrete form and expression. This is particularly true of the moral values listed first.

These and similar lists always contain in a concentrated form an expression of positive and negative individual and social experiences (*q.v.*). This implies that every affirmation concerning a value or values has a social emphasis which is individually convincing and effective and which has to be fulfilled creatively in each separate situation. These moral values also act as norms, regulating the aims of and motives for man's moral actions (see *Norm*), although they are not themselves moral norms (*q.v.*), which present us with indications for our behaviour in the concrete. Moral norms are always, moreover, directed towards the fulfilment of moral values.

2. The philosophical problem which preoccupies most specialists in this sphere today is that of the existential quality and knowability of these values. Values and moral values particularly are not given in the same way as other data or objects and cannot be known, analyzed or described in qualitative terms like empirical, given objects. For this reason, there are certain tendencies, based on different theoretical scientific points of departure, which can only be suggested as examples. One such example is that the phenomenology of values that cannot be known by reason, but only by specific intuition (value sensation). Like several other philosophical tendencies (such as intuitionism and emotivism), then the phenomenology of values is very much in the tradition of R. H. Lotze, according to whom they do not have an existence, but have validity and can be sensed in a special way. Those philosophers who practise meta-ethics mainly in the light of linguistic analysis have examined the problem as to whether values have a basis and motivation in the theory of knowledge (they have concerned themselves, in other words, with the relationship between the indicative state of being and the imperative optimum).

Sociologists are, of course, still engaged in the debate

about value-judgments brought about by Weber's call for a value-free science. In the study of sociology, then, values are regarded as social facts which can be investigated, but towards which it is not possible to take up a permanent position. Finally, values are becoming increasingly interesting to psychologists as factors providing motivation for action and pointers to free choice.

In all this, no part at all is played nowadays by the classical scholastic practice of linking moral values with the premoral transcendental good. The earlier tendency to derive moral values from a given order of being is now severely criticized as a wrong conclusion based on natural reasoning, since the factual state of the valid order is regarded uncritically as existentially conditioned and has therefore been abandoned as a moral demand or norm. It is clear that the single view of the world presupposed in scholastic thought has become ineffectual and that the ontological derivation of moral values has at the same time lost its plausibility. It has, however, to be pointed out in connexion with this new approach, that a measurable, analyzable presence is not the only mode of being.

3. *An attempted analysis.* The definition of the social and individual anthropological function of moral values can be applied to all the various theories. The reality encountered by man has to be refashioned again and again. Man himself has not only to find his form, but also constantly correct and refashion. In this, there is a need, among other things, for moral decisions, since moral convictions and values are a part of man's form and his world (*q.v.*), which is fashioned by him. This is mainly a question of meaningful moral aims, but man does not simply find these as something given, nor does he fashion them out of nothing. On the contrary, he 'takes' them in acts which involve his whole person both spiritually and emotionally on the basis of given presuppositions. They can be understood as personality, intersubjectivity and historicity. Their fashioning results in the establishment, recognition and continuation of values such as freedom, the spirit of partnership and human fellowship (love, *q.v.*) and specifically moral values such as justice, solidarity and faithfulness. Both the 'taking' of values and their fashioning are basically

a free personal commitment that takes place not at random, but according to certain presuppositions. This commitment to moral values is part of the task of controlling his existence which man has continuously to undertake as an individual and as a member of society and which is determined by the polarities of success and failure, freedom and coercion. In this way, he establishes for himself what is 'good' and what is 'bad', an activity that is always accompanied by the risk of error and failure (freedom of will) and therefore by a need of correction on the basis of insights that are again and again being acquired.

The validity of moral values cannot be justified or proved. It can only be made plausible by evidence that is produced by discursive reasoning and verified inter-subjectively. Berger's and Luckmann's three stages of sociological development, that is, the theory of exter-nalization, objectivization and internalization, may help us to understand the establishment of values and the chal-lenging existence of moral values. The first of these stages, externalization, includes the 'taking' and the fashioning of values in the sense outlined above. The second stage of objectivization takes place as soon as the moral values are intersubjectively recognized (by small or large groups or by society or part of society). At this stage, the values encounter the individual as challenging data of the moral order of mutual association, the order of impulses and drives, and the order of social institutions (such as marriage, q.v.) or else as motives for responsible self-fulfilment. They can enter into a systematic relationship with each other, complement each other and support each other. In this way, they form part of any understanding of man and the world and are to this extent conditioned by religion and cultural influences. Finally, the objectivization of moral values, in other words, their universal validity, helps groups, societies and individual members of groups and societies to find their identity. An ideological fixation of values is a possible disadvantage that sometimes emerges in this process. This results in moral values being defended as unchangeable data that are beyond criticism and in their being determined by powerful interests. Such objectivized moral values are encountered by man in his group or society and are given as data for his socialization. He

267

VALUE

acquires them through the language and the behaviour of his environment and makes them his own through understanding them, accepting them and affirming them.

4. *Faith and moral values.* Values are, as we have seen, an integral part of our understanding of man and the world. In this type of relationship, moral values acquire a certain functional rôle, and religion and Christian faith in particular have a special significance here. Christian faith (*q.v.*) is a total commitment directed towards Jesus and requiring an attitude towards moral values that is in turn orientated towards an understanding of God and man. In thinking and speaking about Jesus, insights can be gained into moral values and into the morality of each situation. As a commitment to Jesus and the God proclaimed by him, faith also has a critical function, since it calls for a consciousness of moral values and a mode of behaviour that is in accordance with the teaching of Jesus (for example, an acceptance of one's fellow men without reservations and resistance to the exercise of totalitarian power).

5. *The acquisition of moral values.* The internalization of moral values mentioned above is basically a learning process. Such values are learnt in the family, in the school, in groups and in the Christian community. It is possible to speak of convictions regarding and attitudes towards moral values (see *Virtue*) in the full sense of the word only if a person has fashioned his own concepts concerning these values both in the course of his own development and generally in the whole of his life on the basis of insights into and consent to these values (decision) and in the light of his own acquired knowledge of the same values. These values contain in a concentrated form the various cognitive and effective aspects of the human personality and man's readiness to act. An essential prerequisite is an attitude which is open, ready to co-operate and to accept responsibility and critical, but not constantly correcting experiences and especially experiences of moral values derived from the environment, or ignoring them blindly and unfeelingly, but accepting their claims as valid. This is closely linked with an equally necessary readiness to test all the claims made by moral values for possible corruption or

268

ideological illusion (see, for example, the ambivalent significance of obedience and self-sacrifice).

6. *Conflicting values.* It is possible, in certain situations where an attitude has to be taken towards moral values, for conflicts (*q.v.*) to occur. This is particularly likely to happen when several moral values cannot be satisfied at the same time and only the most urgent can in fact be realized. It may also happen that a choice has to be made between two equally important values—a choice, for example, between loyalty to a friend and truthfulness or justice in the need to expose the possibility of harm to a third party. It is not possible to formulate general rules of behaviour applicable to all cases of this kind. Such conflicts have to be resolved by a sensible and responsible approach to the situation and its particular circumstances. The aim should be to establish a scale of values applicable to the concrete situation. In every case of conflict, however, a separate, individual decision has to be made regarding the most urgent of the moral values in question.

7. *Individual questions.* Education (*q.v.*), the educational environment and the social level of the individual have a very important influence on the choice of values and the content of individual and social concepts of alue. In this, an essential part is played by the individual's education in linguistic skills and his ability to express himself in words and actions emotionally and in situations calling for affection. The psychological preconditions are very important here. A strong fixation in mechanisms of law-reward-punishment will make a person incapable of experiencing values personally and intersubjectively and will give rise to a morality that lacks freedom. This applies particularly to cases of neurosis. A loving and tolerant upbringing in a spirit of partnership and with the aim of promoting freedom is one of the basic preconditions for a creative capacity for values.

Finally, it is necessary for people to make sure again and again of their ideas and convictions concerning values. They can do this best in groups, including Christian groups, by exchanging experiences and by criticizing (see *Conscience*) and correcting what is superseded, ideologically

269

corrupt or repressive. (Examples of this are an adaptive obedience leading to a loss of freedom or a devaluation of sexuality, *q.v.*, to the level of a consumer article.) On the other hand, however, there is always a danger, which has to be combatted, of collective blindness to values or of developing collectively a repressive ideology of values.

In pluralistic societies, many different systems of values exist side by side and often come into conflict with each other. On the basis of shared traditions and needs, basic common values are, of course, established (for example, by the setting up of constitutional laws). It is still necessary, however, in most modern pluralistic societies, to come to terms with all that is different or alien individually and collectively and to co-operate with all sections of society with the aim of achieving the highest possible level of humanity *(q.v.)* in the greatest possible spirit of toleration *(q.v.)*. There is, however, a limit to which tolerance can go when powerful interests and ideologies constitute a serious threat.

V. Eid

Virginity. See *Celibacy; Marriage.*

VIRTUE

1. Virtue out of favour. Even in his time, Hegel was struck by the fact 'that people nowadays do not talk of virtue as much as they used to' (*Philosophy of Right* §150). Nowadays the word 'virtue' seems to be actually derided and obsolete, 'survives almost only in an ironical sense' (Gadamer). There are various reasons for this loss of force—the philosophy of morality constructed by Kant, which placed all the stress on duty, obligation, conscience, intention and subjectivity; and then the eighteenth and nineteenth century middle-class, economic view of virtue directed towards well-regulated domesticity, clear-cut attitudes such as orderliness, cleanliness, punctuality and industry, as though these things constituted the decisive moral and even Christian excellences. Virtue inevitably came to look like a coercive system which strangles man and keeps him from his intensest and most vital possibilities. Hence Nietzsche's vividly presented objections which caricatured virtue as a renunciation of power and an insidious compensation for human inferiorities. So it is not surprising if, more recently, the functions which were formerly assigned to virtue are thought to be performed incomparably better by a behaviourist technology (Skinner, Koestler).

2. *Analysis of the phenomenon of virtue.* If despite all this, virtue is to be rehabilitated, it will have to be convincingly shown, i.e. by rational communication, that virtue is an ultimate value-determined basic attitude in regard to all that is specifically human. And it will have to be shown to be indispensable if that specifically human good is to be achieved. In the first place this calls for a clear distinction between virtue and what are called 'good manners' (social conventions, traditional habits and customs) and from rôles (as the sum-total of expectations, as to how the holder of a position in society or a group should behave). Virtue must no longer be used to denote secondary and peripheral modes of conduct. Otherwise marginal domains of human behaviour are given an emphasis which by right should be reserved for central moral attitudes.

3. *Virtue as a fundamental and value attitude.* On its subjective side, virtue belongs to the category of attitudes or dispositions to action. This expresses the fact that man's ethical existence is dependent on a certain continuity and selectivity. He would be over-burdened if in a concrete situation he had to perform the right action from scratch, as it were, each time, without the aid of appropriate acquired dispositions. Now since this shows that virtue is a fundamental attitude, it is evident that virtue in every case consists of a personally integrated attitude anchored in the very centre of human personality. As such, it points to resoluteness, to perseverance in decision, and consequently to 'active strength of the ego' (Erikson). This feature preserves it from decline into mechanical routine and psycholgical compulsion. As a fundamental attitude, virtue is ultimately value-determined. This distinguishes it from the purely functional human endowments which confer

proficiency, but are not of themselves ethically important qualities. Viewed in this light, to every *value* (*q.v.*) there is a corresponding morally good quality (often bearing the same name), which consists in the propensity to act in conformity with that value (Frankena). *Orientation towards the human is essential.* As a fundamental and value attitude, virtue is immediately directed to building up, shaping and maintaining everything that is specifically human. Since, of course, these human things are both social and individual, virtue can never be achieved in an exclusively self-contained existence, but only in shared existence, based on human communication (see *Freedom*). This also matches the fact that the idea of virtue was originally worked out to describe a *model* (*q.v.*) to be imitated on a religious basis (Wyss). An ethics of virtue is therefore essentially based on a model to follow. And as, furthermore, what is specifically human is not something abstract and static but is only to be attained in a living temporal, historical process, and is therefore subject to the law of gradual development, change and modification, virtue by its very nature has to be open to innovations, further development and reshaping of the particular forms it assumes. The dynamic element cannot be eliminated from the very idea of virtue. Directed in this way toward specifically human developments, and affected by the form they take, virtue is immune from suspicion of making exacting demands which hinder human beings from being human. Only if it is cut off from human fulfilment as a whole and turns into an ideology, does it assume inhuman features.

From the historical, genetic point of view, genuine virtues always have to be developed 'as the logical prescriptive postulation of what actual morality claims to be, but not yet is' (Kehrer). Impetus to their discovery is therefore provided above all by certain deficiencies in general moral character (see *Ethos*), the kind of *experiences* (*q.v.*) which spontaneously appear morally defective even prior to reflection on them.

4. *Virtue today.* A decisive influence in shaping the western Christian ethos was the table of the four cardinal virtues (*justice, courage*–fortitude, *moderation* — temperance—in the sense of 'healthy control of the

senses', and prudence [q.v.]—practical *wisdom*). They are first found in Aeschylus, which points to the fact that originally they belonged to a programme of the early Greek aristocratic ethos. Plato defended them, deepened them by scientific reflection, and at the same time universalized them by bringing them into connexion with the parts of the human soul and so presented them as a concern for what is specifically human in life (E. Schwartz). It is due to Ambrose, Augustine and Aquinas that this quadripartite scheme (enriched with the three theological virtues of *faith, hope* and *love, q.v.*), has survived intact down to the present day. In view of the special conditions of human life nowadays, however, it is no longer possible to be content to hand on the traditional doctrine about virtue without reflection or criticism. What is needed is a comprehensive reinterpretation and further development of the traditional account. If, for example, we consider the dangers to which full human development is exposed by the phenomena of infantile regression, the disturbance of the pleasure-pain economy (see *Pleasure*), the growing disinclination for deliberate abstinence of any kind, there is much to be said for reminding people of the virtue of moderation as the value-virtue opposing the temptation to regression which unleashes instinctual drives, and as answering the need for psychological progression and maturity. Furthermore, if it is true that people today can scarcely summon up enough spirit and strength to resist the nerve-racking thrust of ever-increasing speed (A. Toffler) and of the inherent dynamism of the secondary system, it certainly seems reasonable to present the virtue of *courage (q.v.)* as the capacity which guarantees the 'personal zones of stability' for mastering these risks. Similarly our present-day world needs a large measure of sobriety, discretion, sense of reality and existential humility if it is to check ominous tendencies to ideological and voluntarist presumption. Assistance could be given here by a new account of the virtue of practical wisdom or prudence. Finally, in view of the threat of an omnipresent levelling collectivism and functionalism, an attitude of respect for man and human dignity needs to be revived, a task which would fall within the domain of justice, as its historical origin itself shows.

5. *The Christian contribution to the doctrine of the virtues.*
Exegetes points out that the New Testament hardly uses
the classical concept of virtue (*arete*) at all, because this is
too concerned with self-perfecting and also completely
ignores the complex of the four cardinal virtues. Consequently it is also considered highly dubious to attempt to
combine the classical doctrine of virtue with Christian
theology. In fact, virtue as human achievement does not,
in the New Testament ethos, occupy at least the central
position which belonged to it in classical ethical theory.
Virtue was also to some extent reduced to merely relative
importance through the theology of salvation (cf. Phil 4. 8).
Nevertheless the New Testament does not lay a total
embargo on virtue. It certainly admits of a fundamental,
though critically reserved trust in specifically human
attitudes to values. Furthermore, a decisive reversal of
values is to be observed (reshaping of the classical catalogue
of virtues into markedly altruistic modes of conduct). In this
way, attitudes that in the ethics of those days were actually
maligned, for instance 'eleos' (pity) and 'tapeinophrosyne'
(self-abasement), as well as the previously insignificant
term 'agape', were transformed into highly significant
programmes for moral life.

In principle, the Christian doctrine of virtue has a
threefold task to perform. It has to make perfectly clear that
the really central virtue, from which all other virtues derive
their meaning and to which they are always related,
consists in unconditional respect for the dignity and
inviolability of every human being, even the weakest and
most helpless (hence the emphasis on pity and humility).
At the same time it must emphasize that this attitude itself
cannot adequately be shown to be absolutely obligatory by
a purely rational ethics (see *Evidence*), but can only be
convincingly defended on the presupposition of faith in the
radical love for man of the God revealed in Christ. Seen in
relation to God in that way, the respect due to every
human being appears as the anthropocentric obverse of the
three theological virtues of faith, hope and love. Its
fundamental task is to protect man's personal dignity,
which is ultimately grounded in the mystery of God,
against all measures and manipulations which threaten to
reduce human beings to the level of a merchandise

disposable at will on the impersonal market, or of a mere object of presumptuous scientific theories. If one then recalls the extreme importance which the New Testament attributes to imitation and the idea of discipleship for the formation of moral character (see *Biblical ethics* [NT], it seems essential for a Christian virtue ethics to take the form of an ethics of model imitation. This would enable it to stand out in contrast to an ethics of norms and imperatives and convincingly to present the genuinely virtuous man as the primary instrument for eliciting moral commitment.

Christian ethics has not least to fend off the error that the path of human virtue is the same thing as the way of salvation. For Christian ethics, virtue belongs among the penultimate things of man. Consequently virtue must not be practised as if it were man's be-all and end-all. In view of the widespread tendency nowadays to exaggerate moral obligation, and give it the stamp of a myth of salvation and redemption, reference to the limits of virtue in the theology of salvation is not without importance. As Pascal had noted: 'If one insists on pushing virtues to extremes in this or that direction, vices emerge . . .' (*Pensées*, 357).

B. Stoeckle

W

Wages. See *Capitalism; Marxism; Socialism; Theft; Work.*

War. See *Conflict; Military service.*

Witness. See *Evidence.*

Worship. See *Biblical ethics; Spirituality.*

WORK

1. Definition. Work is the purposeful effort by which man uses, develops and forms the potentialities of a partly incomplete and unruly world.

Through work he makes his living and—not always successfully—shapes himself, his environment and his history in the search of happiness (*q.v.*).

At first sight work seems to be an unpleasant limitation of human freedom, but at the same time it is an attempt to surmount this limitation. Work can contain a satisfying, playful element, which finds expression in enjoyment and in the preference for a particular job.

Work done in a spirit of positive acceptance drives away boredom and a feeling of uselessness. But for real fulfilment in life work alone is not enough. It must be related in a meaningful way to leisure (*q.v.*). A person incapable of work is far from being worthless, for it is love which fulfils life.

2. Rights and duties of work. The first work of every

276

individual consists in appropriating to himself that which is presented by his family (*q.v.*) and his cultural circle (learning, discovering, experience).

Helping in this process is an important part of a mother's work—often underrated.

Just as work and education are today made possible largely by society, society is in turn dependent on responsible work by the individual. There is a right to work and to education and a corresponding duty.

Good work gives the requisite feeling of self-esteem and makes the goodness of creation tangible (see *World*). Aiming for achievement and high quality is justified, as long as achievement does not become man's sole criterion and providing that the socially inadequate are not ostracized as a result.

Work requires a fair wage, which should be enough to live on reasonably and to provide education, care of the sick and the old and a fair share of worldly goods. For a long time this was not so in now 'developed' countries, and it is still not the case in the Third World today.

When industrialization began at the start of the nineteenth century many people had to sell their labour like a commodity and lacked the most elementary social safeguards. This resulted to a great extent in ruthless exploitation by the owners of capital, produced the industrial proletariat, and forced women and children to work in the harshest conditions.

Relief came only with the creation of an 'organized counterforce' (labour unions, trade unions) and the sensitization of public awareness.

Today 'labour' is becoming stronger and stronger in relation to 'capital'. The trade unions take part in wage negotiations as equal partners.

Their strongest resource of power is the strike. Because of its damaging effect on the whole of society it can be used only as a last resort when all the other legal ways of making successful demands—for a fair wage, humane working conditions, or in extreme cases to stop things going badly wrong—have been exhausted.

The demand for codetermination (*q.v.*) in business firms is justified. It accords with human dignity (*q.v.*), the higher level of education and the growing social influence of

277

employees today.

3. *Further questions*. Technical developments are tending to raise work productivity (i.e. output of work in relation to working hours and capital investment).

This has resulted in a number of new and interesting jobs but has also led to highly monotonous work processes (e.g., assembly line work). But the present state of technology (*q.v.*) makes it increasingly possible to use further rises in productivity to improve working conditions and environmental protection and to give more development aid—instead of raising material living standards.

But this means turning away from exclusive consumer thinking and implies a willingness to give up some of the direct benefit from working output.

Because work is so important for the individual, full employment is an essential aim of economic policy. The various forms of rationalization in particular branches of business release the labour force in different ways.

This labour surplus can be taken up either through shorter working hours or increased production. Furthermore, people today must be willing to change their workplace and their job sometimes, to adapt constantly any professional qualifications to current needs.

Occupational training should therefore concentrate less on providing specialist knowledge which quickly goes out of date, and more on a broad knowledge of principles and techniques.

The right to work does not include the right to a particular workplace. But where there is involuntary unemployment, there is a duty of society and the business world—and particularly of the state—to keep as many people at work as possible. This should be done not only through economic policies but also by allocating suitable emergency jobs.

4. *Responsibility before God*. Work, like the whole of human living, must be answered for to God. It can be seen as a way to share in the work of creation and should therefore be organized so that everyone, if possible, may develop his creative abilities.

The humanitarian value of any work is in proportion to

the extent to which work helps to perfect the individual and improve man's corporate life. That goes also for a humane working atmosphere, which greatly influences the individual's enjoyment of work and his whole personal life.

If everyone applies his abilities to his own work in an appropriate way, even the most unlikely types of work take on their full human value and can be fruitful for the kingdom of God.

It is often not immediately obvious whether a particular job helps to make the world more humane. To decide on this we need to take into account *all* those affected—with patience, quiet competence and a willingness to take risks.

It comes down to 'the ability to distinguish between spirits' (spirituality, *q.v.*) in the light of Christ, and a readiness to co-operate in earnest with all who seek the Good.

Bibliography: **Katz, D. & Kahn, R. L.**: The Social Psychology of Organizations. New York, 1966. **Maier, N. R. F.**: Psychology in Industry. Boston, 1955. **Preston, R. H. (Ed.)**: Technology and Social Justice. London, 1971. **Rahner, H.**: Man at Play. London & New York, 1968. **Roethlisberger, F. J. & Dixon, W. J.**: Management and the Worker. Cambridge, Mass., 1940.

H.-J. Schulte-Vieting

WORLD

It is really only since the beginning of modern times that the Christian ethos and, even more, theological ethics, have had to meet the reproach that whatever their protestations to the contrary, they bear the indelible stamp of a distorted relation, or rather lack of relation, to the world. They are alleged to regard the world as 'this world' as opposed to the 'other world', 'the beyond', as a vale of tears. Christian precepts are supposed to inculcate flight from the world, yet refusal of hostility towards the world. This is said to have burdened Christians with a specific ethos alien to the world, which makes them unfitted for the tasks of this world or, at best, only to a limited extent capable of frankly accepting and pursuing them with full commitment. It cannot be denied that there is some justification for these allegations. Nevertheless it must be realized that such objections against the attitude of Christians to the world are decisively determined by the concept of a radically autonomous and secularized world, which the Christian by his very principles cannot share (see *Asceticism*). In view of this fact, what is decisive is to work out an ethos in regard to the world which does maximum justice to reality by being neither acosmic in its preoccupation with the beyond, nor world-bound through purblind neglect of anything but the present.

1. The fundamental concept of the world. The general spontaneous and reflective idea of the world contains three elements. World is the sum total of all objective perceptible and deducible realities, empirical and 'metaphysical'. As such, world does not stand contrasted with man as something different in kind. It includes man as a part of itself. World is therefore defined as a reality that in history man can influence, shape and direct towards certain goals. In this sense it is 'man's world'. Finally, 'the world' can also denote mankind as a whole. All three possible interpretations unmistakably indicate that it is fundamentally impossible to divorce man and world, that the world is just as inconceivable without man as man is without the world. Man cannot break this link with 'being in the world'. Consequently the concept of world always implies the concept of man as part of it, and the converse is equally true. Discourse about the world is never solely cosmological, but always bears anthropological and historical overtones.

For a Christian, the world as field of operation and not least of moral problems, exists only as *this* world, as the world of the present, of temporality and historical change. Such a world of here and now is clearly not final; it shows in fact that it is penultimate and provisional. That follows from belief in the 'eschaton to come'—the reality of the new heaven and the new earth, created by God alone. Consequently any conceivable future within the world and even the most successful evolutionary process or progress, cannot go beyond the status of this world as that of existence in a 'tent' (2 Cor 5. 1), which means, on sufferance. Limited in this way, with a proviso as it were, the world is not the blind product of chance (Monod), but in a radical sense God's creation, and as such it bears the seal of indestructible goodness, a plan and a meaning. Nevertheless it is unfinished in character, even apart from the question of eschatological fulfilment. For it is entrusted to man to work at, shape and use. Man is to make 'more' world out of the world. Furthermore the world of the present as a whole is a wicked world; it is a broken, fallen created thing, attacked by the power of evil. It does not inherently possess this feature, which in the New Testament overlays the idea of creation as well as the idea of the human world (Schnackenburg). It does not belong to the world simply on the ground of its ontological finitude or corporeality. It owes it to the guilt and failure of man (Rom 8. 20 f). See *Eschatology*.

3. *Basic attitude to the world.* The Christian must know that he cannot get away from this world just as it is and will continue to be until the end of time. He must know he may not act as if he can only attain his salvation if he ignores the world and takes as little notice of it as possible. To run away from the world in this fashion and strive to be no part of it, would in men's eyes be flight from oneself, and, in regard to God's will, constitute a refusal to be a creature and to carry out the mandate to be creatively active. The Christian has, rather, to learn to live in this world with this world and for this world in accordance with the meaning of his own human reality. This commitment, however, can only be achieved on condition of a radical and total openness towards everything in the world; not only in regard to the values which the world has to offer, and the possibilities which it holds out for a fruitful shaping of human existence, but also towards the signs of its imperfection, bewilderment and sinfulness. Only where the light and darkness, promise and danger of the world are equally perceived, equally weighed and accepted, can an objectively right attitude to the world be attained. Ultimately this openness can only be achieved on the basis of the Christ event and the interpretation of the world it constitutes (incarnation, cross, resurrection). Thus based on the rela-

tion between Christ and the world, the Christian's mental attitude towards the world will inevitably be dialectical: 'Affirmation and denial combine in concrete action in the world' (Bonheoffer). According to Paul (1 Cor 7. 29–31), the Christian deals with the world as though he had no dealings with it. He combines entering into with leaving off relations with it, affirmation with negation, integration with *renunciation* (see *Abstinence*). Such 'contact at a distance' not only prevents selfish enjoyment and evil fascination with the world, it also alone opens out the possibility of working at the world calmly, and therefore fruitfully.

3. *Specific attitude to the world as God's creation (the world of nature) and as human reality (the world of culture).* In this respect the world includes both the existent cosmos of material, biological, psychological and intellectual facts (Nature) and the things that man himself has created (structures of social order, of *politics* (*q.v.*), material civilization, projects, utopias). Because world in this sense is something constructed and therefore constitutes a non-divine, autonomous domain, secular things cannot be thought of as having divine attributes. Divinization of earthly realities and mythologizing the cosmos (Col 2.8, 20) must be rejected equally with the apotheosis of the contrivances men have devised to make life easier, such as technology. Equally, however, any attribution of malign enchantment or diabolical character to secular things (e.g. pleasure, aggression, the present, the past, things of the body) is to be resisted. These demarcations liberate man from all cosmic constraints and compulsions. In this light, two further aspects of a Christian attitude to the world require special consideration.

Since confession of the goodness of the world as God's creation profoundly marks all discourse in biblical revelation about the present aeon, the Christian's moral responsibility includes certain important elements. Above all, the Christian must be glad at the greatness and beauty of this world and its good things, admire them and recognize them all as a gift which even prior to any human use and interpretation is expressive and has a message for man. Furthermore, the Christian should thankfully make his own the good things of the world, for they were created for his sake. From this point of view nothing is withheld from him, for 'everything is clean' (Rom 14.14, 20), 'everything created by God is good' (1 Tim 4.4). No created value is taboo (1 Tim 4.3). This means that things should be called by their names, discussed, and a free choice made among them. Another consequence is that human reason and language are required in a unique way as instruments of man's appropriation of the world. Yet despite the fact that the world as God's creation is subordinated to man, an indissoluble solidarity links man with all non-human creatures. His *environment* (*q.v.*) is at once native element and social milieu. Human sociability is not really possible without companionable sharing in the world. There is therefore a duty to love Nature and to care for the maintenance of those natural created resources that ensure that the world of today and tomorrow will still be inhabitable for man. How pressing that duty is, is only too obvious now. The really urgent problem is no longer that of winning power over the world, but rather to use that power with a sense of responsibility for Nature and therefore for man himself. In face of what are now almost universal technological possibilities, organs of responsible human decision are still rudimentary. What is needed is a moral agreement to renounce unscrupulous exploitation and damage to the earth, the devastation of living space, and for man only to allow himself what he in fact needs and the earth can bear. That would require in particular the elimination of those expenditures which on a present short term view promise to make life more agreeable but in the long run involve effects which would drastically limit the vital chances of mankind for the future. Since man, unlike the brute animals, is not predetermined, but open to the world around and therefore has a history, he cannot evade the task of a continual transformation of pre-existing nature into structures and institutions which serve his life (= culture). They alone furnish indispensable conditions for his temporal, historical existence by which he fulfils his own nature. Consequently man has to affirm his temporal character, his obligation to make history, as well as his debt to history. That includes the recognition of *work* (*q.v.*), achievement, *progress*, the arts and sciences, *politics* (*q.v.*), culture and material civilization. This vocation in the

283

world is contradicted by all endeavours which under the influence of dualist and gnostic ideologies foment hatred of the 'flesh', and seek forcibly to withdraw mankind from the conditions of historical existence and to reconstruct it as a being of pure intellect. This is not to say that the structures created by man for his own convenience, since they are imperfect and never definitive, do not need constant overhaul and improvement, so that people have to be ready to envisage reforms. Yet only if these run in continuity with the course of history, do they promote a better future.

4. Attitude to the 'wicked' world. Scripture leaves us in no doubt that there is evil in the world and that the forms it takes justify its being called a wicked world. But Scripture makes it just as clear that this state of the world has its origin in the heart, the inner mind of man (see *Biblical ethics*). According to 1 Jn 2.15, the calamitous state of the world is caused by insatiable egotistical covetousness, as well as by the presumptuous claim of man's will to absolute autonomy. The wicked world would consequently denote an expressly moral, but not an ontological quality (Schnackenburg). In this sense, too, we are to understand the 'elements (RSV: elemental spirits) of the world', which hold man in mortal bondage and from which Christ has freed him (Col 2.20), as products of man, to which he clings as though he could find his whole *salvation* in them. Wherever man's empirical or even mental constructs are treated as absolutes in this way, made idols of, man sinks into slavish dependence on his own creations, and the wicked world emerges. In Heidegger's philosophy, this state is characterized as 'fallenness', inauthenticity and existence in the 'They'. Marcuse means much the same by his 'one-dimensional man' who has unconditionally subordinated himself to his own market commodities and achievements. The Christian cannot identify himself with that kind of world. He must not be conformed to it (Rom 12.2), he has to renounce it. Whever that happens he demonstrates not only friendship with God, but also friendship with the world as God's good creation and his own inalienable portion.

Bibliography: **Metz, J. B.**: Theology of the World. London, 1967. **Schnackenburg, R.**: The Moral Teaching of the New Testament. London & New York, 1965.

B. Stoeckle

Worship. See *Biblical ethics* (OT); *Spirituality*.